Politics 1B: Comparative Po

University of Glasgow

Australia • Brazil • Japan • Korea • Mexico • Singapore • Spain • United Kingdom • United States

Politics 1B: Comparative Politics
Second Custom Edition
Mark Kesselman, Joel Krieger, William A. Joseph

Publishing Director: Linden Harris
Production Controller: Eyvett Davis
Custom Editor: Isabel Florence

© 2013, Cengage Learning EMEA

ALL RIGHTS RESERVED. No part of this work covered by the copyright herein may be reproduced, transmitted, stored or used in any form or by any means graphic, electronic, or mechanical, including but not limited to photocopying, recording, scanning, digitizing, taping, Web distribution, information networks, or information storage and retrieval systems, except as permitted under Section 107 or 108 of the 1976 United States Copyright Act, or applicable copyright law of another jurisdiction, without the prior written permission of the publisher.

While the publisher has taken all reasonable care in the preparation of this book, the publisher makes no representation, express or implied, with regard to the accuracy of the information contained in this book and cannot accept any legal responsibility or liability for any errors or omissions from the book or the consequences thereof.

Products and services that are referred to in this book may be either trademarks and/or registered trademarks of their respective owners. The publishers and author/s make no claim to these trademarks.
The Author has asserted the right under the Copyright, Designs and Patents Act 1988 to be identified as Author of this Work.

For product information and technology assistance,
contact **emea.info@cengage.com**.

For permission to use material from this text or product,
and for permission queries,
email **clsuk.permissions@cengage.com**.

British Library Cataloguing-in-Publication Data
A catalogue record for this book is available from the British Library.

ISBN: 978-1-4080-7879-2

Cengage Learning EMEA
Cheriton House, North Way, Andover, Hampshire. SP10 5BE. United Kingdom

Cengage Learning products are represented in Canada by Nelson Education Ltd.

For your lifelong learning solutions, visit
www.cengage.co.uk

Purchase your next print book, e-book or e-chapter at
www.CengageBrain.com

Printed in the UK by TJ International
2 3 4 5 6 7 8 9 10 – 16 15 14

Acknowledgements

The content of this text has been adapted from the following product(s):

Introduction to Comparative Politics, Brief Edition
Kesselman, Krieger and Joseph (978-0-495-80112-2)

Introduction to Comparative Politics, 5th Edition
Kesselman, Krieger and Joseph (978-0-495-79741-8)

Full copyright details and acknowledgements will appear in the aforementioned pulications.

The content of this text has been adapted from the different products listed above and therefore may have slight variances in the formatting throughout

Table of Contents

1. Introducing Comparative Politics 1
   Originally chapter 1 from Introduction to Comparative Politics ~ Brief Edition

2. Germany 39
   Originally chapter 4 from Introduction to Comparative Politics ~ 5th Edition

3. Russia 93
   Originally chapter 5 from Introduction to Comparative Politics ~ Brief Edition

4. China 155
   Originally chapter 9 from Introduction to Comparative Politics ~ Brief Edition

CHAPTER 1

Introducing Comparative Politics

Those who know only one country, know no country.

—**Seymour Martin Lipset,** *American Exceptionalism*

Mark Kesselman
Joel Krieger
William A. Joseph

SECTION 1	What—and How—Comparative Politics Compares
SECTION 2	Comparative Politics and the Challenge of Globalization
SECTION 3	Themes for Comparative Analysis
SECTION 4	Classifying Political Systems
SECTION 5	Organization of the Text

Cold War the hostile relations that prevailed between the United States and the Soviet Union from the late 1940s until the demise of the USSR in 1991.

When did our current political era begin? Although a precise moment is hard to identify, many people would say it began with the collapse of the Berlin Wall in 1989. Until then, the Wall separated communist-controlled East Berlin from democratic West Berlin. More broadly, it separated the two Germanies: the German Democratic Republic, allied with the Soviet Union, and the Federal Republic of Germany, allied with the United States. At the most general level, the Wall was a powerful symbol of the **Cold War**, a tense era of sometimes deadly struggle and potentially catastrophic nuclear conflict that pitted communist nations against the so-called free world. The fall of the Berlin Wall was followed by a series of mostly peaceful revolutions that overthrew the communist regimes of East Central Europe and the Soviet Union. The new governments that emerged after these revolutions were all committed to the market rather than state control of the economy and to multiparty

Chapter 1: **Introducing Comparative Politics**

Two events symbolically mark the major changes in world politics in the late twentieth and early twenty-first century: The fall of the Berlin Wall (left) in November 1989, ushered in the post–Cold War era, while the terrorist attack on the World Trade Center towers in New York City on September 11, 2001 (right), reflected a particularly violent form of the forces of globalization that now affect politics in all countries. *(Sources: (Left) Lionel Cironneau/AP Images. (Right) Gulnara Samoilova/AP Images.*

democracy rather than communist control of all political life. The Cold War was over, and the post–Cold War era, in which we now live, had begun.

While these history-shaking changes were occurring, a book with the bold title *The End of History?*[1] was published. The author, Francis Fukuyama, argued that the failure of communism signaled the end of any real alternative to the regimes of Western-style liberal democracies, that is, systems of government that combine democracy with a capitalist economy based on free markets. Was Fukuyama correct?

Clearly, history has not ended. It is still very dynamic: the period since the end of the Cold War has not been calm or without serious conflict. The years since 1989 have been turbulent and, in many ways, have dashed the hopes of those who thought the end of the Cold War would usher in extended peace and prosperity. In the most recent decades, the world has witnessed horrifying epidemics, famine, and an endless cycle of brutal clashes that have often pitted one ethnic group in a country against another. We have seen financial crises that wiped out years of economic development and the growing marginalization of whole regions of the globe. We have seen a new war, the war on terrorism, whose beginning was marked by another collapse, this time a terribly tragic one: the disintegration of the twin towers of the World Trade Center in New York City in the attacks of September 11,

Introducing Comparative Politics 3

2001. Since 9/11, fear of more attacks and concern for security have dominated politics within many countries and reshaped international relations. Compared to the scourge of global terrorism, the Cold War may not look so bad!

Yet there have been positive developments that suggest Fukuyama's analysis might have some merit. Today there are more democracies or countries moving in that direction than at any previous time in history. Many of the world's less developed countries, like China and India, have made impressive economic progress.

The only thing that is certain about where the world is headed politically is uncertainty! That's one of the things that can make the study of comparative politics so interesting. For example, since the 1990s, a distinctive new focus for analyzing politics both within and among countries—**globalization**—has grabbed attention and stirred debate. *Globalization* refers to the unprecedented worldwide flow of trade, investment, production, communications, technology, culture, ideas, and other influences. There is a wide range of views among political scientists, politicians, social activists, and concerned citizens about whether globalization will promote opportunity and enhance human development around the world, or whether it will only make the richer countries richer, and exclude the poorer regions from its benefits, or disadvantage them even further. These may seem like economic questions, but they are profoundly political, as well.

globalization The intensification of worldwide interconnectedness associated with the increased speed and magnitude of cross-border flows of trade, investment and finance, and processes of migration, cultural diffusion, and communication.

They are also very much at the center of the political agenda of every country in the world and they are central to framework of this book. Globalization has become such a key concept in understanding politics in the contemporary world that we devote a whole section of this chapter to it.

The attacks of 9/11 also remind us that history is full of uncertainties, surprises, and shock that have far-reaching political implications. We have to acknowledge that we can never fully explain, much less predict, politics. But this doesn't mean we should throw our hands up in the air and give up the attempt to bring order and understanding to the world of politics—just the opposite! We can best understand politics, not by getting lost in the rush of headlines and sound bites, but by using a framework that gives us a handle on what's important about politics in a particular country and points us toward similarities and differences within and between groups of countries. *Introduction to Comparative Politics* uses such a framework, based on four central themes to describe and analyze the politics of eight countries from around the world:

- *A World of States:* the historical development and political organization of individual countries and the interaction of countries within the international order
- *Governing the Economy:* the role of the government in economic management
- *The Democratic Idea:* the spread of democracy around the world and the challenges of democratization
- *The Politics of Collective Identities:* the political impact of diverse class, gender, ethnic, and religious identities.

We believe that these four themes provide valuable tools for making sense of politics in our tumultuous times. They will be more fully described later in this chapter.

The contemporary world is an amazing laboratory for the study of comparative politics, and current events give unusual significance to the subject. We turn now to explore what comparative politics actually compares and how comparative study enhances our understanding of politics in general.

SECTION 1

What—and How—Comparative Politics Compares

FOCUS QUESTIONS

What does it mean to compare things? What are two examples of how a comparison can bring to light features that might otherwise have been overlooked?

To compare and contrast is one of the most common human mental exercises. In the study of politics, the use of comparisons dates in the Western world at least from Aristotle. He categorized Greek city-states in the fourth century BCE according to their form of political rule: rule by a single individual, rule by a few, or rule by all citizens. He also distinguished "good" from "bad" versions of each type, according to whether those with power ruled in the interest of the common welfare of all citizens or only in their own interests. The modern study of comparative politics refines and systematizes the age-old practice of evaluating some feature of

A by comparing it to the same feature of B in order to learn more about A than an isolated study of it would permit.

Comparative politics is a subfield of the larger academic discipline of political science.² As you have probably already learned, political science is particularly concerned with the study of power: how it is gained, lost, used, abused, organized, distributed, and contested. The focus of comparative politics is the domestic, or internal, politics of different countries. In addition to comparative politics, most political science (or government) departments in the United States include courses and academic specialists in three other subfields: political theory, international relations, and American politics.

In the United States, the study of American politics is often considered a separate subfield from comparative politics. The pattern of distinguishing the study of politics at home from the study of politics abroad is also common in other countries. Students in Canada study Canadian politics as a distinct specialty, and Japanese students are expected to have particularly in-depth knowledge of Japanese politics.

However, there is no logical reason why the study of the United States should not be included within the field of comparative politics even in the United States—and many good reasons to do so. In fact, many important studies (and an increasing number of courses) integrate the study of American politics with the study of politics in other countries.³ Comparative study can place U.S. politics into a much richer perspective and at the same time make it easier to recognize what is distinctive and most interesting about other countries. Indeed, as the prominent political scientist and **comparativist**, Seymour Martin Lipset once wrote, "Those who know only one country, know no country."⁴

The Central Importance of Countries

We believe the best way to study comparative politics is to focus on countries. Countries comprise distinct, politically defined territories. They usually have their own political institutions, cultures, economies, and ethnic and other social identities. Most people see themselves as citizens of a particular **country**, and national citizenship is one of the most important, but not the only, source of the way people around the world connect to politics.

Within a given country, the most powerful cluster of institutions is referred to as the **state**. In the United States, the word *state* usually refers to the fifty states in the federal system—California, Illinois, New York, Texas, and so on. But in comparative politics, the "state" refers to the key political institutions responsible for making, implementing, enforcing, and adjudicating important policies:⁵ for instance, the "German state" and the "Mexican state." In this context, the state roughly means the same thing as the "government." For example, we might talk about the declining role of the state (or government) in managing the economy in China over the last two or three decades.

The most powerful state institutions in most countries are those that are part of the national **executive** branch—usually headed by the president

---

Sidebar definitions:

What are two more examples of how comparison can distort how we look at political systems?

comparative politics the study of the domestic politics, political institutions, and conflicts of countries.

comparativist a political scientist who studies the similarities and differences in the domestic politics of various countries.

country a territorial unit controlled by a single state.

state the most powerful political institutions in a country, including the executive, legislative, and judicial branches of government, the police, and armed forces.

executive the agencies of government that implement or execute policy.

cabinet the body of officials (e.g., ministers, secretaries) who direct executive departments presided over by the chief executive (e.g., prime minister, president).

bureaucracy an organization structured hierarchically, in which lower-level officials are charged with administering regulations codified in rules that specify impersonal, objective guidelines for making decisions.

legitimacy a belief by powerful groups and the broad citizenry that a state exercises rightful authority.

state formation the historical development of a state, often marked by major stages, key events, or turning points (critical junctures) that influence the contemporary character of the state.

collective identities the groups with which people identify, including gender, class, race, region, and religion, and which are the "building blocks" for social and political action.

and/or prime minister and the **cabinet**, which is made up of individuals who are in charge of the most important government departments and agencies. In some cases, the chief executive leader might be the head of the communist party (China), a military officer (Nigeria until 1999), or the supreme religious leader (Islamic Republic of Iran). The executive branch also includes the administrative **bureaucracy** that carries out laws and regulations. It also includes institutions that are legally allowed to use force, such as the police and military. Other important state institutions are the legislature, courts, and local governments.

All states claim the right to issue rules—notably, laws, administrative regulations, and court decisions—that people within the country must obey. Even democracies can survive only if they use force as a backup to make sure that citizens obey the law. However, in democratic regimes, representatives elected by citizens pass laws. As a result, there is by and large a much greater degree of voluntary compliance with laws in democracies than in nondemocratic states. In dictatorships, the state relies more heavily on the military and police to maintain order. But even then, long-term stability requires that the rulers have some measure of political **legitimacy**. A large percentage of the population, in particular, more influential citizens and groups, must accept that the state has the right to issue commands and to use force against those who do not obey them. Political legitimacy is a crucial concept in the study of comparative politics. It is determined by many factors, including, as we will emphasize, the state's ability to deliver satisfactory economic performance and an acceptable distribution of goods, services, and resources among its citizens.

There are big differences in the ways that states are organized from one country to another. The eight country studies in this book are each written by a comparativist who specializes in studying the politics of that country. The studies devote considerable attention to the description of national political institutions and processes. Each country study begins with an analysis of **state formation**, that is, how the state has evolved historically to reach its present form.

Our country studies also explore the extent to which citizens in a country share a common sense of nationhood, that is, a belief that the state's geographic boundaries coincide with citizens' **collective identities**, particularly ethnicity, language, and religion. When state boundaries and collective identities coincide, political stability is usually easier to maintain. But often they do not coincide. The result may be instability and even violence.

In some countries, nationalist movements seek to secede from the existing state and form their own state, sometimes in alliance with movements from neighboring countries with whom they claim to share a common heritage. The Kurds, for instance, have large populations in both Turkey and Iraq, and have long sought and fought to establish an independent nation-state of Kurdistan.

When a nationalist movement has distinctive ethnic, religious, and/or linguistic ties opposed to those of other groups in the country, conflicts are likely to be especially intense. Nationalist movements may pursue their separatist goal peacefully within the established political system, as has generally been the case with those who support independence for the French-majority province of Quebec from English-majority Canada. Or they may act outside established institutions and engage in illegal, sometimes violent activity. This has often happened in countries around the world, including Spain (the Basque region), Russia (Chechnya), Sri Lanka (the Tamil north), China (Tibet), and Ethiopia (Eritrea). Separatist movements tore apart the once-united country of Yugoslavia. One result of this was the "ethnic cleansing" slaughter in the Balkans region of Southern Europe.

The Comparative Approach to the Study of Politics

How do those of us who study comparative politics—we call ourselves comparativists—go about comparing? What do we compare? Because *countries* are the basic building blocks of the international system and *states* are the most significant political institutions within countries, these are the two critical units for comparative analysis. The comparativist measures and tries to explain similarities and differences among countries or states. One influential approach in comparative politics involves developing what are called **causal theories** that try to explain why "If X happens, then Y is the result." In other words, how does X (the **independent variable**) cause (or influence) Y (the **dependent variable**). This is a basic method of any study that claims to be scientific, whether in the natural, or "hard," sciences like physics and chemistry, or the social, or the "soft" sciences, which include anthropology, economics, and sociology, as well as political science.

To illustrate what causal theories mean in the political science, let's say that we wanted to understand what causes conflict (Y) to intensify among various kinds of groups in a particular country. Many scholars have noted that if a country's economic pie (X) suddenly shrinks, the competition between groups for pieces of that pie will intensify, and conflict is likely to be the result. In other words, a decrease in X (economic pie) will *cause* an increase in Y (conflict). This kind of causal relationship might be tested by statistical analysis of a very large number of cases, a project facilitated in recent years by the creation of data banks that include extensive historical and contemporary data. Another way to study this issue would be to focus on one country, or several, to analyze how the relevant relationships between X and Y have varied over time and with what effect. Comparativists look at a variety of cases and try to identify similarities and differences among countries and discover significant patterns that will, hopefully, help us to better understand what causes important political outcomes.

It is important to recognize the limits on just how "scientific" political science—including comparative politics—can be. Two important differences exist between the natural and the social sciences. First, social scientists study people with free will. Because people have a margin for free choice, even if one assumes that they choose in a rational manner, their choices, attitudes, and behavior cannot be fully explained or predicted. This does not mean that people

---

causal theories an influential approach in comparative politics that involves trying to explain why "if X happens, then Y is the result."

independent variable an important part of social (and natural) scientific research. The cause in a cause-and-effect question.

dependent variable an important part of social (and natural) scientific research. The effect in a cause-and-effect question.

The Internet and the Study of Comparative Politics

The Internet can be a very rich source of information about the politics of countries around the world. Following are some of the types of information you can find on the Web. We haven't included URLs since they change so often. But you should be able to find the websites easily through a key word search on Google or another search engine.

- **Current events.** Most of the world's major news organizations have excellent websites. Among those we recommend for students of comparative politics are the British Broadcasting Corporation (BBC), Cable News Network (CNN), the *New York Times*, and the *Washington Post*.
- **Elections.** Results of recent (and often past) elections, data on voter turnout, and descriptions of different types of electoral systems can be found at: the International Election Guide (IFES), Elections by country/Wikipedia, and the International Institute for Democracy and Electoral Assistance.
- **Statistics.** You can find data that is helpful both for understanding the political, economic, and social situation in individual countries and for comparing countries. Excellent sources of statistics are the Central Intelligence Agency (CIA), the Inter-parliamentary Union (IPU), the United Nations Development Program (UNDP), and the World Bank.

  There are some websites that bring together data from other sources. These not only allow you to access the statistics, but also to chart or map them in a variety of ways. See, for example, Nationmaster.com and Globalis.com.
- **Rankings and Ratings.** There is a growing number of organizations that provide rankings or ratings of countries along some dimension based on comparative statistical analysis. We provide the following examples of these in the Data Charts that appear at the end of this chapter: the UNDP **Human Development Index**; the **Global Gender Gap**; the **Environmental Performance Index**; the **Corruption Perceptions Index**; and the **Freedom in the World ratings**. Others you might look are UNDP's Gender-Related Development Index (GDI) and Gender Empowerment Measure (GEM); the Global Economic Competitiveness Index; the Globalization Index; the Index of Economic Freedom; the World Audit of Freedom and Democracy; and the Press Freedom Index. *A note of caution: Some of these sites may have a certain political point of view that influences the way they collect and analyze data. As with any Web source: be sure to check out who sponsors the site and what type of organization it is.*
- **Official information and documents.** Most countries maintain websites in English. The first place to look is the website of the country's embassy in Washington, D.C., Ottawa, or London. The United Nations delegations of many countries also have websites. Governments often have English language versions of their official homepages,

---

Human Development Index (HDI) a composite number used by the United Nations to measure and compare levels of achievement in health, knowledge, and standard of living.

Global Gender Gap a measure of the extent to which women in 58 countries have achieved equality with men.

Environmental Performance Index a measure of how close countries come to meeting specific benchmarks for national pollution control and natural resource management.

Corruption Perceptions Index A measure developed by Transparency International that ranks countries in terms of the degree to which corruption is perceived to exist among public officials and politicians.

Freedom in the World rating an annual evaluation by Freedom House of the state of freedom in countries around the world measured according to political rights and civil liberties.

including governments with which the United States may not have official relations, such as Cuba and North Korea.
- **The United States Department of State.** The State Department's website has background notes on most countries. American embassies around the world provide information of selected topics about the country in which they are based.
- **Maps.** The Perry-Castañeda Library Map Collection at the University of Texas is probably the best currently available on-line source of worldwide maps at an educational institution.
- **General Comparative Politics.** Several American and British universities host excellent websites that provide links to a multitude of Internet resources on comparative politics (often coupled with international relations), such as those at Columbia University, Emory University, Keele University, Princeton University, Vanderbilt University, and West Virginia University. ❖

choose in a totally random fashion. We choose within the context of economic constraints, institutional dictates, and cultural prescriptions. Comparative politics systematically analyzes how such factors shape political preferences and choices; indeed, one recent study claimed that political beliefs are, to a significant degree, genetically determined,[6] that is, our political values and opinions (for example, on capital punishment or abortion) are, at least partly, inherited biologically from our parents.

A second difference between the natural and social sciences is that in the natural sciences, experimental techniques can isolate how distinct factors contribute to a particular outcome. In a laboratory setting, it is possible to change the value or magnitude of a factor—for example, the force applied to an object or mix of chemicals—and measure how the outcome has consequently changed. But political scientists and comparativists rarely have the opportunity to apply such precise experimental techniques.

Some political scientists have conducted experiments with volunteers in controlled settings to test, for example, the influence of political advertisements on voter opinions. But laboratories provide crude approximations of natural settings, since only one or a few variables can be manipulated. The real world of politics, by contrast, consists of an endless number of variables, and they cannot easily be isolated or manipulated. It simply is not possible to predict with absolute certainly how someone will vote once he or she gets into the voting booth; nor is it possible to know fully why voters cast their ballots the way they do.

Some political scientists try to get deeper into the question of cause and effect by using statistical techniques to identify the specific weight of different factors in explaining variations in political outcomes. But it is difficult to measure precisely how, for example, a person's ethnicity, gender, or income influences her or his voting choices. Nor can we ever know exactly what mix of factors—conflicts among elites, popular ideological appeals, the weakness of the state, the organizational capacity of rebel leaders, or the discontent of the masses—leads to the success or the failure of a revolution. Indeed, similar outcomes of different revolutions may result from different combinations of factors. No single theory, therefore, can explain the outcomes of all revolutions—or why people vote the way they do.

Comparative Politics and the Challenge of Globalization

FOCUS QUESTIONS

What do we mean by globalization? How does increased cross-border contact among countries and peoples affect political, social, and cultural life?

Comparative politics has traditionally focused on studying single countries or domestic institutions and processes in several countries. Comparativists considered that studying the international system fell within the subfield of international relations. However, as mentioned near the beginning of this chapter, for nearly two decades, globalization has been a critical factor in analyzing politics within and among countries. Today, business and trade, information technology, mass communications and culture, the environment, immigration and travel, as well as politics, forge deep connections—and often deep divisions—among people worldwide. To appreciate the complexity of politics in any country, comparativists now recognize that we must look beyond and across borders at the growing interdependence among nations. We have learned that we must develop a truly global perspective in order to understand the politics of individual countries and to compare them.

The terms *globalization* and *global era* identify the growing depth, extent, and diversity of today's cross-border connections. Discussion of globalization usually begins with economic activities—the great increase in international trade, finance, and overseas investment, as well as the worldwide reorganization of production and redistribution of the work force that has led to the creation of the so-called global factory in which very few manufactured products are, in fact, produced in just one country. Globalization also involves the movement of peoples through migration, employment, business, tourism, and educational opportunities.

The Internet and other new applications of technology now blur distinctions between what is around the block and what is around the world. These technologies link producers and contractors, headquarters, branch plants, suppliers, and consumers in real time anywhere in the world. Employees may be rooted in time and place, but they can take advantage of the ebb and flow of a global labor market. On the flip side: a secure job today may be gone tomorrow if an employer decides to move a business to another country.

Globalization has provoked challenges from grassroots movements in every region of the world that are concerned with its negative impact on, for example, poor people, the environment, and labor rights. Conferences convened by governments and international organizations to develop rules for global commerce have been the sites of demonstrations by coalitions of environmental, labor-based, and community activists. Activists from around the world have recently assembled in places such as Mumbai, India, and Porto Alegre, Brazil, to exchange ideas and develop alternatives to the current form of economic globalization.[7]

Globalization in its many forms challenges the ability of even the strongest countries to control their destinies. In today's world, no country can be an island unto itself and protect its national culture from outside influences, seal off its economy, or isolate its people. Many of the most important problems confronting individual states are related to globalization, including pandemics like AIDS, global climate change, financial panics, the arms trade, and international terrorism. The study of comparative politics has, in many ways, become the study of global politics.

The events of September 11, 2001, made it painfully clear that international terror networks, such as Al Qaeda, are an evil form of globalization. Terrorists, and the causes that motivate them, move around the world. They can attack anywhere. But such issues have not replaced concerns about economic globalization, which has an impact on many more countries and peoples than does terrorism. Rather these issues remind us how multifaceted globalization has become and underline the urgency of developing a more complex understanding of globalization and how it influences both politics throughout the world and the study of comparative politics.

SECTION 4 Themes for Comparative Analysis

FOCUS QUESTIONS

Of the themes presented for comparative analysis, which one seems the most important? Why? The least important? Why?

Give an example of how, in one particular country, features of one theme can affect the features of another theme.

We have already emphasized the need to apply a clear framework to the study of comparative politics in order to make sense of major and often confusing developments that have shaped the contemporary political world. We have also explained the subject matter of comparative politics and described some of the tools of comparative analysis.

This section describes the four themes we use in *Introduction to Comparative Politics* to organize the information on state institutions and political processes in the country chapters. These themes help explain similarities and differences among countries. We also suggest a way that each theme highlights a particularly important question—or puzzle—in comparative politics.

Theme 1: A World of States

Our first theme, *a world of states*, is a bit of a play on words. It is meant to reflect the facts that individual states are the most important actors on the world stage and that all states must be understood from the perspective of their place among other states on the world stage.

For about 500 years, states have been the basic building block of global politics. International organizations (such as the United Nations) and private actors like transnational corporations (such as Microsoft)—and ordinary citizens organized in political parties and social movements—have certainly come to play a crucial role in world politics. But it is still, for the most part, states that determine the decisive outcomes in international affairs. It is the rulers of states who send armies against other states. The legal codes of states make it possible for businesses to operate within their borders and beyond. States are the main source—to greatly varying degrees—of resources for human welfare by providing assistance for the sick, poor, elderly, orphaned, or unemployed. States regulate the movement of people across borders. States negotiate and sign (or reject) treaties or agreements on the most critical issues facing individual countries and the world as a whole, be they war and peace, nuclear proliferation, trade, or pollution.

A state's position in the world of states has a powerful impact on its domestic politics. In 1796, George Washington warned the United States not to "entangle our peace and prosperity" in alliances with other nations. He believed the United States would be more successful if it could remain detached from the global power politics of the time. That kind of disengagement might have been possible then. But not today, particularly in this post–9/11 era of globalization.

Thanks to radio, television, and the Internet, people nearly everywhere can become remarkably well informed about international developments. This knowledge may lead citizens to demand that their governments intervene to stop atrocities in faraway Kosovo, Rwanda, or Dafur, or rush to aid the victims of natural disasters, as happened after the great tsunami struck South and Southeast Asia in late 2004.

Heightened global awareness may encourage citizens to hold their own government to internationally recognized standards of human rights and democracy. The recent spread of the so-called color or flower revolutions illustrates how what happens in one state can influence popular movements in other states, particularly in this era of globalized media and communications. Such movements have adopted various symbols to show their unity of purpose: the "Rose Revolution" (2003) in Georgia (a country located between Russia and Turkey, not the southern U.S. state), the "Orange Revolution" (2004) in Ukraine, the "Tulip Revolution" (2005) in Kyrgyzstan all led to the toppling of dictatorial leaders. The "Cedar Revolution" in Lebanon (2005) didn't force a change of political leadership, but it did cause the withdrawal of unpopular Syrian troops from that country, and the "Blue Revolution" in Kuwait has emerged as an important movement in support of granting women greater political rights.

States may collapse altogether when challenged by powerful rivals for power. And a similar outcome may occur when leaders of the state violate the rule of law and become predators, preying on their own people. Political scientist Robert Rotberg suggested the term **failed states** to describe this extreme situation, and cited as examples Sierra Leone, Somalia, and Afghanistan before and under the Taliban.[8] *Foreign Policy*, a highly respected journal on current affairs, compiles an annual ranking of failed states. In 2007, Sudan headed the list. Iraq, even under American military occupation, was ranked second.[9] The seventeenth-century English philosopher Thomas Hobbes, who lived in a time of great political disorder that included the beheading of a king, warned in his classic book, *Leviathan*, that the absence of effective state authority produces a war of every person against every other person. This desperate situation, he observed, involves "continual fear, and danger of violent death; and the life of man [is] solitary, poor, nasty, brutish, and short." For the nearly two billion people that *Foreign Policy* estimates live in states that are in serious danger of failing, Hobbes' dire warning may be all too true.

Although few states collapse into complete failure, all states today are experiencing intense pressures from external influences. But international political and economic factors do not have the same impact in all countries, and a few

failed states states in which the government no longer functions effectively.

powerful and privileged states have the capacity to shape the international system as much as they are shaped by it. The more advantages a state possesses, the more global influence it will have. At the same time, countries with fewer advantages are more extensively molded by other states, international organizations, and transnational corporations.

Our case studies also emphasize the importance of similarities and contrasts in state formation and organization among countries. We discuss how states have developed historically: key events like colonial conquest, defeat in war, economic crises, or revolutions that had a durable impact on the character of the state.

Furthermore, the world-of-states theme draws attention to the importance of variations in the organization of states. This is the overall mix of their political institutions that distinguishes, for example, democratic from authoritarian regimes (see below for a discussion of the meaning of **authoritarianism**). This theme also highlights variations in institutions within a given regime type, such as the contrast between presidential (as in Mexico) and parliamentary (as in Britain) systems of government in democratic states.

> **authoritarianism** a system of rule in which power depends not on popular legitimacy but on the coercive force of the political authorities.

A World-of-States Puzzle

How do states today deal with the many challenges to their authority from both internal and external forces? Increasingly, the politics and policies of states are shaped by diverse international factors from "above" often lumped together under globalization. At the same time, many states face groups within their borders who confront the power and legitimacy of central governments from "below." In reading the country case studies, try to assess how pressures from both above and below—outside and inside—affect the state in carrying out its basic functions. To what extent are even the most powerful states influenced by global and social forces that they cannot fully control? In what ways are the poorer and less powerful countries especially vulnerable to the pressures of globalization and disgruntled citizens? In this world marked by globalization and increasing interdependence, can states any longer achieve desirable outcomes on their own?

Theme 2: Governing the Economy

The success of states in maintaining the support of their people depends to a great degree on their ability to meet the economic needs and desires of their populations. An important reason for the rejection of communism and the disintegration of the Soviet Union was the poor performance of the Soviet economy. People simply became fed up with long lines to buy daily necessities, with the shoddy quality or even total lack of consumer products, crowded housing, unavailable or outrageously expensive foreign goods—to name just a few of the economic woes inflicted on its people by the Soviet state. In contrast, communist rule has survived in China in large part because of the stunning growth of the Chinese economy and the rapidly rising standard of living for the large majority of the people.

How a state organizes production and the extent and character of its intervention in the economy—that is, how it "governs the economy"[10]—reflects one of its most important functions and is a key element in its overall pattern of governance and political legitimacy. It is important to analyze, for example, how the economies of various countries differ in the balance between agricultural and industrial production, why some countries do so well in competing with other countries that offer similar products in international markets, and the relative importance of private market forces versus government direction of the economy.

The term **political economy** refers to how government policy affects economic performance and how economic performance in turn affects a country's political processes. We believe that politics in all countries is deeply influenced by the relationship between the government and the economy and that a political economy perspective should be part of any thorough approach to the study of comparative politics.

A Governing-the-Economy Puzzle

There is not one right way for a state to govern the economy, nor is there one single standard by which to measure economic success. There is widespread agreement that some state practices *hinder* economic development, for example, when state officials accept bribes, set tax rates so high as to discourage investment, and fail to provide public goods like education and transportation facilities that promote a productive economy. However, there is less agreement on the economic policies that states *should* adopt. As you read the country studies in this book, ask yourself: Why are some states more successful at promoting successful economic performance than others?

A related puzzle: Should economic performance be measured solely by how rapidly a country's economy grows? Or are other standards important to keep in mind, such as the quality of life of its citizens, as measured by such criteria as life expectancy, level of education, and unemployment rate? Is equality important? What about the environmental impact of economic growth? There is now much greater attention than just a few decades ago to this question, and more countries are emphasizing **sustainable development**, which promotes ecologically sound ways to modernize the economy and raise the standard of living. What do you think are the appropriate yardsticks to evaluate how well a state is governing its economy?

Theme 3: The Democratic Idea

One of the most important and astounding political developments in recent years has been the rapid spread of **democracy** throughout much of the world. There is overwhelming evidence of the strong appeal of the democratic idea and the desire to live in a democracy. We will define what we mean by *democracy*

---

political economy the study of the interaction between the state and the economy, that is, how the state and political processes affect the economy and how the organization of the economy affects political processes.

sustainable development an approach to promoting economic growth that seeks to minimize environmental degradation and depletion of natural resources.

democracy from the Greek *demos* (the people) and *kratos* (rule). A type of political system that features the following: selection to important public offices through free and fair elections based on universal suffrage (the right of all adults to vote); political parties that are free to organize, offer their ideas, present candidates for public office, and compete in elections; an elected government that develops policy according to specified procedures that are fair and relatively open to public scrutiny; all citizens possess political rights and civil liberties; an independent judiciary (court system); civilian control of the military.

How Is Economic Development Measured?

As we have already noted, we put particular importance on understanding the relationship between the political system and the economy in the study of the politics of any country and in our overall approach to comparative politics. Each of the country case studies describes and analyzes the role of the government in making economic policy. They also take special note of the impact of the global economy on national politics.

This book makes frequent reference to two commonly used measures of the overall size or power of a country's economy:

- **Gross Domestic Product (GDP):** a calculation of the total goods and services produced by the country during a given year.
- **Gross National Product (GNP):** GDP plus income earned abroad by the country's residents.

A country's GDP and GNP are different, but not hugely so. Both measure the *total output* of a country's economy. In this book, we use GDP calculated according to an increasingly popular method called **purchasing power parity (PPP)**. PPP takes into account the real cost of living in a particular country by calculating how much it would cost in the local currency to buy the same "basket of goods" in different countries. For example, how many dollars in the United States, pesos in Mexico, or rubles in Russia does it take to buy a certain amount of food or to pay for housing? Many scholars think that PPP provides a relatively reliable (and revealing) tool for comparing the size of an economy and among countries. In terms of annual total output, the world's ten largest economies are: the United States, China, Japan, India, Germany, Britain, Italy, France, Russia, and Brazil.

But a better way to measure and compare the level of economic development and the standards of living in different countries is to look at annual GDP *per capita* (per person), in other words, to look at total economic output divided by total population. Although China has the world's second-largest economy in terms of total output, from the annual GDP *per capita* perspective China ($7700) falls to 109th out of 229 countries measured between 2004–2006, and India ($3800) falls to 154th place. Luxembourg ($71,400) with its small population, ranks first while the United States is ninth ($44,000). This approach gives us a better idea of which countries in the world are rich (developed) or poor (developing).

The comparative data charts at the end of this chapter provide total GDP and GDP *per capita* as well as other economic, geographic, demographic, and social information for our eight country case studies. The data charts also provide several ways of ranking or rating countries in order to compare them along various dimensions of their economic, political, or public policy performance. One of the most important of these is the Human Development Index (HDI), which the United Nations uses to evaluate a country's level of development that considers more than just economic factors. The formula used to calculate a country's HDI takes into account *longevity* (life expectancy at birth), *knowledge* (adult literacy and average years of schooling), as well as *income* (according to PPP).

Based on this formula, countries are annually ranked and divided into three broad categories by the United Nations Development Program (UNDP): "High" "Medium," and "Low" human development. Out of 177 countries ranked according to HDI in 2006, the top three were Norway, Iceland, and Australia; the bottom three were Mali, Sierra Leone, and Niger. Look at the data charts to see how the countries in this book are ranked, and as you read the case studies try to see what connections there may be between a country's state policies, politics, and its human development ranking. ❖

---

gross domestic product (GDP) the total of all goods and services produced within a country that is used as a broad measure of the size of its economy.

gross national product (GNP) GDP plus income earned by the country's residents; another broad measure of the size of an economy.

purchasing power parity (PPP) a method of calculating the value of a country's money based on the actual cost of buying goods and services in that country rather than how many U.S. dollars they are worth.

TABLE 1.1

The Spread of Democracy

Year	Free Countries	Partly Free Countries	Not Free Countries
1973	43 (35%)[1]	38 (18%)	69 (47%)
1983	54 (36%)	47 (20%)	64 (44%)
1993[2]	75 (25%)	73 (44%)	38 (31%)
2006	90 (46%)	58 (17%)	45 (37%)[3]

Notes:

1. The number of countries in each category is followed by the percentage of the world population.
2. In 1993, the large increase in the number of *free* and *partly free* countries was mostly due to the collapse of communist regimes in the Soviet Union and elsewhere. The main reason that there is a significant drop in the percentage of world population living in *free* countries in 1993 is that India was classified as *partly free* from 1991 through 1997. It has been ranked as *free* since 1998.
3. The increase in the number of countries and percentage of people rated as *not free* countries in 2006 compared to 1993 reflects the fact that several countries, most notably Russia, were shifted from *partly free* to *not free*.

more precisely later in this chapter. For now, it can be taken to mean a political system in which leaders and officials are held accountable in meaningful ways to those over whom they exercise power. In democracies, citizens also have some control and influence over the decisions made by their states and governments.

Freedom House (a research organization based in the United States) annually collects and analyzes data on civil and political liberties in countries around the world and then rates them as "Free" (democratic), "Partly Free," and "Not Free." The table above is based on data from Freedom House reports[11], and shows just how dramatic the spread of democracy has been since the early 1970s.

We do not mean to claim that all countries are or inevitably will become democracies. There is a vigorous scholarly debate about whether China will democratize.[12] Furthermore, countries that have adopted democratic institutions may experience reversals. An important recent example is Russia. Following the disintegration of communist rule in the 1990s, there was a trend toward democracy. However, many democratic liberties and procedures were undermined under the rule of Vladimir Putin in the first decade of the twenty-first century. In fact, Freedom House now classifies Russia as "Not Free," although we still classify it as a "transitional democracy" (see below). Thus, a trend toward democracy is only a trend, not a certainty.

What explains why some countries become democratic? For all the attention this question has received, there is no scholarly consensus on how and why democratization occurs. Or rather, we have learned that there is not one path to democracy, just as there is not one path to economic success.

Is it possible to identify conditions that are critical for democracy to flourish? Comparativists have proposed that among such conditions are secure national boundaries, a stable state, an adequate standard of living, a large middle class, the widespread acceptance of democratic values, agreement to play by the rules of the democratic game among those who contend for power. One might extend the list, but the point should be clear. There are infinite possible factors that might explain why democratic institutions are adopted. Democracy can and has flourished in unlikely settings—for example, in India, a country with a vast population whose per capita income is among the lowest in the world. And it has failed where it might be expected to flourish—for example, in Germany in the 1930s when Hitler came to power in a country that was a very rich and modern country for the times. Democracies vary widely in terms of how they came into existence and in their specific historical, institutional, and cultural dimensions.

Toppling authoritarian regimes and then holding elections does not mean that democracy will prevail or endure. A wide gulf exists between what comparativists have termed a *transition* to democracy and the *consolidation* of democracy. A transition involves toppling an authoritarian regime and adopting the basic ingredients of a democratic state (see below); consolidation requires fuller adherence to democratic procedures, a deeper commitment to democratic values, and democratic institutions that are sturdy and durable. The process of democratic consolidation may take decades.

At the same time, the democratic idea fuels political conflicts in even the most durable democracies, because a large gap usually separates democratic ideals and the actual functioning of democratic political institutions. **Social movements** may target the democratic state because they judge that it does not respond to their demands. Such movements have organized in varied spheres including environmental regulation, reproductive rights, and race or ethnic relations. Even in countries with impressive histories of democratic institutions, citizens may demand that their government be more responsive and accountable to the ideals of democracy.

social movements
large-scale grass-roots action that demands reforms of existing social practices and government policies.

A Democratic-Idea Puzzle

What is the relationship between democracy and political stability? On the one hand, democracy by its very nature permits political opposition, which can make political life in democracies turbulent and unpredictable. On the other hand, it is rarely violent. The very fact that political opposition and competition are legitimate in democracies appears to deepen support for the state, even among opponents of a particular administration. The democratic rules of the game may promote political stability by encouraging today's losers to remain in the game because they may win peacefully in future competition. As you learn about different countries, look for the stabilizing and destabilizing consequences of recent democratic transitions (Mexico, South Africa); the reasons for the reversal of democracy (Russia); the pressures (or lack of pressure) for democratization in authoritarian states (China, Iran); and the persistence of undemocratic elements even in established democracies (Britain, France, India).

Chapter 1: **Introducing Comparative Politics**

A Puzzle That Combines the Democratic Idea and Governing the Economy

Is there a relationship between a democratic state and successful national economic performance? This is a question that students of political economy have long pondered—and which continues to provoke debate. All economies, even the most powerful, experience ups and downs. But the United States, Britain, and France—all long-established, durable democracies—have been notable economic success stories. Does this suggest that democracy assures economic success (that there is a causal relationship)? But, then, how do we explain that several East Asian countries, such as the Republic of Korea (South Korea), Taiwan, and Singapore, achieved remarkable development in the 1960s and 1970s while under authoritarian regimes. China is a repressive **communist party–state** ("Not Free" according to Freedom House) that has enjoyed the highest growth rate in the world since the early 1990s. It provides a vivid case of development without democracy. The fact that both South Korea and Taiwan subsequently became democracies has led some scholars to conclude that an authoritarian state may be suitable for promoting rapid economic development for a while, but that economic development itself creates pressures for democratization. China is a very interesting case study about whether that hypothesis is valid.

Nobel Prize–winning economist Amartya Sen has argued, "There is no clear relation between economic growth and democracy in *either* direction."[13] As you read the country studies, try to identify why some states have been more successful than others in "governing the economy," that is, fostering successful economic performance. Do you think democracy is a factor?

Theme 4: The Politics of Collective Identity

How do individuals understand who they are in political terms? National citizenship is one of the broadest sources of what we call collective political identities. On what other collective identities do people form groups to advance common political aims?

Social scientists once thought they knew. In the 1940s and 1950s, many argued that the age-old loyalties of ethnicity, religious affiliation, race, gender, and locality were on the decline and were being replaced by identities shaped by economic, political, and cultural modernization. Comparativists (as well as many others who observe and analyze society) thought that **social class**—solidarities based on the shared experience of work or, more broadly, economic position—had become the most important source of collective identity. They believed that most of the time, identity-based groups would pursue their interests in ways that were not politically destabilizing. We now know that the formation of group attachments is far more complex.

In many long-established democracies such as the United States, Britain, and Japan, the importance of identities based on class membership has declined, although class and economic sources of collective political identity remain

---

communist party–state a type of nation-state in which the communist party attempts to exercise a complete monopoly on political power and controls all important state institutions.

social class a group whose members share common economic status determined largely by occupation, income, and wealth.

significant in political competition and economic organization. In many countries, identities not based on class have assumed growing, not diminishing, significance. Such affiliations may include shared language, region, religion, ethnicity, race, nationality, or gender.

The politics of collective identity involves struggles to form politically influential groups and to increase and assert their power against other groups or the state. Such politics also involves the struggle to define which groups are significant or favored players in the political process and which are marginalized, excluded, or even repressed. These issues are never fully settled, although they may rage with greater or lesser intensity in particular countries and at particular times. The issue of race relations in the United States is a powerful reminder of this basic fact of political life.

Religion is another especially important source of collective identity—as well as of severe political conflict, both within and among religious communities. Violent conflict among religious groups has recently occurred in many countries, including India, Sri Lanka, Nigeria, and Britain in Northern Ireland (an agreement in 2007 offers hope that the conflict in Northern Ireland has ended). Such conflicts may spill over national boundaries. For example, Al Qaeda claimed that the presence of non-Muslim Western forces in the sacred Islamic territory of Saudi Arabia was an important reason for its violent attacks against the United States and related targets. At the same time, we want to emphasize that the political orientation of a particular religious community is not predetermined, but is rather a product of efforts of leaders to mobilize the community to support their views. The political posture associated with Christian, Jewish, Muslim, or Hindu beliefs cannot simply be read from sacred texts of that religion. There is intense conflict *within* most religious communities—often over the meaning of the same sacred texts—that pits more liberal, secular elements against those who defend what they claim is a more orthodox, traditional interpretation.

A Collective-Identities Puzzle

distributional politics the use of power, particularly by the state, to allocate some kind of valued resource among competing groups.

How does collective identity affect a country's **distributional politics**, that is, the process of deciding how resources are distributed among different groups? Collective identities operate at both the level of symbols, attitudes, values, and beliefs and at the level of material, or economic, resources, and both are important when it comes to distributional politics.

In a situation of extreme scarcity, it may prove nearly impossible to reach any compromise among groups with conflicting material demands. But if an adequate level of material resources is available, such conflicts may be easier to resolve through distributional politics because groups can negotiate at least a minimally satisfying share of resources.

However, the nonmaterial demands of ethnic, religious, and nationalist movements may be very difficult to satisfy by distributional politics. The distributional style may be quite ineffective when, for example, a religious group demands that the government require all citizens to conform to its social practices or when a dominant linguistic group insists that a single language be used in education and government throughout the country. In such cases, political conflict tends to move from the distributive realm to the realm where compromises cannot be achieved by simply dividing the pie of material resources. As the important British weekly *The Economist* pointed out in a mid-2007 review of the crisis in the Middle East, one of the main reasons for the lack of progress in finding a solution to the Israeli-Palestinian conflict is that "What started as a national struggle between two peoples for one land is gradually, and often willfully, being transformed into a war of religion. . . ."[14] Look in the country studies for examples of identity conflicts over distributional issues that can be resolved by the normal give and take of political bargaining—and those that lead, instead, to political violence.

These four themes provide the analytic scaffold on which this book is built. With an understanding of the methods of comparative politics and the four themes in mind, we can now discuss how we have grouped the country studies that comprise *Introduction to Comparative Politics* and how the text is organized for comparative analysis.

SECTION 4

Classifying Political Systems

FOCUS QUESTIONS

What are some difficult problems involved in establishing a useful way of classifying political systems?
Can you think of another way from the one suggested in this chapter?

typology a method of classifying by using criteria that divide a group of cases into smaller numbers.

There are about 200 states in the world today, each with a political system that is distinctive in some ways. How can we classify them in a manageable fashion? It makes sense to highlight clusters of states that share important similarities, just as it is useful to identify what distinguishes one cluster of relatively similar states from other clusters. When comparativists classify a large number of cases into a smaller number of types or clusters, they call the result a **typology**.

Typologies make comparison easier both within the same type as well as between types of states. For example, Britain and the United States are long-established democracies, but they have very different institutional architecture. Britain has a parliamentary system, in which parliament (the legislature) chooses the prime minister, that is, the official who heads the executive. Parliament and the prime minister have considerable power over each other. Parliament can force the prime minister to resign by voting a motion of no confidence. And the prime minister can dissolve parliament and call new elections. The United States has a presidential system, in which the president and the legislature (Congress) are separately elected. Further, the two branches have extensive powers independent of each other. Neither branch can force the other to resign, although Congress can impeach the president. What political significance is there in the fact that Britain and the United States organize state power in such different ways? This kind of question about the different mix of state institutions within similar political systems is the kind of issue that is at the heart of comparative politics.

How do we construct typologies of states? Typologies are artificial constructs, made rather than occurring naturally. They are based on certain features that comparativists decide are important as the basis for classification. Typologies are helpful to the extent that they permit us to engage in useful comparisons that further our understanding of politics.

The typology that we use in this book classifies regimes into three groups: *consolidated democracies*, *transitional democracies*, and *authoritarian regimes*. This typology reveals the bedrock distinction between democratic and undemocratic regimes. To understand why we have chosen to classify countries in this fashion, it is first necessary to take a closer look at what is meant by democracy.

The Meaning—or Meanings—of Democracy

It is generally agreed by political scientists that democracy includes the following features:

- Selection to important public offices on the basis of free and fair elections based on universal suffrage (the right of all adults to vote). For an election to qualify as fair, votes must be counted accurately, with the winning candidate(s) determined according to preexisting rules about the kind of majority or plurality that is needed to gain electoral victory.

- Political parties are free to organize, offer their ideas, present candidates for public office, and compete in elections. The opposition party or parties—those not in power—enjoy adequate rights to organize and to criticize the incumbent government.

- The elected government develops policy according to specified procedures that are fair and relatively open to public scrutiny. Elected executives are held accountable for their decisions and actions at the next election, through the courts, and by the legislature. In turn, the legislature is held most directly accountable to the citizens through a system in which voters choose who will represent them in the legislature.

- All citizens possess civil and political rights—the right to participate and vote in elections periodically held to select key state officeholders—and civil liberties—the rights of free assembly, conscience, privacy, and expression, including the right to criticize the government. In theory, these rights must be available to all citizens equally.

- The political system contains a judiciary (court system) with powers independent of the executive and legislature, charged with protecting citizens' rights and liberties from violation by the state and other citizens, as well as with ensuring that governmental officials respect the constitution and other laws.

- The military must accept, without question, that it is subordinate to the elected government and that its commander-in-chief is an civilian responsible to voters.

consolidated democracies democratic political systems that have been solidly and stably established for an ample period of time and in which there is relatively consistent adherence to the core democratic principles.

transitional democracies countries that have moved from an authoritarian government to a democratic one.

Our typology of political systems distinguishes between those countries whose political regimes are democratic according to the above criteria and those that are not. The typology involves a further distinction between long-established, or **consolidated democracies**, and newly established, or **transitional democracies**. We believe that there is an important difference in kind, and not just of degree, between these two types of democratic states. We distinguish between consolidated and transitional democracies in two ways.

First, the *longevity* and *durability* of democratic institutions and practices. Have they been solidly and stably established for an ample period of time? Precisely how much time is open to question. Consolidated democracies are long-standing democracies: the countries in this book that fall in this category (Britain, France, and India) have been democracies for a minimum of about sixty years (India). There is very little likelihood that a consolidated democracy will experience a reversal and become undemocratic. Transitional democracies are those that have relatively recently adopted the essential features of democracy, and their futures as democracies may be less certain.

The second criterion for distinguishing between consolidated and transitional democracies is the *extent* of their democratic practice. In consolidated democracies, there is relatively full compliance with the democratic principles specified above. We do not mean to claim that consolidated democracies always respect democratic principles. That would be naïve. For example, police abuse and unequal treatment of citizens who are poor or from a racial or ethnic minority are all too common in democracies like Britain, France, and the United States. However consolidated democracies generally practice the democracy they preach.

The reason we highlight the extent of democracy becomes apparent when we turn to the category of transitional democracies. In such countries, formal democratic institutions and procedures often conceal informal practices that violate the checklist of core features of democracy.[15]

To be sure, there is greater legal protection of citizen rights and liberties, a more independent judiciary, and more independent political parties in transitional democracies than in authoritarian regimes—the third category that is part of our typology. But these and other democratic features are less extensive and stable than in consolidated democracies. In transitional democracies, democratic forms of governance coexist with and are often compromised by undemocratic elements. Compared to consolidated democracies, political authorities in transitional systems are much more likely to engage in corruption, control of the media, intimidation and violence against opponents, vote rigging, and other measures to make sure they get reelected. Despite what the constitution of the country may specify, the courts are often packed with judges loyal to the ruling party, and top military officers often exercise extraordinary political power behind the scenes. The countries in *Introduction to Comparative Politics* that we classify as transitional democracies are Mexico, Russia, and South Africa.

How do we define authoritarian regimes? The simplest way would be to say that they fail to meet all or most all of the characteristics of a democracy listed above. Authoritarian regimes lack meaningful procedures for selecting political leaders through competitive elections based on universal suffrage; there are no secure procedures for holding political leaders accountable to the citizens of the country; the right to criticize the government is severely restricted; people of different genders, racial groups, religions, and ethnicities do not enjoy equal rights; and the judiciary is not an independent branch of government capable of checking the power of the state or protecting the rights of citizens; and finally the military may not be effectively subject to civilian political control.

Clearly, then, authoritarian states are not democracies. But it isn't good social science to define something only by what it is not. The term *authoritarianism* refers to political systems in which power (or authority) is highly—perhaps almost totally—concentrated in a single individual, a small group of people, or a single political party or institution (such as the military). Furthermore, those with power claim an exclusive right to govern and use various means, including force, to impose their will and policies. Another way to put it: in authoritarian systems, the state is more powerful than the citizens it governs and is not accountable to them.

There is an enormous variety of authoritarian regime types: communist party–states (China and Cuba); **theocracies** in which sovereign power is held by religious leaders and law is defined in religious terms (Iran); military governments (Pakistan and Burma); absolute monarchies (Saudi Arabia); and personalistic dictatorships (Iraq under Sadaam Hussein). These types of authoritarianism differ from one another in many ways, including fundamental beliefs (**ideology**) and the degree and methods of force used to suppress opposition and control society. The countries classified as authoritarian in *Introduction to Comparative Politics* are China and Iran.

Although there are fundamental differences between democracy and authoritarianism, these categories are not airtight.

For example, in most authoritarian countries, there are elements of democratic practices. In Iran (a theocratic authoritarian regime), there are vigorously contested multiparty elections, although the extent of political debate and opposition is defined and limited by the Islamic clergy. For the last decade or so in China, a form of grassroots democracy has been implemented in the more than 700,000 rural villages, where a majority of the population lives. Even though the communist party still makes sure that dissent does not get out of hand, China's rural dwellers now have a real choice when they elect their local leaders, and their choices have often resulted in the ouster of corrupt and unpopular officials. Such democratic elements in Iranian and Chinese politics certainly make a difference in important ways to the citizens of those countries, but they do not fundamentally alter the essential authoritarian character of the state in these two countries.

As another example of the gray zone between democracy and nondemocracy, we consider India a consolidated democracy because it has generally respected most of the democratic procedures on our checklist since it gained independence from Britain in 1947. There is intense political competition in India, elections are usually free and fair, and the Indian judiciary is quite independent. However, India has repeatedly experienced scenes of communal

---

theocracy a state dominated by the clergy, who rule on the grounds that they are the only interpreters of God's will and law.

ideology a set of fundamental ideas, values, or beliefs about how a political, economic, or social system should be organized.

violence, in which Muslim, Sikh, and Christian minorities have been brutally massacred, sometimes with the active complicity of state officials. Horrific political violence has occurred so often and sometimes on such a wide scale that India's claim to live up to the democratic idea is certainly open to question. When it comes to democracy there are many different shades of gray, but in every country a gap remains between the aims and achievements of democratic governance.

We hope that the timely information and thematic focus of this book will not only help you understand better politics in several different countries from around the world but also inspire you to explore further the comparative approach to the often troubling, sometimes inspiring, but always changing and endlessly fascinating world of politics.

SECTION 5: Organization of the Text

FOCUS QUESTIONS

If you could choose one other country to study in a comparative politics course besides the eight included in this book, what would it be? Why?
What would you like to know about politics in that country?

The core of this book consists of eight country case studies. We selected them for their significance in terms of our comparative themes and because they provide an interesting sample of types of political regimes, levels of economic development, and geographic regions. Although each of the country studies makes important comparative references, the studies primarily provide detailed descriptions and analyses of the politics of individual countries. At the same time, the country studies have common section and subsection headings to help you make comparisons and explore similar themes across the various cases. The following are brief summaries of the main issues and questions covered in the country studies.

1: The Making of the Modern State

Section 1 in each chapter provides an overview of the forces that have shaped the political development of the state up to the present. Understanding the contemporary politics of any country requires some understanding of the historical process through which its current political system took shape. Each chapter opens with a specific event to illustrate "Politics in Action" at a particularly important moment in the country's recent history and to highlight some of the critical political issues facing the country. "Geographic Setting" locates the country in its regional context and discusses the political implications of this setting. "Critical Junctures" looks at some of the major stages and decisive turning points in the state's development. This discussion shows how the country assumed its current political order and how relations between state and society have developed over time.

"Themes and Implications" explores how the past pattern of state development continues to shape the country's current political agenda. "Historical

Junctures and Political Themes" applies the text's four core themes to the making of the modern state. How has the country's political development been affected by its place in the world of states? What are the political implications of the state's approach to economic management? What has been the country's experience with the democratic idea? What are the important bases of collective identity in the country, and how do these affect the country's politics? "Implications for Comparative Politics" discusses the broader significance of the country for the study of comparative politics.

2: Political Economy and Development

Section 2 looks at the issues raised by our core theme of governing the economy and analyzes the interaction between economic development and political change. We put this section near the beginning of the country study because we believe that understanding a country's economic situation is essential for analyzing its politics. "State and Economy" discusses the basic organization of the country's economy. It emphasizes the relationship between the government and other economic actors, such as business firms and labor unions, and the state's role in managing economic life. How do the dynamics and historical timing of the country's entry into the world economy—and its current position and competitiveness within the globalized economy—affect domestic politics? This section also analyzes the state's social welfare policies, such as health care, housing, and social security programs. "Society and Economy" examines the social implications of the country's economic situation and their political impact. It asks who benefits from the state's economic policies and looks at how economic development creates or reinforces class, ethnic, gender, regional, or ideological divisions in society. "The Global Economy" considers the country's relationship to the international economy. How have patterns of trade and foreign investment changed over time? What is the country's relationship to regional and international economic organizations? How have international economic issues affected the domestic political agenda?

3: Governance and Policy-Making

Section 3 focuses on the state's major policy-making institutions and procedures. "Organization of the State" lays out the fundamental principles—reflected in the country's constitution, its dominant ideology, and its historical experience—on which the political system and the distribution of political power are based. It also sketches the basic structure of the state, including the relationship among different levels and branches of government. "The Executive" encompasses the key offices (for example, presidents, prime ministers, communist party leaders) at the top of the political system. We focus on how political leaders are selected, and how they use their power to make policy. This section also looks at the national bureaucracy and its relationship to the chief executive, and its role in policy-making. "Other State Institutions" looks at the military, the judiciary and the legal system, and at semipublic agencies, and subnational government. "The Policy-Making Process" provides an overview of how public policy gets made and implemented. It describes the roles of formal institutions and procedures, as well as informal aspects of policy-making, such as the influence of lobbyists and interest groups.

4: Representation and Participation

The relationship between a country's state and society is the topic of Section 4. How do different groups in society organize to further their political interests? How do they participate and get represented in the political system, and how do they influence policy-making? Given the importance of the U.S. Congress in policy-making, American readers might expect to find the role of the legislature described in Section 3 ("Governance and Policy-Making") rather than Section 4. But the United States is quite exceptional in having a legislature that has almost a coequal role with the executive in its policy-making role. In most other political systems, the executive dominates the policy process, even when it is ultimately responsible to the legislature, as in a parliamentary system. In these countries, the legislature functions primarily to represent and provide a forum for the political expression of various interests in government. It is only secondarily (and in some cases, such as China, only marginally) a policy-making body. Although this section does deal with the legislature's role in policy-making, its primary focus is on how the legislature represents or fails to represent different interests in society.

"Political Parties and the Party System" describes the overall organization of the country's party system and its major parties. "Elections" reviews the election process and trends in how people voted and why in recent elections. It also considers the significance of elections (or lack thereof) as a vehicle for citizen participation in politics and in bringing about changes in the government. "Political Culture, Citizenship, and Identity" examines how people perceive themselves as members of the political community: it considers such things as the nature and source of political values and attitudes, who is considered a citizen of the state, and how different groups in society understand their relationship to the state. The topics covered may include political aspects of the educational system, the media, religion, and ethnicity. "Interests, Social Movements, and Protests" discusses how various groups pursue their political interests both within and outside the political system. When do they use formal organizations (such as unions) or launch movements (such as environmental, antiglobalization, or peace movements)? What is the relationship between the state and such organizations and movements? When and how do citizens engage in acts of antistate protest? How does the state respond to such protests?

5: Politics in Transition

In Section 5, each country study returns to the book's four main themes and the major challenges reshaping the world and the study of comparative politics. "Political Challenges and Changing Agendas" lays out the major unresolved issues facing the country and assesses which are most likely to dominate in the near future. Many of the country studies address issues that have generated intense conflicts—conflicts involving globalization, collective identities, human rights and civil liberties, and the consequences of America's exercise of global power. "Politics in Comparative Perspective" highlights the implications of the country case for the study of comparative politics. How does the history—and how will the fate—of the country influence developments in a regional and global context? What does this case study tell us about politics in other countries that have similar political systems or that face similar kinds of political challenges?

Key Terms and Suggested Readings

At the end of each chapter, including this one, is a list of key terms that we think are especially important for students of comparative politics to know. Each term is in boldface the first time it appears in the text and is briefly defined on the page on which it appears and in the Glossary that appears near the end of the book. Each chapter also has a list of suggested readings: we have tried to emphasize books that we think would be both interesting and accessible to undergraduates. If you find yourself particularly interested in one or more of the countries covered in this text, we urge you to take a look at some of the suggested titles.

What's in the Comparative Data Charts?

The following charts and tables present important factual and statistical information about each of the countries included in this book, plus the United States. We hope most of this information is self-explanatory, but a few points of clarification may be helpful.

- The social and economic data largely comes from the CIA *World Factbook*, the World Bank *World Development Indicators*, and the United Nations *Human Development Report*, all of which are issued annually.
- The data presented is as up-to-date as possible. Unless otherwise indicated, it is from 2004–2007.
- Several important terms used in the data, including Gross Domestic Product (GDP), Gross National Product (GNP), Purchasing Power Parity (PPP), and Gini Index, are explained in the Glossary and/or the feature called "How Is Economic Development Measured?" on page 15.

These reports and other statistics are available from the national statistics or census agencies of individual countries and from the following websites:

- www.cia.gov/cia/publications/factbook/
- www.worldbank.org/data/
- hdr.undp.org/
- ipu.org/english/home.htm/ ❖

Chapter 1: Introducing Comparative Politics

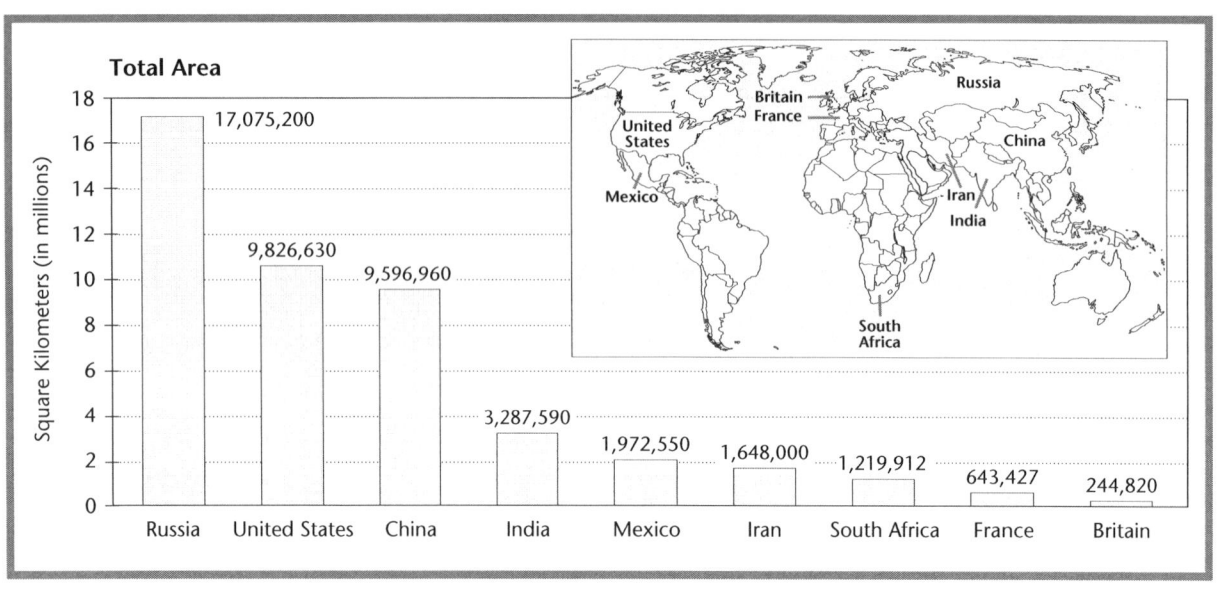

	Britain	China	France	India
Official Name	United Kingdom of Great Britain and Northern Ireland	People's Republic of China	French Republic	Republic of India
Capital	London	Beijing	Paris	New Delhi
Comparative Size	Slightly smaller than Oregon	Slightly smaller than the U.S.	Slightly smaller than Texas	Slightly smaller than one-third the size of the U.S.
Population Growth Rate (2007)	0.27%	0.61%	0.59%	1.61%
Major Ethnic Groups	White, 92.1% (comprising English, 83.6%; Scottish, 8.6%; Welsh, 4.9%; Northern Irish, 2.9%) Black, 2%; Indian, 1.8%; Pakistani, 1.3%; mixed, 1.2%; other, 1.6%	Han Chinese, 91.9%; other nationalities, 8.1% (including Zhuang, Uygur, Hui, Yi, Tibetan, Miao, Manchu, Mongol, Buyi, Korean)	French-born, 91%; other European, 3%; North African, 4% (mostly Algerian); other, 2%	Indo-Aryan, 72%; Dravidian, 25%; Mongoloid and other, 3%
Religions	Christian, 71.6% (Anglican, Roman Catholic, Presbyterian, Methodist); Muslim, 2.7%; Hindu, 1%; other, 1.6%; unspecified or none, 23.1%	Note: officially atheist; Daoist (Taoist), Buddhist, Christian, 3%–4%; Muslim, 1%–2%	Roman Catholic, 83–88%; Protestant, 2%; Jewish, 1%; Muslim, 5–10%; unaffiliated, 4%	Hindu, 80.5%; Muslim, 13.4%; Christian, 2.3%; Sikh, 1.9%; other, 1.8%; unspecified, 0.1%
Languages	English, Welsh (about 26% of the population of Wales), Scottish form of Gaelic (about 60,000 in Scotland)	Standard Chinese or Mandarin based on the Beijing dialect; other major dialects include Cantonese and Shanghaiese. Also various minority languages, such as Tibetan and Mongolian.	French	Hindi is the national language and primary tongue of 30% of the people; there are 14 other official languages. English enjoys associate status but is the most important language for national, political, and commercial communication.

Land and People

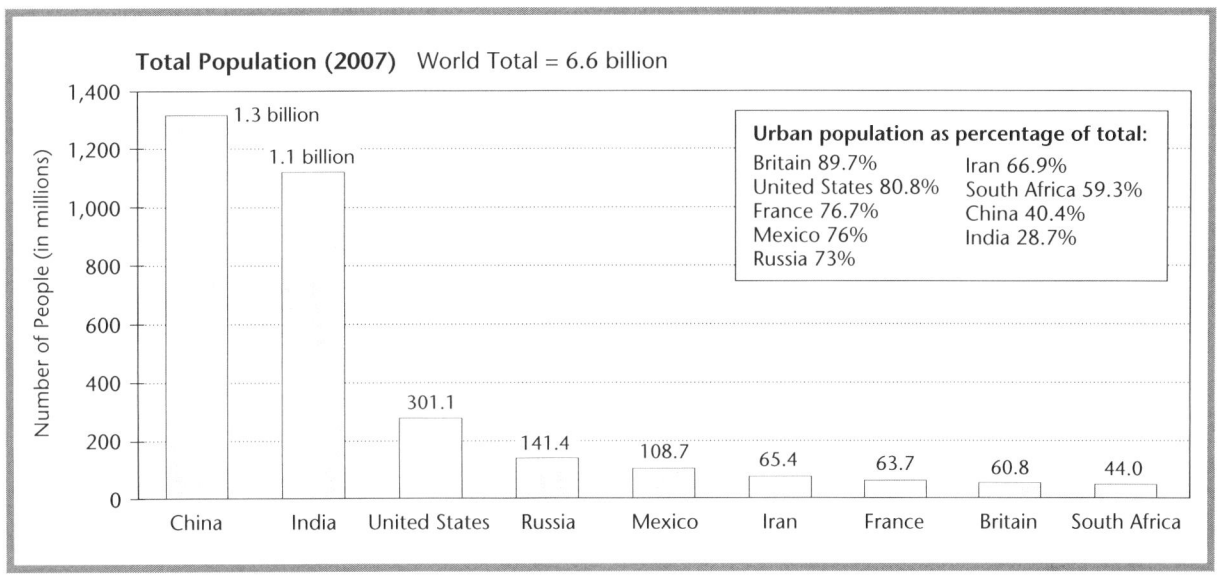

Iran	Mexico	Russia	South Africa	United States
Islamic Republic of Iran	United Mexican States	Russian Federation	Republic of South Africa	United States of America
Teheran	Mexico City	Moscow	Pretoria	Washington, D.C.
Slightly larger than Alaska	Slightly less than three times the size of Texas	Approximately 1.8 times the size of the U.S.	Slightly less than twice the size of Texas	About half the size of Russia
0.66%	1.15%	−0.48%	−0.46%	0.89%
Persian, 51%; Azeri, 24%; Gilaki and Mazandarani, 8%; Kurd, 7%; Arab, 3%; Lur, 2%; Baloch, 2%; Turkmen, 2%; other, 1%	Mestizo (Amerindian-Spanish), 60%; Amerindian or predominantly Amerindian, 30%; White, 9%; other, 1%	Russian, 79.8%; Tatar, 3.8%; Ukrainian, 2%; Bashkir, 1.2%; Chuvash, 1.1%; other/unspecified, 12.1%	Black African, 78.4%; White, 9.6%; Colored, 8.9%; Indian/Asian, 2.5%	White, 75.1%; Hispanic or Latino, 12.5%; Black/African American, 12.3%; Asian, 3.6%; American Indian and Alaskan Native, 0.9%; Native Hawaiian and other Pacific Islander, 0.1%; some other race, 5.5%; two or more races, 2.4%
Muslim, 98% (Shi'a, 89%; Sunni, 9%); other, 2% (includes Zoroastrian, Jewish, Christian, and Baha'i)	Roman Catholic, 76.5%; Protestant, 6.3% (Pentecostal, 1.4%; Jehovah's Witnesses, 1.1%; other, 3.8%); other, 0.3%; unspecified, 13.8%; none, 3.1%	Russian Orthodox, 15–20%; Muslim, 10–15%; other Christian, 2%; large number of non-practicing believers and non-believers	Christian, 32.6% (including Anglican, Methodist, Presbyterian, Lutheran, Roman Catholic, Dutch Reformed); African Independent, 31.8%; Pentecostal/Charismatic, 5.9%; other Christian, 9.5%; other, 3.8% (including Hindu, Muslim, Jewish); unspecified, 1.4%; none, 15.1%	Protestant, 52%; Roman Catholic, 24%; Mormon, 2%; Jewish, 1%; Muslim, 1%; other, 10%; none, 10%
Persian and Persian dialects, 58%; Turkic and Turkic dialects, 26%; Kurdish, 9%; Luri, 2%; Balochi, 1%; Arabic, 1%; Turkish, 1%; other, 2%	Spanish; various Mayan, Nahuatl, and other regional indigenous languages	Russian, many minority languages	IsiZulu, 23.8%; IsiXhosa, 17.6%; Afrikaans, 13.3%; Sepedi, 9.4%; English, 8.2%; Setswana, 8.2%; Sesotho, 7.9%; Xitsonga, 4.4%; other, 7.2%	English, 82.1%; Spanish, 10.7%; other Indo-European, 3.8%; Asian and Pacific Island, 2.7%; other, 0.7%

Chapter 1: Introducing Comparative Politics

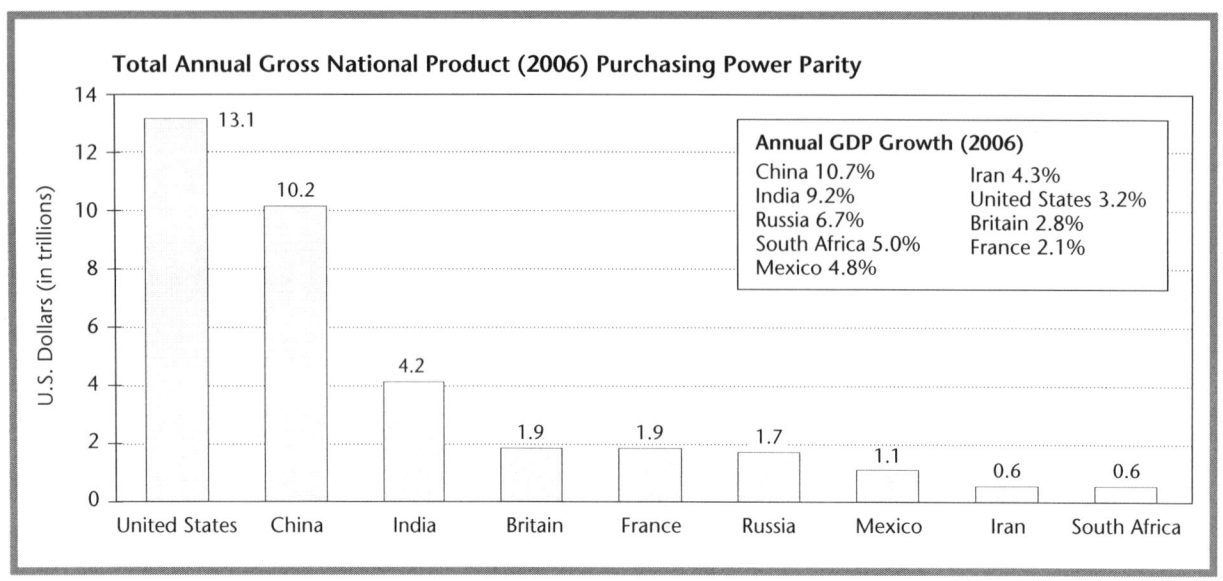

	Britain	China	France	India
GDP per capita average annual growth rate, 1990–2004	2.2%	8.9%	1.7%	4.0%
GDP by sector of the economy (2006)	Agriculture: 1% Industry: 25.6% Services: 73.4%	Agriculture: 11.9% Industry: 48.1% Services: 40%	Agriculture: 2.2% Industry: 20.6% Services: 77.2%	Agriculture: 19.9% Industry: 19.3% Services: 60.7%
Employment by sector of the economy (1999–2006)	Agriculture: 1.4% Industry: 18.2% Services: 80.4%	Agriculture: 45% Industry: 24% Services: 31%	Agriculture: 4.1% Industry: 24.4% Services: 71.5%	Agriculture: 60% Industry: 12% Services: 28%
Exports and imports as % of GDP (2004–2005)	Exports: 26.1% Imports: 30.0%	Exports: 37.5% Imports: 31.9%	Exports: 26.1% Imports: 27.1%	Exports: 20.5% Imports: 24.2%
Inequality Share of income or consumption • Poorest 20% • Richest 20% GINI Index (Year) *(higher = more unequal)*	 6.1% 44.0% 36.8 (1999)	 4.7% 50.0% 44.0 (2002)	 7.2% 40.2% 26.7 (2002)	 8.9% 43.3% 32.5 (2000)
Estimated income (PPP) (2004)	Male: $37,506 Female: $24,448	Male: $7,159 Female: $4,561	Male: $35,922 Female: $23,105	Male: $4,723 Female: $1,471

Economy

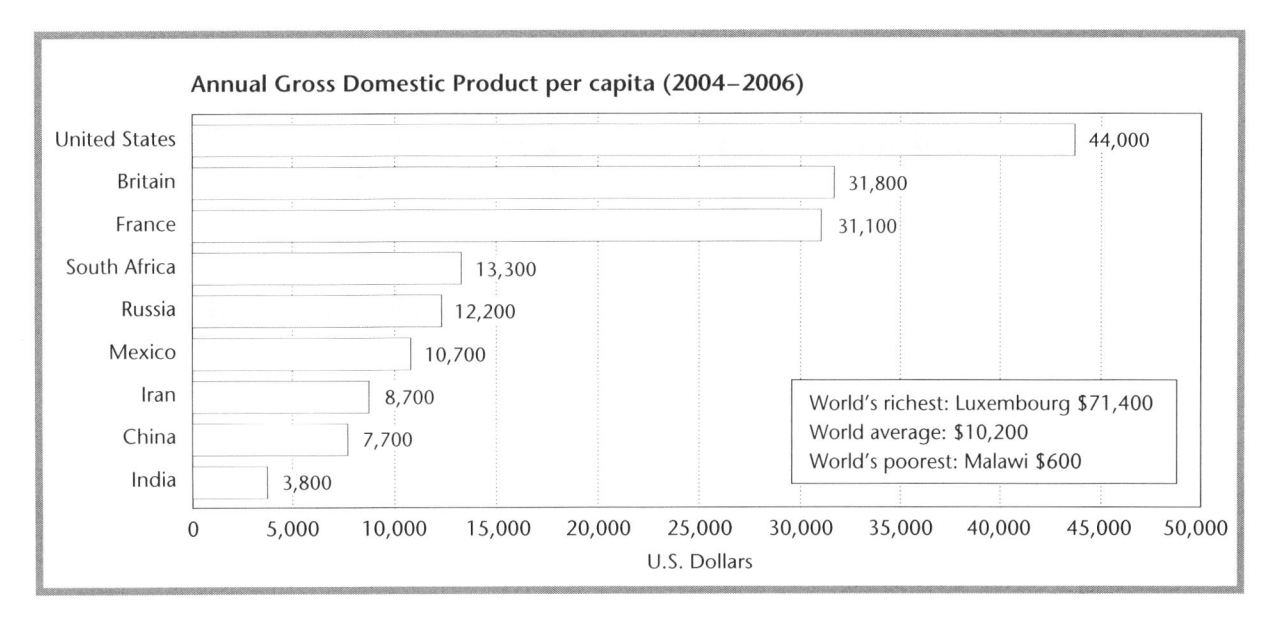

Annual Gross Domestic Product per capita (2004–2006)

Country	GDP per capita (U.S. Dollars)
United States	44,000
Britain	31,800
France	31,100
South Africa	13,300
Russia	12,200
Mexico	10,700
Iran	8,700
China	7,700
India	3,800

World's richest: Luxembourg $71,400
World average: $10,200
World's poorest: Malawi $600

Iran	Mexico	Russia	South Africa	United States
2.3%	1.3%	−0.6%	0.6%	1.9%
Agriculture: 11.2%	Agriculture: 3.9%	Agriculture: 5.3%	Agriculture: 2.6%	Agriculture: 0.9%
Industry: 41.7%	Industry: 25.7%	Industry: 36.6%	Industry: 30.3%	Industry: 20.4%
Services: 47.1%	Services: 70.5%	Services: 58.2%	Services: 67.1%	Services: 78.6%
Agriculture: 30%	Agriculture: 18%	Agriculture: 10.8%	Agriculture: 30%	Agriculture: 0.7%
Industry: 25%	Industry: 24%	Industry: 29.1%	Industry: 25%	Industry: 22.9%
Services: 45%	Services: 58%	Services: 60.1%	Services: 45%	Services: 76.4%
Exports: 38.8%	Exports: 29.9%	Exports: 35.1%	Exports: 27.1%	Exports: 10.1%
Imports: 30.2%	Imports: 31.5%	Imports: 21.6%	Imports: 28.6%	Imports: 15.4%
5.1%	4.3%	6.1%	3.5%	5.4%
49.9%	55.1%	46.6%	62.2%	45.8%
43.0 (1998)	49.5 (2002)	40.5 (2005)	57.8 (2002)	45.0 (2004)
Male: $10,830	Male: $14,202	Male: $12,401	Male: $15,521	Male: $49,075
Female: $4,122	Female: $5,594	Female: $7,735	Female: $7,014	Female: $30,581

Life Expectancy at Birth (years)

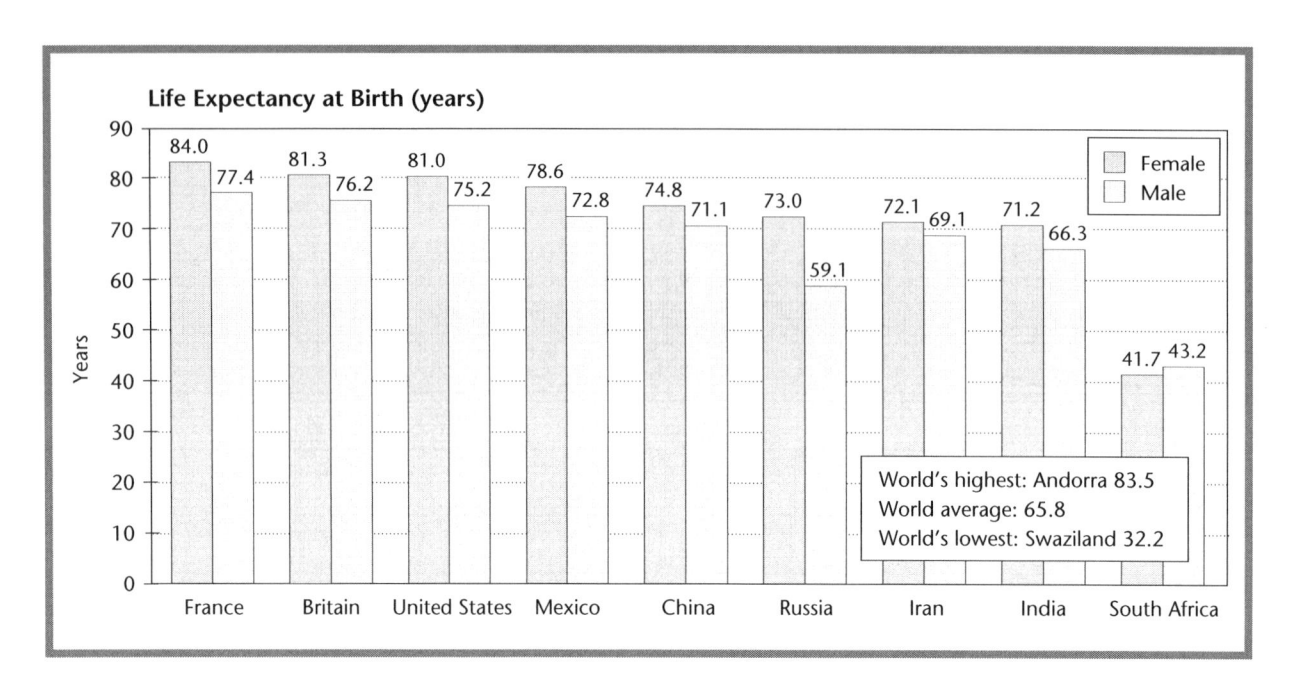

Country	Female	Male
France	84.0	77.4
Britain	81.3	76.2
United States	81.0	75.2
Mexico	78.6	72.8
China	74.8	71.1
Russia	73.0	59.1
Iran	72.1	69.1
India	71.2	66.3
South Africa	41.7	43.2

World's highest: Andorra 83.5
World average: 65.8
World's lowest: Swaziland 32.2

	Britain	**China**	**France**	**India**
Adult literacy (2002–2006)	Male: 99% Female: 99%	Male: 95.1% Female: 86.5%	Male: 99% Female: 99%	Male: 73.4% Female: 47.8%
Percentage of age-eligible population in secondary school and college	Secondary: 95.4% College: 59.7%	Secondary: 74.3% College: 20.3%	Secondary: 99.1% College: 52.8%	Secondary: 56.6% College: 11.4%
Communications and technology per 1,000 people (2004–2005)	Telephones: 528 Cell phones: 1,088 PCs: 600 Internet users: 474	Telephones: 287 Cell phones: 302 PCs: 41 Internet users: 85	Telephones: 587 Cell phones: 790 PCs: 575 Internet users: 430	Telephones: 46 Cell phones: 82 PCs: 15 Internet users: 55
Physicians (per 100,000 people) (1990–2004)	23.0	10.6	33.7	6.0
Women as percentage of national legislature	Lower: 20% Upper: 19%	Single: 20%	Lower: 12% Upper: 19%	Lower: 8% Upper: 11%

Society

Infant Mortality per 1,000 Live Births (2007)

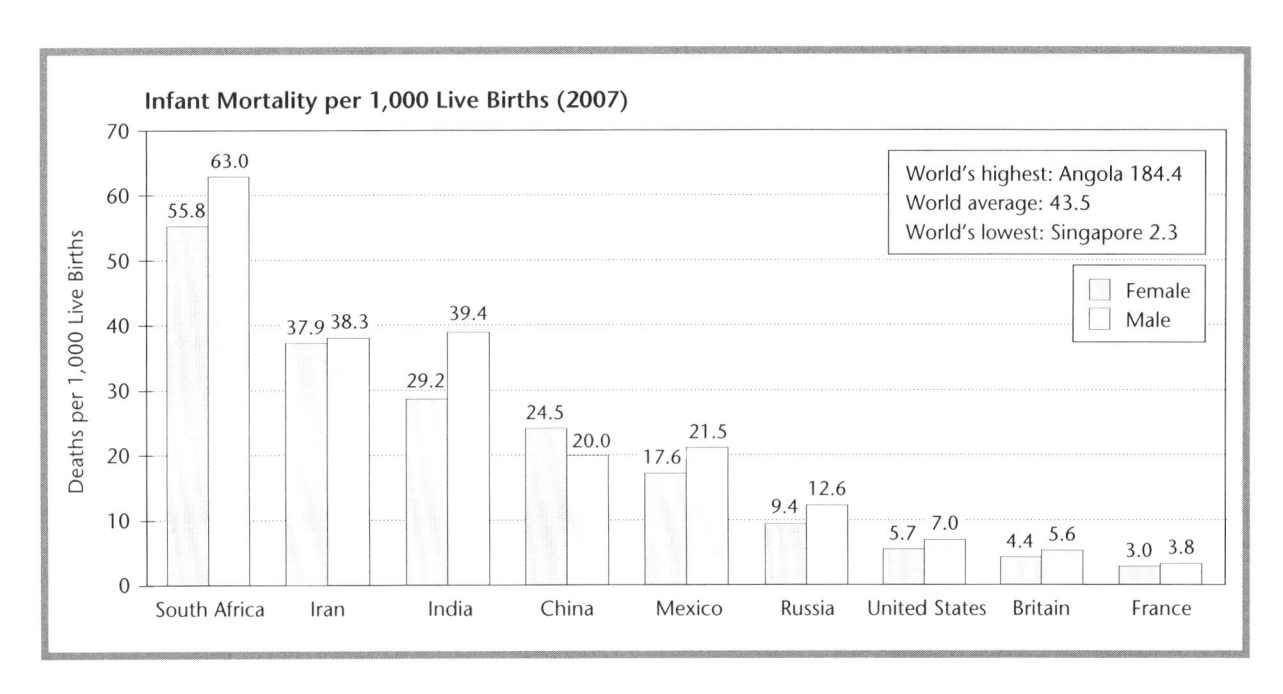

Country	Female	Male
South Africa	55.8	63.0
Iran	37.9	38.3
India	29.2	39.4
China	24.5	20.0
Mexico	17.6	21.5
Russia	9.4	12.6
United States	5.7	7.0
Britain	4.4	5.6
France	3.0	3.8

World's highest: Angola 184.4
World average: 43.5
World's lowest: Singapore 2.3

Iran	Mexico	Russia	South Africa	United States
Male: 83.5%	Male: 92.4%	Male: 99.7%	Male: 87%	Male: 99%
Female: 70.4%	Female: 89.6%	Female: 99.2%	Female: 85.7%	Female: 99%
Secondary: 83.1%	Secondary: 80.2%	Secondary: 91.9%	Secondary: 93.4%	Secondary: 94.7%
College: 23.9%%	College: 24.0%	College: 51.3%	College: 15.3%	College: 82.7%
Telephones: 278	Telephones: 189	Telephones: 280	Telephones: 101	Telephones: 606
Cell phones: 106	Cell phones: 460	Cell phones: 839	Cell phones: 724	Cell phones: 680
PCs: 109	PCs: 136	PCs: 122	PCs: 85	PCs: 762
Internet users: 103	Internet users: 181	Internet users: 152	Internet users: 109	Internet users: 630
4.5	19.8	42.5	7.7	25.6
Single: 4%	Lower: 23%	Lower: 10%	Lower: 33%	Lower: 16%
	Upper: 17%	Upper: 3%	Upper: 33%	Upper: 16%

Comparative Rankings of Selected Categories

International organizations and research institutions have developed statistical methods to rate and rank different countries according to various categories of economic, social, political, and environmental performance. Such rankings can be controversial, but we think they provide an interesting approach to comparative analysis. Five examples of this approach are listed below. In addition to the countries included in this book and the United States, the top and bottom five countries (and in the case of the Freedom House ratings, examples of each level) are also listed.

Human Development Index (HDI) is a measure used by the United Nations to compare the overall level of well-being in countries around the world. It takes into account life expectancy, education, and the standard of living.

2006 HDI Rankings

1. Norway
2. Iceland
3. Australia
4. Ireland
5. Sweden
8. United States
16. **France**
18. **Britain**
53. **Mexico**
65. **Russia**
81. **China**
96. **Iran**
121. **South Africa**
126. **India**
173. Guinea-Bissau
174. Burkina Faso
175. Mali
176. Sierra Leone
177. Niger

Source: http://hdr.undp.org/hdr2006

Global Gender Gap measures "the extent to which women in 58 countries have achieved equality with men in five critical areas: economic participation, economic opportunity, political empowerment, educational attainment, and health and well-being."

2005 Gender Gap Rankings

1. Sweden
2. Norway
3. Iceland
4. Denmark
5. Finland
8. **Britain**
13. **France**
17. United States
31. **Russia**
33. **China**
36. **South Africa**
52. **Mexico**
53. **India**
54. South Korea
55. Jordan
56. Pakistan
57. Turkey
58. Egypt

Note: Iran was not included in this study, but it ranked 71 out of 75 in the UNDP's 2004 Gender Empowerment Index.
Source: www.weforum.org

Environmental Performance Index (EPI) measures how close countries come to meeting specific benchmarks for national pollution control and natural resource management.

2006 EPI Rankings

1. New Zealand
2. Sweden
3. Finland
4. Czech Republic
5. **Britain**
12. **France**
28. United States
32. **Russia**
53. **Iran**
66. **Mexico**
76. **South Africa**
94. **China**
118. **India**
129. Ethiopia
130. Mali
131. Mauritania
132. Chad
133. Niger

Source: http://www.yale.edu/epi

International Corruption Perceptions Index (CPI) defines corruption as the abuse of public office for private gain and measures the degree to which corruption is perceived to exist among a country's public officials and politicians in 163 countries.

2006 CPI Rankings

1. Finland
2. Iceland
3. New Zealand
4. Denmark
5. Singapore
11. **Britain**
18. **France**
20. United States
51. **South Africa**
70. **China**
70. **India**
70. **Mexico**
105. **Iran**
121. **Russia**
156. (4 tied)
160. Guinea
163. Iraq
163. Myanmar
163. Haiti

Source: http://www.transparency.org/
Similar numbers indicate a tie in the rankings.

Freedom in the World ratings measure how free a country is according to an analysis of its civil and political liberties. 1 = most free; 7 = least free.

2006 Freedom House Rankings

"Free" (1.0–2.5)
Britain (1.0)
France (1.0)
United States (1.0)
South Africa (1.5)
Mexico (2.0)
India (2.5)

"Partly Free" (3.0–50)
Colombia (3.0)
Tanzania (3.5)
Bangladesh (4.0)
Singapore (4.5)
Afghanistan (5.0)

"Not Free" (5.5–7.0)
Russia (5.5)
Iran (6.0)
China (6.5)
Cuba (7.0)

Source: http://www.freedomhouse.org

Key Terms

- Cold War
- globalization
- comparative politics
- comparativist
- country
- state
- executive
- cabinet
- bureaucracy
- legitimacy
- state formation
- collective identities
- causal theories
- independent variable
- dependent variable
- Human Development Index (HDI)
- Global Gender Gap
- Environmental Performance Index (EPI)
- Corruption Perceptions Index (CPI)
- Freedom in the World rating
- failed states
- authoritarianism
- political economy
- sustainable development
- democracy
- gross domestic product (GDP)
- gross national product (GNP)
- purchasing power parity (PPP)
- social movements
- communist party–state
- social class
- distributional politics
- typology
- consolidated democracies
- transitional democracies
- theocracy
- ideology

Suggested Readings

Friedman, Thomas. *The World Is Flat: A Brief History of the Twenty-first Century* New York: Farrar, Straus and Giroux, 2005.

Kesselman, Mark. *The Politics of Globalization: A Reader*. Boston: Houghton Mifflin, 2006.

———. *Readings in Comparative Politics: Political Challenges and Changing Agendas*. Boston: Houghton Mifflin, 2005.

Krieger, Joel. *Globalization and State Power: A Reader*. Boston: Longman, 2005.

———. *Globalization and State Power: Who Wins When America Rules?* Boston: Longman, 2004.

Soe, Christian. *Annual Editions: Comparative Politics 07/08*, 25th ed. New York: McGraw Hill/Dushkin, 2007.

Zakaria, Fareed. *The Future of Freedom: Illiberal Democracy at Home and Abroad*. New York: W.W. Norton, 2003.

Oxford University Press (New York) publishes a series of "Very Short Introductions" that includes many books on topics related to the study of comparative politics:

- Andrew Clapham, *Human Rights* (2007)
- Bernard Crick, *Democracy* (2002)
- James Fulcher, *Capitalism* (2004)
- Steven Grosby, *Nationalism* (2005)
- Stephen Howe, *Empire* (2002)
- Khalid Koser, *International Migration* (2007)
- Robert J. McMahon, *Cold War* (2003)
- Kenneth Minogue, *Politics* (2000)
- Amrita Narlikar, *World Trade Organization* (2005)
- Michael Newman, *Socialism* (2005)

- Kevin Passmore, *Fascism* (2002)
- Malise Ruthven, *Fundamentalism* (2007)
- Manfred B. Steger, *Globalization* (2003)
- Charles Townshend, *Terrorism* (2002)

Notes

[1] Francis Fukuyama, "The End of History?" *The National Interest* 16 (Summer 1989). The article is reprinted in Mark Kesselman and Joel Krieger, eds., *Readings in Comparative Politics: Political Challenges and Changing Agendas* (Boston: Houghton Mifflin, 2006).

[2] See Philippe Schmitter, "Comparative Politics," in Joel Krieger, ed., *The Oxford Companion to Politics of the World*, 2nd ed. (New York: Oxford University Press, 2001), 160–165. For a more extended discussion and different approach, see David D. Laitin, "Comparative Politics: The State of the Subdiscipline," in Ira Katznelson and Helen V. Milner, eds., *Political Science: The State of the Discipline* (New York: Norton, 2002), 630–659. For a collection of articles in the field of comparative politics, see Kesselman and Krieger, eds., *Readings in Comparative Politics*.

[3] See Anthony Marx, *Making Race and Nation: A Comparison of the United States, South Africa, and Brazil* (Cambridge: Cambridge University Press, 1998).

[4] Seymour Martin Lipset, *American Exceptionalism: A Double-Edged Sword.* (New York: W. W. Norton, 1996), 17. Fukuyama cotaught at George Mason University with Lipset, who was first and foremost a scholar of American politics. In his appreciation of Lipset's life and work following his death in 2006, Fukuyama wrote that his colleague often began their course on American public policy with some variation on this quote; see *Journal of Democracy*, 18, no. 2 (2007) 185–188.

[5] For reviews of recent literature on the state, see Margaret Levi, "The State of the Study of the State"; Miles Kahler, "The State of the State in World Politics"; and Atul Kohli, "State, Society, and Development," in Katznelson and Milner, eds., *Political Science: State of the Discipline*, 84–117.

[6] John R. Alford, Carolyn L. Funk, and John R. Hibbin, "Are Political Orientations Genetically Transmitted?" in *American Political Science Review*, 99, no. 2 (2005), 153–167.

[7] For descriptions by sympathetic participant-observers, see John Cavanagh and Jerry Mander, eds., *Alternatives to Economic Globalization: A Better World Is Possible*, 2nd ed. (San Francisco: Berrett-Koehler, 2004); and Robin Broad, ed., *Global Backlash: Citizen Initiatives for a Just World Economy* (Lanham, Md.: Rowman & Littlefield, 2002). For spirited defenses of globalization, see Jagdish Bhagwati, *In Defense of Globalization* (New York: Oxford University Press, 2004) and Martin Wolf, *Why Globalization Works* (New Haven, Conn.: Yale University Press, 2004).

[8] Robert I. Rotberg, "Failed States in a World of Terror," *Foreign Affairs* 81, no. 4 (July–August 2002). The article is reprinted in Kesselman and Krieger, *Readings in Comparative Politics*.

[9] "The Failed State Index," www.foreignpolicy.com.

[10] This term is borrowed from Peter A. Hall, *Governing the Economy* (New York: Oxford University Press, 1986).

[11] This table is based on data from Adrian Karatnycky, "Liberty's Expansion in a Turbulent World: Thirty Years of the Survey of Freedom," *Freedom in the World, 2003: The Annual Survey of Political Rights and Civil Liberties* (Lanham, Md.: Rowman & Littlefield, 2003) and Arch Puddington, "Freedom Stagnation Amid Pushback Against Democracy," *Freedom in the World 2007: The Annual Survey of Political Rights and Civil Liberties* (Lanham, Md.: Rowman & Littlefield, 2007). Both reports are available at www.freedomhouse.org.

[12] See, for example, Bruce Gilley, *China's Democratic Future: How It Will Happen and Where It Will Lead* (New York: Columbia University Press, 2004) and Minxin Pei, *China's Trapped Transition: The Limits of Developmental Autocracy* (Cambridge, Mass.: Harvard University Press, 2006).

[13] Amartya Sen, "Democracy as a Universal Value," *Journal of Democracy* 10, no. 3 (July 1999): 3–17 (http://muse.jhu.edu/demo/jod/10.3sen.html). This article is included in Kesselman and

Krieger, *Readings in Comparative Politics*. An influential study of this question, on which Sen draws, reaches a similar conclusion: Adam Przeworski et al., *Democracy and Development: Political Institutions and Well-Being in the World, 1950–1990* (Cambridge: Cambridge University Press, 2000). For a study that reaches a different conclusion—that there is a positive correlation between democracy and economic growth—see Yi Feng, *Democracy, Governance, and Economic Performance: Theory and Evidence* (Cambridge, Mass: MIT Press, 2005).

[14]*The Economist*, May 24, 2007.

[15]See, for example, Guillermo O'Donnell, "Illusions About Consolidation," *Journal of Democracy* 7, no. 2 (April 1996): 34–51; Thomas Carothers, "The End of the Transition Paradigm," *Journal of Democracy* 13, no. 1 (January 2002): 5–21; and Steven Levitsky and Lucan A. Way, "The Rise of Competitive Authoritarianism," *Journal of Democracy* 13, no. 2 (April 2002): 51–65. All are reprinted in Kesselman and Krieger, *Readings in Comparative Politics*.

Christopher S. Allen

Chapter 2 » GERMANY

Section 1 The Making of the Modern German State
Section 2 Political Economy and Development
Section 3 Governance and Policy-Making
Section 4 Representation and Participation
Section 5 German Politics in Transition

Official Name: **Federal Republic of Germany (Bundesrepublik Deutschland)**

Location: **Central Europe**

Capital City: **Berlin**

Population (2008): **82.3 million**

Size: **357,021 sq. km.; slightly smaller than Montana**

Chapter 2: Germany

Chronology of Germany's Political Development

1806–1871	1871–1918	1919–1933	1933–1945	1939–1945
Nationalism and German Unification	Second Reich	Weimar Republic	Third Reich	World War II

SECTION 1: The Making of the Modern German State

Politics in Action

May Day in Europe—and most of the world—is usually a day of traditional protests and celebratory parades by organized labor movements and democratic left wing political parties, but in Hamburg in 2008 there was a sharper edge to the demonstrations. Challenging the social forces of the democratic left were groups of far right-wing nationalists who provoked the most radical of the left to engage in sometimes violent clashes in the streets. The German weekly *Der Spiegel* reported that 1,100 neo-Nazis and members of the extreme right-wing National Democratic Party (NPD) confronted over 7,000 anti-fascist left wing groups in a day-long series of demonstrations, barricades, and fires.

When such street protests lead to violence in Germany, they usually cause observers to raise the spectre of the turbulent Weimar Republic years in the 1920s, when Nazis and Communists had much larger conflicts as Germany's first experiment in democracy gave way to Hitler's Third Reich. These contemporary conflicts are but a pale image of those events. However, they are a disturbing indicator of significantly increased fragmentation of German democratic politics in the early 21st century compared to the more consensual politics in the years since the end of the World War II in 1945.

For almost all of the post–World War II period, the Federal Republic of Germany (FRG) admirably developed a stable, democratic government run by two large parties, the Social Democratic Party (*Sozialdemokratische Partei Deutschlands*, SPD) on the moderate left, the Christian Democratic Union and its sister party the Christian Social Union (CDU/CSU) on the moderate right, and one smaller party in the center, the pro-free market but socially liberal Free Democratic Party (FDP). In what came to be called a "two and a half party system" the FDP, depending on the issues, would join one of the two larger parties to form stable governments for the first forty-plus years of the FRG.

The emergence of the environmental Green Party, gaining seats in the *Bundestag* for the first time in 1983, was one harbinger of change. The other was the increasing growth of the Left Party (*die Linke*), once a mostly eastern German former communist party that began to develop considerable strength in the west in 2004. The 2005 election confirmed that the days of the "two and a half party" system were long gone, as the FDP and the two new parties received almost 26 percent of the total vote.* The electoral arithmetic had become much more complicated because the three smaller parties won enough seats to prevent one of the two large parties coalescing with only one of the smaller ones. The only other possible

---

*Significantly, no far right party has ever achieved the 5 percent threshold for winning seats in the *Bundestag*, but the NPD has recently surpassed 5 percent of the vote and won seats in two eastern German state parliaments.

1945–1990	1990–1998	1998–2001	2001–
A Divided Germany	The Challenge of German Unification	Germany in the Euro Era	Germany after September 11

result—other than a three-party coalition—was what in fact occurred: a "Grand Coalition" between the SPD and CDU/CSU. Since 2005, however, this compromise coalition has produced considerable disagreement, ineffective governance, and enabled the three smaller parties—as the only opposition—to increase their support in opinion polls to almost 35 percent of the electorate by mid-2008.

The increasing fluidity of the party system has made coalition possibilities much more difficult. The longer that the SPD and CDU/CSU remained in a coalition in which agreement on major issues was difficult, the more support increased for the three smaller parties. Since the 2005 election, the "natural" coalitions of CDU/CSU and FDP on the moderate right, and SPD and Greens (who comprised the government from 1998–2005) on the moderate left, have been unable to form because neither potential coalition controlled 50 percent of the seats. The Left Party's 8.7 percent share of the vote in 2005—and its increasing popularity to between 12 percent and 14 percent in opinion polls in mid-2008—made coalition possibilities difficult: none of the other parties wanted to join in coalition with the Left due to its status as a former communist party.

By the third year of the SPD-CDU/CSU Grand Coalition, German politics had become more stable, thanks to a popular chancellor in Angela Merkel and

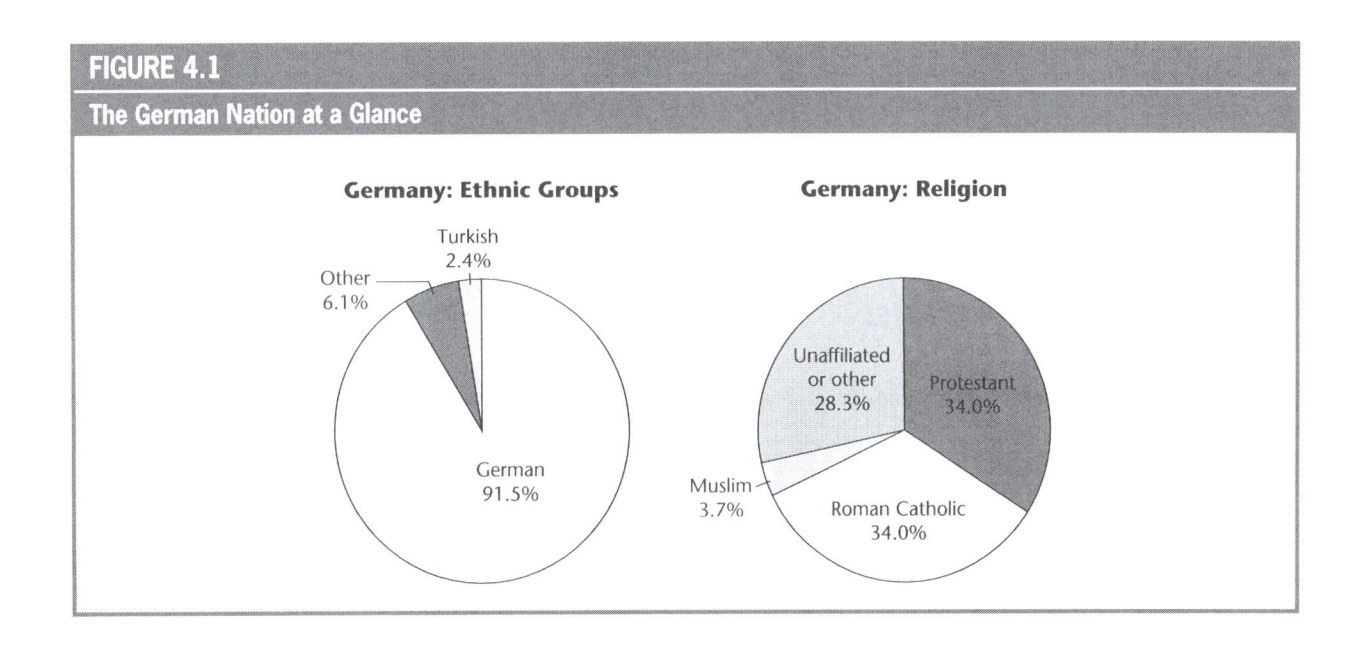

FIGURE 4.1

The German Nation at a Glance

Germany: Ethnic Groups
- Turkish 2.4%
- Other 6.1%
- German 91.5%

Germany: Religion
- Unaffiliated or other 28.3%
- Protestant 34.0%
- Muslim 3.7%
- Roman Catholic 34.0%

Table 4.1	
Political Organization	
Political System	Parliamentary democracy.
Regime History	After the Third Reich's defeat, Germany was partitioned and occupied by Allies in 1945. In 1949 the Federal Republic of Germany (FGR) was established in the west, and the German Democratic Republic (GDR) was established in the east. The two German states unified in 1990.
Administrative Structure	Federal, with 16 states. Germany does not have sharp separation between levels of government.
Executive	Ceremonial president is the head of state, elected for a five-year term (with a two-term limit) by the Federal Convention. Chancellor is head of government and is a member of the *Bundestag* and a leader of the majority party or coalition.
Legislature	Bicameral. *Bundestag* (614 members at 2005 federal election) elected via dual-ballot system combining single-member districts and proportional representation. Upper house (*Bundesrat*) comprised 69 members who are elected and appointed officials from the 16 states.
Judiciary	Autonomous and independent. The legal system has three levels: Federal High Court, which is the criminal-civil system; Special Constitutional Court, dealing with matters affecting Basic Law; and Administrative Court, consisting of Labor, Social Security, and Finance courts.
Party System	Multiparty. Major parties are Social Democratic Party (SDP), the Greens, Christian Democratic Union (CDU), Christian Social Union (CSU), Free Democratic Party (FDP), and Left Party (*die Linke*. PDS).

modest economic growth. But it had also become more unpredictable than it had been during most of its democratic history since the end of WWII. While Germany was certainly not about to descend again into the pre–Third Reich chaos of the 1920s, German democracy faced some of its sharpest challenges and unpredictable outcomes in decades.

Geographic Setting

Germany is located in central Europe and has been as much a western European nation as an eastern European one. It has a total area of 137,803 square miles (slightly smaller than the state of Montana). Its population of 82 million, comprising over 85 percent ethnic Germans, all of whom speak German as the primary language, is roughly evenly divided between Roman Catholics and Protestants. It has the largest population of any country in western Europe and is second only to Russia in all of Europe. Germany has been relatively homogeneous ethnically; however, ethnic diversity has been increased by the presence of several million Turks in Germany, first drawn to the Federal Republic in the 1960s as **Gastarbeiter** (guest workers)—foreign workers who had no citizenship rights. Furthermore, increased migration across borders by EU citizens is further decreasing cultural homogeneity.

For a densely populated country, Germany has a surprisingly high proportion of its land in agricultural production (54 percent). It is composed of large plains in northern Germany, a series of smaller mountain ranges in the center of the country, and the towering Alps to the south at the Austrian and Swiss borders. It has a temperate climate with considerable cloud cover and precipitation throughout the year. For Germany, the absence of natural borders in the west and east has been an important geographic fact. For example, on the north, it borders both the North and Baltic seas and the country of Denmark, but to the west, south, and east, it has many neighbors: the Netherlands,

Belgium, Luxembourg, France, Switzerland, Austria, the Czech Republic, and Poland. Conflicts and wars with its neighbors were a constant feature of German life until the end of World War II.

Germany's lack of resources—aside from iron ore and coal deposits in the Ruhr and the Saarland—has shaped much of the country's history. Since the Industrial Revolution in the nineteenth century, many of Germany's external relationships, both commercial and military, have revolved around gaining access to resources it lacks within its national borders. Germany is divided into sixteen **federal states** (*Bundesländer*), many of which correspond to historic German kingdoms and principalities (such as Bavaria, Saxony, and Hesse) or medieval trading cities (such as Hamburg and Bremen).

Critical Junctures

Nationalism and German Unification (1806–1871) *First Reich = HRE*

The first German "state" (or more accurately, entity) was the Holy Roman Empire, founded by Charlemagne in 800 A.D. (sometimes referred to as the First Reich). But this loose and fragmented "*Reich*" (empire) bore little resemblance to a modern nation-state; it was composed of up to 300 sovereign entities including the territories of present-day Germany, Austria, and the Czech Republic.

Two main factors hindered German state formation: uncertain geographic boundaries and religious (Protestant vs. Catholic) division.[1] As a result of these divisions, the German language, as well as German physical and cultural traits, played a larger role in defining national identity than such features did in other European states. For many nineteenth-century Germans, the lack of political unity stood in sharp contrast to the strong cultural influence of such literary and religious figures as Goethe, Schiller, and Luther.

The victories of the French emperor Napoleon against Prussia and Austria brought an end to the Holy Roman Empire in 1806. But the defeat and occupation aroused strong German nationalist sentiment, and in 1813–1814 the Prussians—the largest and most powerful of the German-speaking states—led an alliance in a "War of Liberation" against Napoleon's France, culminating in a new German confederation created in 1815.

In 1819, authoritarian Prussian leaders confidently launched a tariff union with fellow German states that by 1834 encompassed almost all of the German Confederation except Austria, greatly expanding Prussian influence. But free-market capitalism and democracy did not take root in the Prussian-dominated Germanic principalities. Instead, there surfaced qualities such as a strong state, the dominance of a reactionary group of noble landlords in eastern Prussia called **Junkers,** a patriotic military, and a political culture dominated by honor, duty, and service to the state.

The European revolutions of 1848 sparked many prodemocracy uprisings, including those of Berlin and Vienna, respectively, the Prussian and Austrian capitals. But these revolutionary democratic movements in Germany and Austria were violently and quickly suppressed. Germany was united instead by a "revolution from above" led by Count Otto von Bismarck, who became minister-president of Prussia in 1862.[2] A *Junker* who reflected the values and authoritarian vision of his class, Bismarck realized that Prussia needed to industrialize and modernize its economy to compete with Britain, France, and the United States. He created an unlikely and nondemocratic coalition of northeastern rural *Junker* lords and northwestern Ruhr Valley iron industrialists, known as the "marriage of iron and rye." Unlike the French and American revolutionaries, the coalition leaders relied on the support of wealthy elites rather than on the democratic working class and peasant/farmers. Very simply, Bismarck was contemptuous of democracy, preferring "blood and iron" as his primary political tools. He was also as good as his word, launching three short wars—against Denmark (1864), Austria (1866), and France (1870)—that culminated in the unification of Germany. The so-called Second Reich, excluding Austria and with the King of Prussia as *Kaiser* (emperor), was proclaimed in 1871.

The Second Reich (1871–1918)

The Second Reich was an authoritarian regime controlled by industrial and landed elites. It was symbolically democratic in that the Iron Chancellor allowed for universal male suffrage for the lower house (*Reichstag*) of the bicameral legislature, but real decision-making authority lay in the hands of the upper house (*Landtag*), which Bismarck controlled.

The primary goal of the Second Reich was rapid industrialization, supported by state power and a powerful banking system geared to foster large-scale industrial investment rather than by the trial-and-error methods of free markets.[3] This path was so successful that Germany had become a leading industrial power by 1900, emphasizing such industries as coal, steel, railroads, dyes, chemicals, industrial electronics, and machine tools. The state pushed the development of such heavy industries at the expense of those producing consumer goods. Lacking a strong domestic consumer-goods economy, Germany had to export a substantial portion of what it produced on world markets.

Rapid transformation from a largely agrarian society in the 1850s to an industrial one by the turn of the twentieth century created widespread social dislocation and growing opposition to the conservative regime. A small middle class of professionals and small-business owners with rising expectations pressured the government—mostly unsuccessfully—to democratize and provide basic **liberal** (that is, free-market) rights. Industrialization also promoted the growth of a manually skilled working class and the corresponding rise of a militant Social Democratic Party (*Sozialdemokratische Partei Deutschlands,* SPD). The Social Democrats' primary goals were economic rights in the workplace and democratization of the political system. The party was greatly influenced by the founders of socialism, the Germans Karl Marx and Friedrich Engels. Socialist philosophy argues that workers, as producers of society's goods and services, should possess the country's economic and political power.

As German **chancellor** (head of government) from 1871 to 1890, Bismarck alternately persecuted and grudgingly tolerated the democratic and socialist opposition. He banned the Social Democratic Party yet created the beginnings of the first welfare state as a way to blunt the effects of rapid economic growth. Social welfare benefits included health insurance and the first forms of state-sponsored old-age pensions. This combination of welfare with political repression is sometimes referred to as Bismarck's "iron fist in a velvet glove."

Bismarck also significantly influenced German political culture by creating a strong and centralized German state. The *Kulturkampf* (cultural struggle) he initiated was a prime example of Prussian and Protestant dominance. Essentially a movement against the Catholic Church, it sought to remove educational and cultural institutions from the church and place them under the state. This action, which alienated the church and many Catholic Germans, left a powerful political legacy.

By 1900, Germany's primary economic challenge consisted of obtaining necessary raw materials and accessing world markets to sell its finished goods, in order to sustain rapid economic growth. Germany then embarked on an imperial adventure sometimes called "the scramble for Africa." However, as a latecomer on this continent, Germany could colonize only resource-poor southwestern and eastern Africa. From 1871 until World War I, Germany tried and failed to extend its colonial and economic influence. This failure inflamed German nationalists and pushed German leaders to rapidly develop the shipbuilding industry and a navy to secure German economic and geopolitical interests.

An undemocratic domestic political system, the lack of profitable colonies, an exposed geopolitical position in central Europe, and increasingly inflamed nationalism heightened Germany's aggression toward other nations and ultimately prompted it to declare war in 1914.

German leaders expected World War I to be brief and victorious. It turned into a protracted conflict, however, and cost Germany both its few colonial possessions and its imperial social order. The Second Reich collapsed in November 1918, leaving a weak foundation for the country's first attempt to establish a parliamentary democracy.

The Weimar Republic (1918–1933)

Kaiser Wilhelm II abdicated after Germany's defeat in World War I, and the Weimar Republic (the constitution was drafted in that eastern German city) replaced the Second Reich. The SPD, the only remaining party not discredited by the failed war, found itself in charge of Germany's first democracy. Its first unwelcome task was to surrender to the Allies—an action that was later used to discredit the party.

The new government was a **procedural democracy** (formal political institutions without broad public support), holding regular elections and comprising multiple parties from the far left to the far right. Yet it had a fatal flaw: the many right-wing political parties and social forces, as well as the Communists on the left, refused to accept the legitimacy of democratic government.

From the beginning, the SPD leadership was on shaky ground: it foolishly asked the undemocratic military to guarantee order and stability. Because SPD leaders signed the Treaty of Versailles and its onerous reparations payments for war costs that the victorious Allied coalition demanded from Germany, the right accused the government of having "stabbed Germany in the back." Further, the SPD-led government failed to address the ruinous inflation of 1923, when the government was forced to print worthless *Reichmarks* to pay the huge war reparations.

Into this turmoil stepped Adolf Hitler, a little-known, Austrian-born former corporal in the German army, who became the leader of the Nazi Party in 1920 (**Nazi** is a German abbreviation for National Socialist German Workers' Party). Taking advantage of a deepening economic crisis, the Nazis mobilized large segments of the population by preaching hatred of the left and of "inferior, non-Aryan races"—especially Jews, whom Hitler accused of defiling racial purity, betraying German patriotism, and enjoying illegitimate economic privilege.

After the Great Depression spread to central Europe in 1931, Germany became more unstable, with none of the major parties able to win a majority or even form durable government coalitions. Frequent elections produced ever-shakier minority governments, party fragmentation and lack of a stable majority. The Nazis relentlessly pressed for political power from a population that continued to underestimate Hitler's real intentions and viewed his hate-filled speeches as merely political rhetoric. The Nazis were rewarded in early 1933 when they and their conservative allies maneuvered President Paul von Hindenburg, a former World War I general, into appointing Hitler chancellor in a Nazi-Nationalist coalition government sworn in on January 30. Once in power, the Nazis began to ban political parties and took advantage of a fire at the Reichstag that they tried to blame on the Communists to engage in sweeping repression of the opposition. Hitler then pressured President Hindenburg to grant—by "emergency" executive order—broad, sweeping powers to the Nazi-dominated cabinet. This act made the Reichstag irrelevant as a representative political body and enabled the Nazi regime to consolidate its hold on power.

The Third Reich (1933–1945)

After the Nazis had obtained the chancellorship, establishing social control was their next major priority. This took the form of banning political parties and then all civic and religious institutions. Ultimately, the Nazis employed propaganda and demagoguery—along with the military, paramilitary, and police through arbitrary and brutal suppression of the opposition—to mobilize large segments of the German population. Using mesmerizing speeches and a relentless propaganda ministry led by Joseph Goebbels, Hitler exercised total control of political power and the media to reshape German politics to his party's vision. This vision allowed no opposition, even within the party.

Initial Nazi domestic policy was focused on two major areas: centralization of political power and the rebuilding of an economy devastated by the depression of the early 1930s. The Nazis concentrated all political authority in Berlin, removing any regional political autonomy. The main purpose of this top-down system was to ensure the repression of political opposition, Jews and other minorities.

The Nazis' economic program was also autocratic in design and implementation. Because free trade unions had been banned, both private and state-run industries forced workers, including slave laborers during World War II, to work long hours for little or no pay. The program emphasized heavier industries that required massive investment from the large manufacturing cartels, the banking system, and the state itself. Although some segments of big business had initially feared Hitler before he took power, most of German industry eventually endorsed Nazi economic policies. The Nazis also emphasized massive public works projects, such as building the *Autobahn* highway system, upgrading the railroad system, and constructing ostentatious public buildings. Almost all favored Nazi industries had direct military application.

During the Third Reich, Hitler fanned the flames of German nationalism by glorifying the warrior tradition in German folklore and exulting in imperial Germany's nineteenth-century victories. Extolling a mythically glorious and racially pure German past, he made scapegoats out of homosexuals, ethnic minorities, and, especially, Jews. Anti-Semitism proved an important political force that Hitler deployed to blame any political problems on this "external" international minority and to target them as enemies who should be relentlessly persecuted and suppressed. Thus, in the first years of Nazi rule, Jews were excluded from professions, including teaching, law, medicine, and the

Hitler strides triumphantly through a phalanx of Nazi storm troopers (SA) in 1934. *Source:* Ullstein Bilderdienst.

civil service, and prohibited from marrying non-Jews. As described below, much worse was yet to come.

The Nazis refused to abide by the provisions of the Treaty of Versailles. Germany began to produce armaments in large quantities, and remilitarized the Rhineland. The Nazis also rejected the territorial divisions of World War I, since Hitler claimed that a growing Germany needed increased space to live (*Lebensraum*) in eastern Europe. He engineered a union (*Anschluss*) with Austria in March 1938 and the occupation of the German-speaking Sudetenland section of Czechoslovakia in September 1938. The Third Reich's attack on Poland on September 1, 1939, finally precipitated World War II.

Hitler's grandiose visions of world domination were dramatically heightened by the German conquests of much of Europe during 1939 and 1940. In 1941, Hitler attacked the Soviet Union, assuming that defeating the Soviet Union would be as easy as his other conquests. The attack was an enormously costly failure, and foreshadowed the Third Reich's defeat almost four bloody years later.

The most heinous aspect of the Nazi regime was the systematic extermination of 6 million Jews and the imprisonment in concentration camps of millions of other civilians. Concentration camps were first created in 1933 for Jews, political opponents, homosexuals, and gypsies. Prisoners were treated with extreme

"Enemies of the Third Reich" *Source:* Courtesy of the Trustees of the Boston Public Library, Rare Books and Manuscripts. Reproduced with the permission of Alexandra Szyk Bracie, daughter of Arthur Szyk, in cooperation with The Arthur Szyk Society/Historicana, www.szyk.com.

brutality and large numbers were shot or died from starvation, disease, or overwork. Several years later, the Nazis created extermination camps in occupied countries like Poland, equipped with gas chambers to murder the Jews and other inmates. Hitler had explicitly stated in *Mein Kampf* (*My Struggle*), written in 1925 while he was imprisoned for leading a failed insurrection, that the Germans were the master race and all those of non-Aryan ethnicity, especially Jews, were inferior. But as with many of his statements during his rise to power, many Germans chose to ignore the implications of this hatred or thought it was mere exaggeration. The magnitude of Nazi plans for other races, religions, opposing political views, gays, and gypsies, among others, became apparent after Hitler came to power, but by then any chance of domestic opposition had passed. Persecution of Jews and other racial and ethnic minorities grew steadily more atrocious until Germany's defeat in 1945.

A Divided Germany (1945–1990)

Germany was occupied by the victorious Allied powers from 1945 to 1949. However, cold war tensions soon led to the formal division of Germany: the Federal Republic of Germany (FRG) in the west, run by the Allies (Britain, France, and the United States), and the communist German Democratic Republic (GDR), directed by the Soviet Union in the east. This division was not expected in 1945, but postwar Germany soon took on the respective postwar visions of the two victorious sides. The major German cold war focal point was the city of Berlin, like Germany itself, divided between Allied- and Soviet-supported governments.

During the years of occupation in West Germany (1945–1949), German and Allied officials reduced the powers of the central state in domestic politics; some of these powers were assumed by regional governments. Western German reformers also rebuilt the party system, helping to create parties with more broad-based interests and ideological considerations. The most significant political development was the merger for the first time in 1946 of Roman Catholic and Protestant interests into the Christian Democratic Party. The result was the emergence of a large center-right party that ruled the FRG, alone or in coalition, for the first twenty years of the new republic.

Formal nation-statehood was restored to the two Germanys in 1949, and the Occupation ended, but neither half of divided Germany was fully sovereign. The FRG deferred to the United States in matters of international relations, as did the GDR to the Soviet Union. Neither of the two Germanys joined the cold war's international alliances—NATO (North Atlantic Treaty Organization) and the Warsaw Pact, respectively—until 1955.

In 1949, the Federal Republic became a democracy, characterized by constitutional provisions for free elections, civil liberties and individual rights, and an independent judiciary. The Federal Republic's democratic system produced rapid economic growth and remarkable political stability for the first forty years of its existence. Alternation from a moderate center-right government to a moderate center-left one, and back again, produced high standards of living and a genuine democratic regime. Under Christian Democratic chancellors Konrad Adenauer (1949–1963) and Ludwig Erhard (1963–1966), the FRG saw the establishment of a new parliamentary regime, an extensive system of social welfare benefits, a politically regulated market economy, and the re-establishment of strong regional governments.

Under Social Democratic chancellors Willy Brandt (1969–1974) and Helmut Schmidt (1974–1982), the FRG first enjoyed robust full employment and a large increase in social services. The SPD also advocated a more equal distribution of income. But later in the 1970s, two economic recessions produced increased unemployment and forced Chancellor Schmidt to introduce moderate cutbacks in social services. Unlike many Western capitalist countries in the 1980s, however, West Germany retained many of the social programs of the postwar welfare state, a stance that enjoyed wide public support.

The Christian Democrats returned to power in 1982 under the leadership of Chancellor Helmut Kohl, who formed a center-right coalition with the Free Democratic Party (FDP), a moderate centrist party that had allied with both of the two major parties in most governments since 1949. The 1949–1990 period established the viability of constitutional democracy in the Federal Republic, as the country maintained a firm commitment to parliamentary government and political stability.

In the meantime, the German Democratic Republic was established in Soviet-occupied East Germany in 1949. The GDR was a one-party state under the control of the Communist Party, which was known as the Socialist Unity Party (SED, *Sozialistische Einheits Partei*). Although the state provided full employment, housing, and various social benefits to its citizens, it was a rigid, bureaucratic, Stalinist regime that tightly controlled economic and political life under the leadership of party chairmen Walter Ulbricht, Willi Stoph, and finally Eric Honnecker. The East German regime stressed the desirability of communism and suppressed public dissent as deviationist and undermining the "true path of socialism." The infamous *Stasi*, or secret police, was an extensive system of surveillance that kept tabs on all German citizens and ruthlessly dealt with those suspected of opposing the regime. East Germans caught trying to escape to the West were executed on the spot. In August 1961, East Germany erected the Berlin Wall to keep its citizens from fleeing to West Germany.

For more than forty years, the international role of the two Germanys was limited. Because of NATO's geopolitical restrictions, West German energies were focused on rebuilding the economy and pursuing European economic integration. East Germany was similarly restricted. Although it became the strongest of the Warsaw Pact's economies, it also loyally toed the Soviet line in international affairs.

The Challenge of German Unification (1990–1998)

Germany's unification in 1990 took place rapidly. When Soviet rule over Germany and other communist regimes in East Central Europe loosened, and the Berlin Wall was opened in November 1989, the two German states envisioned a slow process of increased contacts and cooperation while maintaining separate sovereign states for the short term. Yet a currency reform provided East Germans with valuable West German deutsche marks and fueled massive migration westward in the summer of 1990. The process of German unification proceeded much faster than anyone could have imagined. After a referendum on unification and intense negotiations in the late summer, the former East Germany was incorporated into the FRG as five new West German states (*Länder*).

Formal unification took place in the fall of 1990 as Helmut Kohl, the "unification chancellor," won a strong re-election victory for his center-right Christian Democratic–Free Democratic coalition. But unification euphoria did not last, as its costs strained Germany's budget and democratic institutions. The process proved much more difficult than expected. The communist-planned economy (sometimes called a *command economy*) was much weaker than had been recognized. The production of goods was determined more by rigid government dictates than by real consumer needs, and what was produced was of shoddy quality. The East German level of technology was decades behind, and the unified German government spent huge sums just to rebuild communication networks.

Incorporating the disadvantaged East Germany into the FRG had an adverse impact on a wide range of public policies, including unemployment expenses, structural-rebuilding funds, and the large tax increases necessary to pay for it all. Because the production apparatus in eastern Germany was so deficient, unemployment soared. The proportion of the unemployed in eastern Germany—approximately 20 percent, more than twice the figure in the prosperous west—helped fuel scattered ultra-right-wing political movements. Skinheads and others targeted foreigners (often Turks) as scapegoats, and there were several vicious attacks on minority groups beginning in the 1990s.

The difficulties of unification were complicated by the Kohl government throughout the 1990s. In order to win the support of eastern Germans, he sugarcoated the enormity of the unification process as well as its duration. In order to win the support of western Germans, he had to convince them that the 7.5 percent "unification tax" imposed on them in the early 1990s would be sufficient to achieve economic integration. Unfortunately for Kohl, the longer the unification process remained incomplete, the less willing the German electorate was to give him continued support.

By 1998, Kohl's center-right coalition had run out of both gas and ideas. Successfully convincing Germans that a change was necessary, newly elected SPD Chancellor Gerhard Schröder, a generation younger than Kohl, formed a coalition government with the environmentalist Green Party for the first time in the nation's history. Significant too was the continued high support for the former Communist Party (now called *die Linke*) in eastern Germany (over 20 percent), which enabled it to gain more than 5 percent of the total German vote. With almost 54 percent of the electorate voting for parties of the left, clearly a new era had arrived in Germany.

Germany in the Euro Era (1998–2001)

Germany's leaders—from Konrad Adenauer, the first postwar chancellor, through Schröder—were all strong supporters of European integration. Germany is the economic anchor of the EU, and its membership in the EU has enabled it to do things and to take on needed political responsibilities that it would be unable to carry out alone. Former chancellor Kohl (1982–1998) realized this and was a firm advocate of all measures that would assist in a smooth, stable, and comprehensive EU.

The accelerating pace of European integration, however, produced movement toward a common monetary policy, a European central bank, and a single (virtual) currency in 1999. This, followed by the replacement of eleven European national currencies in favor of the euro on January 1, 2002, placed additional pressures on the Federal Republic. Many Germans wondered whether the EU would provide the same stability as the redoubtable deutsche mark (DM) and the inflation-fighting Deutsche Bundesbank. The fall in value of the euro by some 25 percent in relation to the dollar in 1999 and 2000—and its subsequent rise to more than 50 percent greater than the dollar eight years later—was worrisome to Germans long accustomed to a stable and predictable DM. So too was the loss of domestic control of monetary and fiscal policies, due to the EU requirement that member states not run deficits greater than 3 percent of GDP.

With respect to open borders and seemingly free-flowing immigration, Germans also feared that Europeanization threatened to erode what it meant to be German. At the same time that immigration and political asylum increased in Germany during the 1990s, the birth rate, particularly in the former GDR, dropped precipitously. Far-right and even some moderate right-wing politicians used these demographic changes to whip up nationalist support for decreasing the flow of migrants to the FRG. Ironically, these demographic changes also coincided with the inability of the highly regarded secondary educational system to produce enough skilled workers for the information age. Germany's vocational educational system and integrated apprenticeship system, described in Section 2, have worked exceptionally well for traditionally strong German industries, but they have been less effective in producing highly qualified workers for the information sector. Finally, the issue of democratic governance was an additional European challenge. With fiscal and monetary policy essentially determined by either Brussels or the European Central Bank, where does democratic governance really lie?

Germany after September 11 (2001–)

The terrorist attacks on the United States had several significant effects on German domestic and international politics. Among the most significant were immigration/globalization, antiterrorist measures, and Germany's relationship with the United States.

The enlargement of the EU with the addition of twelve central and eastern European countries since 2004 highlighted the challenge that immigration poses for Germany, since there are no restrictions on movement by citizens of member states to other EU member states. During the *Gastarbeiter* period after World War II, immigration to Germany was comparatively straightforward. Workers came from southern Europe and Turkey, supposedly for limited periods, and would return home when economic conditions no longer required their services. Of course, several generations of Turkish-Germans remain in the Federal Republic. But in the first decade of the twenty-first century, in addition to migrants coming for economic opportunities in a globalizing world, a wave of migrants arrived from unstable and repressive countries in Africa and East Europe seeking political asylum.

The discovery that some of the 9/11 terrorists had lived in Hamburg prior to the attacks only added to the tension. Germany's sensitivity after World War II to the excesses of the Nazi regime was responsible for the liberal asylum laws; postwar German governments viewed with pride the country's openness to oppressed people facing repression. Yet the discovery that several of the terrorists belonged to an Al Qaeda cell in Hamburg before going to the United States created uneasy discussion in Germany on the issue of freedom versus security. In the wake of 9/11, the Schröder and Merkel governments increased domestic surveillance to locate additional terrorist cells, and made a series of arrests and detentions. While such aggressive actions by police and security forces helped identify potential threats to domestic and international security, they rested uneasily with considerable segments of the German population, creating tension between Germany and the United States

Germany's opposition to the Iraq war also drove a large wedge between the United States and the Federal Republic. The tension was exacerbated by the conduct of Gerhard Schröder during his 2002 reelection campaign. His leading issue in the final weeks of the campaign—largely reflecting the preferences of the German public—was in direct opposition to the Bush administration's Iraq policy in the months before the war in early 2003. Although the campaign never degenerated to the level of American–French acrimony regarding the Iraq war, the long-standing strong relationship between Germany and the United States took a significant hit because of this dispute. Further exacerbating these tensions were the acquittals of two Moroccan alleged terrorists in Germany in February 2004. Because the Bush Administration refused to release witnesses—who were being held in detention in the United States—who could potentially exonerate the two Moroccan suspects in Germany, the judges in the two German courts were forced to release the two defendants because they could not present a proper defense.

Themes and Implications

Historical Junctures and Political Themes

Because of the historic importance of militarism and a corresponding authoritarian political culture, Germany's role in the world of states is contentious. For all states, military strength is a basic tool used to shape and consolidate. But in Germany, late unification propelled by war created a state that caused tremendous fear among Germany's neighbors. The conduct of World War I and the crimes of the Third Reich during World War II intensified this fear. Although more than fifty years have passed since the end of World War II and although Germany's independent political actions are constrained by the EU, many Europeans remain wary of Germany's international role.

The second theme, governing the economy, has been colored profoundly by Germany's late unification and the issue of state building. Delayed unification and industrialization in Germany prevented it from embarking on the race for empire and raw materials until the late nineteenth century. The pursuit of fast economic growth and an awakened sense of German nationalism in the late nineteenth century produced an aggressive, acquisitive state in which economic and political needs overlapped. The fusion of state and economic power enabled Hitler to build the Third Reich. Consequently, policy-makers and political leaders after World War II desired to remove the state from actively governing the economy. Thus, the postwar period saw the development of *Modell Deutschland* (the German model), a term often used to describe the Federal Republic of Germany's distinctive political and socioeconomic features. While amazingly successful for decades after World War II, it remains an open question whether these economic institutions will continue to function well in a unified Europe.[4]

The democratic idea, our third theme, is one that developed much later in Germany than in most other advanced industrialized countries. It was not until 1918 and the shaky Weimar Republic that Germany attained democracy at all. Despite a formal democratic constitution, Weimar was a prisoner of forces bent on its destruction. Unlike stable multiparty political systems in other countries, the Weimar Republic was plagued by a sharp and increasing polarization of political parties. And of course Germany's descent into authoritarianism in the 1930s destroyed every vestige of democracy.

The constitution of the Federal Republic in 1949 was designed to overcome Weimar's shortcomings. A system of federalism, constitutional provisions to encourage the formation and maintenance of coalitions, and a streamlined political party system proved solid foundations for the new democracy. Electoral turnout of 80 to 90 percent for almost all elections since 1949 further suggests that Germans have embraced democracy, although skeptics once argued that Germans voted more out of duty than anything else.[5] However, four peaceful electoral regime changes in the past fifty years, in which both the government and the opposition functioned more smoothly than in most other democratic regimes, have finally put doubts about German democracy to rest. The remaining uncertainties involve how fully the democratic culture will penetrate formerly communist eastern Germany and how successfully Germany's politics will adapt to a five-party system since the Left Party now appears to be a permanent fixture.

As for the fourth theme, the politics of collective identity, more than in other democratic countries, German political institutions, social forces, and patterns of life emphasize collective action rather than the individualism characteristic of the United States. This does not imply that German citizens have less personal freedom compared to those in other developed democracies or that there is no conflict in Germany. It means that political expression, in both the state and civil society, revolves around group representation and cooperative spirit in public action.

Certainly, Germany's history from Prussian militarism through Nazism has led many observers to believe that collectivist impulses should be eradicated. However, to expect Germany to embrace an individualistic democracy like that of the United States is misguided. Germany's development of a collective identity since 1945 has relied on a redefinition of Germany in a European context. For example, one of the first provisions of the SDP-Green coalition agreement was to ease Germany's restrictive immigration law to enable those who had lived in Germany for decades to obtain citizenship. German collective identity is changing.

Implications for Comparative Politics

Germany differs from other developed countries in substantial ways. Germany—like Japan—was late to industrialize and late to democratize. But the most significant difference between Germany and other western European states is, of course, the Nazi period and the destruction that the Third Reich wrought. Concerns about this period, however, have been somewhat allayed by Germany's stable democratic experience since 1949.

Germany's significance for the study of comparative politics lies in several areas: the contrast between its nationalistic history and democratization in an integrating Europe; its unique form of organized capitalism that is neither state-led nor laissez-faire; its successful form of representative democracy that combines widespread participation and representation of the entire electorate in a stable parliamentary regime; and a politics of identity that builds on existing collectivities in an increasingly multifaceted political culture.

SECTION 2 Political Economy and Development

State and Economy

Germany's capitalist economy relies on a coordinated network of small and large businesses working together. Most German banks—especially local and regional ones—see their primary role as providing long-term investments to support Germany's internationally competitive manufacturing industries. German banks have been the prime foundation for the country's economic pattern of stable, long-term relationships among economic partners rather than the short-term deals common among banks, investors, and firms in the United States. Although these practices have eroded somewhat among the largest banks (e.g., Deutsche Bank, Dresdner Bank) in the face of globalization, deregulation, and Europeanization, the core principles of this arrangement remain, particularly among small and medium-sized firms and financial institutions.

The Role of the State Before 1945

In the years before unification in 1871, many of Germany's regional governments played a strong role in promoting economic growth and development. They worked directly and indirectly with private economic interests, thus blurring distinctions between the state and the market. The foundations for economic growth were established, and the most spectacular early leaps of industrial modernization happened, before Germany's unification in 1871. The creation of a customs union (*Zollverein*) in 1834 from eighteen independent states with a population of 23 million people propelled industrial modernization by greatly facilitating trade among these states after centuries of economic stagnation.

Bismarck became the dominant symbol for Prussia's hegemonic position in brokering the interests of grain-growing *Junkers* in the east with those of the coal and steel barons in the Ruhr. Bismarck used the development of the railroad as a catalyst for this "marriage of iron and rye."[6] He astutely realized that although railroads were a primary consumer of coal and steel, they also provided an effective way to transport the *Junkers*' grain to market from the relatively isolated eastern part of Germany. The image of Prussian-led, rapid, state-enhanced industrial growth is important, but small-scale agricultural production remained in many parts of the southern states, particularly in Bavaria, and small-scale craft production continued in Württemberg and many other regions.

By 1871, a unified Germany was forced to compete with a number of other countries that had already developed industrialized capitalist economies. German business and political elites realized that a gradual, small-firm-oriented economy would face ruinous competition from countries such as Britain, France, and the United States. To become competitive, the German state became a powerful force in the German economy. The most influential analysis of German industrial growth during the nineteenth century was by economic historian Alexander Gerschenkron. He maintained that Germany's transformation from a quasifeudal society to a highly industrialized one during the latter two-thirds of the nineteenth century was made possible by explicit coordination among government, big business, and a powerful universal banking system (with a given bank handling a variety of financial transactions as opposed to separate banks for savings and commercial activities).

A severe economic crisis in 1923, caused largely by Germany's payment of massive reparations to the Allies as required by the Versailles Treaty that ended World War I, destabilized the economy and produced massive hyperinflation. After the 1929 stock market crash, Hitler used demagoguery and hatred to claim that his leadership could produce the solution for all of Germany's problems. During the Third Reich, between 1933 and 1945, the state worked hand in glove with German industry to repress workers, employ slave labor, and produce military armaments. As a result, a number of leading industrialists, notably those of the Krupp steel works and the IG Farben chemical complex, were tried and convicted of war crimes after the Allied victory.

The Social Market Economy

Unlike Anglo-American laissez-faire policies, or heavy-handed state-led economic policies, German economic policies after World War II were indirect and supportive rather than clumsy and overly regulatory. Although the government sets broad guidelines, it encourages the formation of voluntary associations to coordinate negotiations among employers, banks, trade unions, and regional governments in order to reach the government's policy objectives. Its economic policy-making is flexible in two ways.

First, German regulation establishes a general framework for economic activity rather than providing detailed standards. The government sets broad licensing and performance standards for most professions and industries. Government policy-makers believe that once their core requirements are met and their general objectives known, private actors can be trusted to pursue government goals without detailed regulation. Violating government standards can result in fines or, in some criminal cases, imprisonment. In contrast, the United States has no such core requirements. Instead, it often produces many layers of detailed—and sometimes contradictory—regulations in the wake of banking failures and financial abuses.

Second, among the major European economies, Germany has the smallest share of industry in national government hands; but it allows state governments to have considerable power. This is called cooperative federalism, which delegates to the states (*Länder*) the administrative powers to oversee the implementation of laws and regulations passed at the federal level.

Postwar policy-makers avoided a dominating role for the state in the Federal Republic's economic life. Unlike the French and the Japanese states, which have intervened much more in the economy, the German state has evolved a careful balance between the public and private sectors. Germany has avoided the opposite pattern as well: the frequently antigovernment, free-market policies of Britain and the United States since the 1980s.

In other words, the relationship between state and market in Germany is neither free market nor state dominant. Rather, the state sets clear general ground rules, acknowledged by the private sector, but then allows market forces to work relatively unimpeded within the general framework of government supervision. For example, the Federal Bank Supervisory Office encourages banks to have slightly more capital reserves than the international standard and it certifies the competency of senior management. The German system of **framework regulations** has enabled German economic policy to avoid the sharp lurches between laissez-faire and state-led economic policy that have characterized Britain since World War II. This system often appears externally rigid but internally flexible (in the sense that large institutions and firms are often surprisingly flexible in adapting applied technologies to produce specialized goods). In short, this system regulates not the details, but the general rules of the game under which all actors must play.

Some would criticize such a system as being too cumbersome and inflexible. However, supporters praise its ability to generally produce agreement on major policy direction without major social dislocation. For example, the banks are legally allowed to develop close financial ties with firms in other industries, including owning their stock, granting them long-term loans, having representatives on their boards of directors, and voting as stockholders. The end result is that much private investment is based on "patient capital" geared toward long-term economic success rather than quick profits in the short term. Once agreement has been informally worked out among all the major parties, it is easier to move forward with specific policies and/or legislation. Since the time of the first postwar chancellor, Christian Democrat Konrad Adenauer, the Germans have referred to this approach as the **social market economy** (*Sozialmarktwirtschaft*).

But the contemporary period has been much more stressful for this model. Among the many social components of the German economy once considered bedrocks, but now under pressure, are such diverse public benefits as health care, workers' rights, public transportation, and financial support for the arts. In some respects, these benefits are similar to those provided by other European governments. However, the provision of some public benefits through organized private interests (such as the quasipublic "sickness funds" that provide for health insurance) makes the German social market economy a blend of public and private actions that support and implement public policies. The social market economy blurs state/market distinctions in the hope of producing a socially responsible capitalism. The social component of the social market economy is distinctive to Germany. Several programs, such as savings subsidies and vocational education, contribute to the production of income. The former contributes to a stable pool of investment capital, while the latter helps create a deep pool of human capital that has enabled Germany to produce high-quality goods throughout the postwar period. But as we see below, these programs face daunting challenges.

Germany, for most of its postwar history, has been a high-wage, high-welfare nation that has maintained its competitive world position far better than have most other advanced industrialized states since the oil crises of the 1970s. An emphasis on high skills in key export-oriented manufacturing industries was the special path that German economic policy took to maintain its competitive position. An elaborate vocational education system combined with apprenticeship training underlay this policy, which was implemented through the **works councils,** firm-level institutions elected by every worker in all German companies with five or more employees. This system of training workers in advanced skills enabled Germany for many years to resist the postindustrial service sector emphasis pursued by countries such as the U.S. and Britain.

Relying extensively on its elaborate apprenticeship program, Germany maintained a competitive position in such traditional manufacturing industries as automobiles, chemicals, machine tools, and industrial electronics. By relying on its highly skilled work force, Germany resisted for many years the claim that it must lower its wage costs to match those of newly industrializing countries. Germany's record suggests that a developed country in a globalized world economy can still compete in manufacturing by raising product quality rather than by lowering wage costs. Despite a lack of natural resources, Germany has maintained a trade surplus with a large working-class population that historically has spurned protectionism. With one in every three jobs devoted to exports (one in two in the four manufacturing industries just mentioned), protectionism would be self-defeating for German unions. The skills and productivity of its workers have helped German industry acquire natural resources and pay high wages. This has enabled Germany's highly skilled blue-collar workers to drive expensive German automobiles, obtain high-quality medical care, and enjoy six weeks of paid vacation each year.

Germany's research and development strategy has enhanced these economic policies. Rather than push for specific new breakthroughs in exotic technologies or invent new products that might take years to commercialize, the strategy is to adapt existing technologies to traditional sectors and refine already competitive sectors. This was the exact opposite of U.S. research and development strategy. During the postwar years, this policy has enabled Germany to maintain a favorable balance of trade and a high degree of competitiveness. However, German unification and European integration have forced German industry and policy-makers to reexamine and perhaps modify this model. Taking others' core discoveries and quickly applying them to production requires coordinated policies among all producer groups. The primary challenge since the 1990s has been trying to integrate into this system former GDR workers raised in an industrial culture that encouraged workers to follow orders rather than apply skill and initiative. One of the major tasks for early twenty-first century governments has been to improve Germany's vocational education system, particularly in the five eastern states.

Other than the government, the German institution that, until recently, was most responsible for shaping economic policy was the very independent *Bundesbank* (central bank). *Bundesbank* policy produced low inflation, both because this was a traditional demand of all central bankers and because of Germany's history of ruinous inflation during the Weimar Republic. However, when the government wished to expand the economy by increasing spending or reducing taxes, the *Bundesbank* preferred policies that favored monetary restrictions over fast economic growth. As a result, the government and the *Bundesbank* disagreed on economic policy repeatedly in the years since after unification. Since the introduction of the euro, however, the European Central Bank (ECB) has usurped the *Bundesbank*'s role. Although the ECB is modeled on the *Bundesbank* (and is also located in Frankfurt), it signifies a change in German economic policy from the national to the European level.

Despite the long success of the German model, the early twenty-first century ushered in a period of deep introspection concerning economic stagnation. Upon its election in 1998, the SPD-Green government led by Gerhard Schröder pledged to maintain the core features of the *Sozialmarktwirtschaft*. But it too found each of these traditionally successful policies facing mounting challenges from Europeanization, globalization, and a powerful deregulatory free enterprise ideology. However, the presence of the environmental Greens in the cabinet for the first time gave added weight and attention to climate change and environmental policies.

The expansion of the EU to twenty-seven countries in 2007 had an important impact on German-specific organized capitalist institutions. Now, German firms could go to lower-cost eastern and southern European countries to find the best deals rather than maintain the kind of long-standing business relationships that were the lynchpin of the German model. Continued globalization meant that lower-cost but high-quality goods, such as automobiles from East Asia, threatened the strength of Germany's auto producers such as BMW and Daimler-Chrysler. More fundamentally, the German organized capitalist model was increasingly attacked at the ideational level. For many years, free-market adherents from abroad criticized the German model for its "clubby" relationships among what the Germans called the "social partners" (business associations, labor unions, and federal and state governments). Yet, as long as Germany's economy thrived, German officials could slough off the criticism. As the German economy's troubles mounted, policy-makers had no effective answers to such criticism. Yet as the American financial crisis associated with deregulation and free-market policies spread to Europe in early 2008, some began to wonder whether the German organized capitalist model might still be appropriate after all.

Welfare Provision

Welfare policies can be described as the social part of the social market economy. Although the Federal Republic's social welfare expenditures are not as extensive as those in Scandinavia, public services in the Federal Republic dwarf those in the United States. From housing subsidies to savings subsidies, health care, public transit, and the rebuilding of the destroyed cities and public infrastructure of the former GDR, the Federal Republic is remarkably generous in its public spending. Even under the moderately conservative rule of the CDU-led Adenauer coalition during the 1950s and early 1960s, there was a strong commitment to provide adequate public services. This strategy recalls Bismarck's efforts to use public services to forestall radical demands in the late nineteenth century. For antidemocratic conservatives like Bismarck and for democratic conservatives like Adenauer, comprehensive welfare benefits were attempts to blunt and soften the demands of the Social Democratic Party and the trade unions. Welfare in Germany has never been a gift but a negotiated settlement, often after periods of conflict between major social forces.

During the mid-1970s, when unemployment grew from 1 or 2 percent to roughly 4 percent and when some social welfare measures were capped (but not reduced), citizens of the Federal Republic spoke of the crisis of the welfare state. Yet non-German observers were hard-pressed to find indications of crisis. Clearly, contraction of substantial welfare state benefits in no way approximated the cutbacks of the United States and Britain in the 1980s and 1990s.

Since the 1980s, continued high unemployment (by German standards) and the costs of support for workers who had depleted their benefits presented difficult dilemmas for the welfare state. German jobs tend to be highly paid, so employers have tried to avoid creating part-time jobs, preferring to wait to hire until the need for employees is sustainable. During times of recession, the number of new jobs created can be minuscule.

Current Strains on the Social Market Economy

Throughout the postwar period, unemployment was virtually nonexistent—hovering around 1 percent. Since the onset of economic strains in the 1980s, however, unemployment has not dropped below 6 percent. One persistent problem facing successive German governments has been shouldering the cost of sustaining the long-term unemployed. An even more serious challenge involved devising a way for the Federal Republic's elaborate vocational education and apprenticeship system to absorb all the new entrants into the labor market. This problem could have undermined one of the strengths of the German economy: the continued supply of skilled workers. Despite these threats in the mid-1980s, both the

A cynical western German view of money spent to rebuild eastern Germany.
Source: © Janusz Majewski/Cartoonists and Writers Syndicate, from *Frankfurter Allgemeine Zeitung*.

unemployment compensation system and the vocational education and apprenticeship system survived. However, the issue resurfaced with the large increase in the unemployment rate following unification in 1990, particularly in the eastern German states.

In the early 1990s, the smoothly functioning German economic juggernaut faltered. First, the Kohl government badly misjudged the costs of unification. In 1992, Kohl finally acknowledged that the successful integration of the eastern economy into the western one would cost much more and take longer than originally predicted. Second, the structural challenges that the German political economy faced in the mid-1990s proved far more extensive than anything the Federal Republic had encountered since the 1950s. The amount budgeted in the early 1990s for reconstruction of eastern Germany's infrastructure was approximately 20 percent of the entire national budget. Yet even these huge sums were not enough to help smooth the assimilation process, and a large gap in productivity levels still exists between the two regions. Third, western German democratic corporatist institutions, composed of employers and trade unions with a long history of cooperation, were difficult to transfer to eastern Germany since they had to be created from scratch. In their absence, the *Treuhandanstalt* (the government reconstruction agency—*Treuhand*, for short) took the path of least resistance and simply privatized some 7,000 of the total of 11,000 firms that it had inherited from East Germany. One of the most significant costs of this transition from state to private ownership was high unemployment in the eastern sector. Some 1.2 million workers were officially unemployed, and in the early 1990s, another 2 million enrolled in a government-subsidized short-term program combined with job training (this program's funds were later slashed as part of an austerity budget).

The costs of the social market economy, particularly following unification, stretched the upper limits of Germany's capacity to pay. Massive budget cuts became imperative by the early and mid-1990s. The completion of the EU's single market placed additional strains on the German government. More significant for the German government, the EU has begun to disturb the intricate, mutually reinforcing pattern of government and business self-regulation. In addition, the growing push for deregulation in European finance threatens Germany's distinctive finance-manufacturing links, which depend on long-term relationships between the two parties, not on short-term deals.[7] Thus, the trend toward Europeanization may be incompatible with the consensus-oriented and coordinated nature of Germany's political and social institutions as shown by the worldwide financial crisis in late 2008.

Tensions have also flared up between former East and West Germans. The East German economy was strong by communist standards and provided jobs for virtually all adults who wanted one. But East German industry, as in most other former communist countries, was inefficient by Western standards, and most firms were not able to survive the transition to capitalism. Among the most serious problems were overstaffing and inadequate quality controls. Consequently, many easterners lost their jobs when newly privatized firms had to compete in a capitalist economy.

In short, the magnitude of the problems in eastern Germany threatened to overwhelm the institutional capacity to handle them. It certainly helped defeat Helmut Kohl's CDU/CSU-FDP center-right coalition government in 1998. Some pessimistic observers began to suggest that these stresses placed the German political economy in a precarious position. Germany's economic prowess has depended on certain manufacturing industries that produce eminently exportable goods but whose technologies must constantly be upgraded and whose labor costs continue to rise. Complicating the demands on Germany's economic institutions is the obligation to align Germany's economic policies with those of its European neighbors.

Thus, early in the twenty-first century, the prospects for the German political economy seem dimmer than in previous decades. Poor economic performance created the *Wirtschaftsstandort* debate (literally, location for economic growth), which argued that the combination of domestic and international factors had made Germany a much less attractive place for investment by either international or German capital. In response to this challenge, the Schröder government passed a tax reform package in 2000, followed in 2003 by Schröder's Hartz IV reform package of personal and corporate tax cuts that challenged many traditional labor market institutions to become more "flexible" along Anglo-American lines. These contentious issues helped precipitate the early election (one year ahead of schedule) in September 2005 that produced the SPD's defeat. Although the reforms seemed to mollify the equities markets, they were bitterly opposed by the left-leaning rank and file of Schröder's Red-Green coalition. For many, his programs represented an abandonment of fundamental principles and directly led some SPD members, most notably former SPD Finance Minister Oskar Lafontaine, to join with the former Communist Party of Democratic Socialism (PDS) from eastern Germany to form the new Left Party just before the 2005 election. Schröder's policies divided the left-of-center parties and saw the CDU/CSU emerge as the largest party, forcing Schröder into retirement and leaving the SPD as only the junior partner in the Grand Coalition government.

Society and Economy

Booming economic growth after WWII provided a sound foundation for social development. The social market economy of the Christian Democrats was augmented by governments led by Social Democrats from 1969 to 1982, when the social programs of the 1950s and 1960s were extended and enhanced. The expansion of social policies provided Germany with a solid foundation for forty years. Until the 1990s, Germany provided generous benefits to almost all segments of the population, including support for public transit, subsidies for the arts, virtually free higher and vocational education, and a comprehensive welfare state. There was also a general tolerance for a wide variety of political and artistic opinion. But the costs of unification, adjustment to the EU, and globalization have begun to undercut Germany's perception of itself as a prosperous country with a high standard of living and a well-paid work force. The strong role of trade unions and the consequent unwillingness of employers to confront workers on wage and workplace, once indicators of pride and success, have become sources of criticism. Higher unemployment and social service cutbacks have somewhat increased stratification of the society and the workplace. The primary workplace fault line lies between the core of mostly male, high-skilled blue-collar workers in the largest competitive industries and less-skilled workers, often employed in smaller firms with lower wages and not always full-time work. A significant number of women and immigrants are among the less-skilled workers.

Ethnicity and Economy

The most controversial social issue for German society since the 1990s has been race and ethnicity, with profound implications for Germany's ideology and political culture. Racist attacks against Turkish immigrants and other ethnic minorities have forced Germans to confront the possibility that almost fifty years of democracy have not tamed the xenophobic aspects of their political culture. The issue of ethnic minorities was exacerbated in the 1990s and 2000s by unification and European integration. Nationalism apparently has not disappeared. East Germans were raised in a society that did not celebrate, or even value, toleration or dissent and in which official unemployment did not exist. East Germany was a closed society, as were most other communist regimes, and many of its citizens had little contact with foreign nationals before 1989. In contrast, since the 1960s, West Germany has encouraged the migration of millions of guest workers (*Gastarbeiter*) from southern Europe. The Federal Republic has also provided generous provisions for those seeking political asylum, in an effort to overcome—to some degree at least—the legacy of Nazi persecution of non-Germans from 1933 to 1945.

The *Gastarbeiter* program originated after 1961 when the construction of the Berlin Wall caused a labor shortage because East Germans could no longer emigrate to the West. Thus, temporary workers were recruited from southern Europe with the stipulation that they would return to their native countries if unemployment increased. However, the economic boom lasted so long that by the time the economy did turn down in the mid-1970s, it was difficult for these so-called guests to return to homes in which they had not lived for a decade or more. These foreign workers produced heightened social strain in the 1970s and 1980s, a time of increasing unemployment. Because German citizenship was not granted to the guest workers or their children, the problem remained unresolved. The clash between German and *Gastarbeiter* cultures increased in intensity into the 1980s, particularly in areas where Turkish workers were highly concentrated. However, in a significant departure from past practice, the Schröder-led SPD-Green government in 1999 adopted a slightly easier immigration policy, allowing some second-and third-generation *Gastarbeiter* to obtain German citizenship or maintain dual citizenship.

Upon unification, few former GDR citizens were able to respond positively. Instead of guaranteed lifetime employment, they faced a labor market that did not always supply enough jobs, one where structural unemployment idled up to 25 percent of the work force. And they were expected to embrace completely and immediately a much more open and ethnically diverse society than they had ever known. Thus, immigrants and asylum seekers became scapegoats for the lack of employment, and Germans who were falling through the cracks of the welfare state were susceptible to racist propaganda blaming ethnic minorities for the rapid upheaval that had occurred. Events like these helped precipitate the—still relatively small—growth of the far-right NPD in the mid-2000s.

Germany's changing economy produced a "tech shortage" in the early 2000s that forced the Schröder government to recruit software specialists from India who would be granted "green cards" (that is, permanent residency status) upon their arrival! In other words, a new wave of *Gastarbeiter* was arriving precisely when some Germans were increasingly agitated about the immigration boom. The problem, however, was that the speed with which the German economy needed to embrace the information sector could not wait. The country needed both to increase Germany's presence in this complex sector and enable its traditionally strong industries to adapt to new forms of international competition. The economic pressures did not allow the luxury of waiting for the German secondary educational system to get up to speed.

Gender and Economy

Until the late 1970s, men traditionally dominated all positions of authority in management and the union movement. The union movement has made greater strides than management in expanding leadership opportunities for women, but men still hold the dominant positions in most unions. More than half of all German women were in the work force by the late 1970s, but their participation only reached 66.8 percent in the 1990s, while the male participation rate remained steady at 80 percent (see Table 4.2). Beyond the workplace, the differences between the laws of the former East and West Germany have created a firestorm of controversy. In the East, women had made far greater social and economic progress than in the West, and both women and men had received generous government support for childcare and family leave. During the last Kohl government, one of the

Table 4.2
Labor Force Participation Rates (Ages 15–65)

	1997	1999	2001	2003	2005
Male	80.3%	80.9%	80.1%	79.2%	80.4%
Female	62.8%	63.5%	64.9%	65.1%	66.8%

Source: Federal Statistical Office, Germany, 2007.

most heated debates concerned the cancellation of the more liberal East German policies toward women (including abortion) in favor of the more conservative and restrictive ones of the Federal Republic. In the 2005 election, Angela Merkel's weakness among women voters, especially in the east where she grew up, was due to her changing positions on the abortion issue. Once favoring the liberal eastern policy, she changed her position as she rose within the CDU, a switch that may have helped her gain the chancellorship in 2005.

Perhaps the most significant obstacle that German women have to overcome is not so much the benefits that they receive but the premise on which women's role in German society is defined.[8]

Women's benefits in German society have been tied more to their roles as mothers and wives than as autonomous individuals. This means that within the context of the labor market, individual German women face discrimination and assumptions about their career patterns that American women have largely overcome. As increasing numbers of women enter the German work force, it is harder for them to achieve positions of power and responsibility as individuals than it is for their American counterparts.

A final social cleavage is the generation gap, which has two dimensions. The first of these is the so-called postmaterialist social movement, which focuses on lifestyle concerns rather than bread-and-butter economic issues. It has not hinged on class, since many within this group tend to be university-educated children of the middle class. This group has not, however, been able to create an identity strong enough to challenge the highly skilled working class's dominance in the structure of the Federal Republic. The still-dominant working-class culture of the Federal Republic has acted as a barrier to the postmaterialist social movement's attaining further influence.

The second aspect of the generation gap comprises pensioners and older workers. The German birthrate fell markedly in the last decade of the twentieth century, particularly in the former GDR. This placed great demographic pressure on the German welfare state because the low birthrate and the increasing age of the baby boom generation meant that fewer younger workers now contribute to the welfare and retirement benefits of an increasing elderly population. This time bomb is just hitting German politics in the early 21st century, largely because the Kohl government during the 1980s and 1990s essentially ignored it. Pensions are one of many unresolved issues with which the Angela Merkel-led CDU/CSU-SPD Grand Coalition struggles.

Germany in the Global Economy

Germany's relationship to the regional and international political economy is shaped by two factors: the EU and globalization.

The European Union

The EU was embraced by most Germans and by the political and industrial establishment, especially in the first few years after unification. As Europe's leading economic power, Germany has benefited greatly from European integration. Many actions and policies that might once have been viewed by its neighbors as German domination have become more acceptable when seen as Germany's active participation as a member of the EU. But the cost for Germany was that it had to adapt to an unfamiliar free-market economic model quite different from the organized capitalism that had developed after World War II.

Several difficult issues confront Germany's international position in the early twenty-first century. One concern is whether German-specific institutional arrangements, such as its institutionalized system of worker (and union) participation in management, tightly organized capitalism, and elaborate system of apprenticeship training, will prove adaptable or durable in wider European and global contexts.[9] Before the worldwide economic crisis in late 2008, most observers thought that Germany's institutional, political, or cultural patterns may not successfully transfer beyond

Global Connection

The EU and the Euro

One of the Federal Republic's most lasting legacies at the end of the twentieth century was its commitment to European integration. As early enthusiasts of European unity, Germany's postwar political leaders realized the positive opportunity that a more formally united continent would present. In its relations with other states after World War II, Germany faced two different kinds of criticism. First was the fear of a too-powerful Germany, a country that had run roughshod over its European neighbors for most of the first half of the twentieth century. Second was the opposite problem: what was often described as an economic giant–political dwarf syndrome in which Germany was accused of benefiting from a strong world economy for fifty years while taking on none of the political and military responsibilities. The fact that these are mutually contradictory positions did not spare Germany from criticism. Yet Chancellors Kohl, Schröder, and Merkel since the 1990s hoped that an integrated Europe might solve both problems simultaneously. Germany remains the economic anchor of the EU, while Germany's membership in the EU has enabled it to take on political responsibilities that it would be unable to assume on its own, such as UN peacekeeping operations in eastern Europe. Until then, Germany's aggressive militarist history prevented Germany—and its neighbors—from developing a strong military.

The euro was a crucial part of this broader European goal. Although the deutsche mark (DM) was the very foundation of postwar German economic performance and contributed mightily to German self-confidence, it remained only one currency among many in Europe, thereby giving German and Europe an economic disadvantage in relation to both North America and East Asia. Kohl, Schröder, and now Merkel realized that economic success for both Germany and Europe depended on creating a stronger economic foundation, which is where the euro came in.

The euro was introduced in most countries of the EU in 2002. Gone was the redoubtable DM in favor of a currency that had no human beings on the notes, only nonspecific buildings, bridges, and arches. In the first few months of the "physical" euro, the currency traded below the value of the dollar. Considerable uncertainty among Germans mounted as to whether adopting the new currency was a good idea. Yet by the middle of 2002, financial scandals in the United States caused the euro to rise in value and achieve parity with the dollar. However, its continued rise since then against a sharply weakening dollar raised a different set of concerns: the higher-valued euro now made it more difficult for the export-oriented German economy to sell its goods in the United States.

---

the Federal Republic. Since then, the idea of a more stable form of capitalism received a second look.

Germany in a Globalizing World

Issues such as trade, economic competition with East Asia and North America, the introduction of the euro, the general pace of economic integration, climate change, and patterns of financial regulation have challenged the German postwar policies of finding a stable balance between state and market.

As a goods-exporting nation, Germany has always favored an open trading system. Management and unions realize that exports represent both profits and jobs, and that seeking refuge in protectionism would be self-defeating. Yet international competition has caused unemployment to remain persistently high in the early twenty-first century (near 10 percent). With respect to banking regulation, the Schröder government sponsored a law (since endorsed by the Merkel government) that enabled banks to sell their large ownership shares in German companies. This altered the prevailing postwar policy of encouraging banks to maintain equity holdings in other firms as a form of investment oriented toward the long term. This took the German model perilously close to the Anglo-American world of highly mobile capital investment. Many large German banks now see themselves more as international players than as German ones. Some have suggested that the pressures of competing in a globalized world economy have made the German-specific patterns of the country's political economy more of a liability than an asset. Similar criticisms have occurred since the mid-1970s, but the challenges to the German model in the early twenty-first century seem the most fundamental yet.

However, the worldwide economic crisis of 2008 that originated in the American housing and financial sectors has exploded into western Europe. Many wonder whether the more traditionally regulated form of continental European organized capitalism might be far more preferable than American-style deregulation after all.

SECTION 3 Governance and Policy-Making

The primary goals at the Federal Republic's founding in 1949 were to work toward eventual unification of the two Germanys and, more important, to avoid repeating the failure of the Weimar Republic that resulted in Hitler reaching power and the laying to rest of the legacy of the Nazi regime. When unification was blocked indefinitely, the founders instituted the **Basic Law** (*Grundgesetz*) as a compromise. They preferred to wait until Germany could be reunited before using the term *constitution* (*Verfassung*). After unification in 1990, however, the term *Basic Law* was retained because of the FRG's unqualified success after World War II. In addition, the institutional framework spelled out by the basic law for the FRG was simply applied to the five *Länder* of the former GDR.

The other goal, ensuring a lasting democratic order, presented a more complicated problem. Two fundamental institutional weaknesses had undermined the Weimar government: (1) provisions for emergency powers enabled leaders to arbitrarily centralize authority and suspend democratic rights, and (2) the fragmentation of the political party system prevented stable majorities from forming in the *Reichstag*. This second weakness, instability, encouraged the first: the use of emergency powers to break legislative deadlocks. It was, of course, Weimar's weakness that made possible the Nazi takeover, and so the primary motivation of state rebuilding after World War II was to minimize the risk of extremism. The attempt to deal with these problems involved introducing federalism and a weak presidency to curb the risk of arbitrary power, and instituting reformed electoral procedures and what was named the constructive vote of no confidence to curb instability.

Organization of the State

The Basic Law and Promoting Stability

Under Allied guidance during the occupation, the builders of the postwar government sought to inhibit centralized power by establishing a federal system with significant powers for the states (*Länder*). It is paradoxical that a document that owes so much to the influence of foreign powers has proved so durable. Under the Basic Law of the Federal Republic, many functions that had formerly been centralized during the imperial, Weimar, or Nazi periods, such as the educational system, the police, and the radio networks, now became the responsibility of the states. Although the federal *Bundestag* (lower house) became the chief lawmaking body, the implementation of many laws fell to the state governments. Moreover, the state governments sent representatives to the *Bundesrat* (upper house), which was required to approve bills passed in the *Bundestag*.

There was little opposition from major actors within the Federal Republic to this shift from a centralized to a federal system. The Third Reich's arbitrary abuse of power had created strong sentiment for curbing the state's repressive capacities. Further, the development of a federal system was not a departure but a return to form. Prior to the unification of Germany in 1871, the various regions of Germany had formed a decentralized political system with such autonomous institutions as banks, universities, vocational schools, and state administrative systems.

Several methods were used to surmount party fragmentation and the inability to form working majorities.

The multiplicity of parties, a characteristic of the Weimar Republic, was partly controlled in the FRG by the **5 percent rule:** a political party must receive at least 5 percent of the national vote to obtain seats in the *Bundestag* (and 5 percent of the vote in state or municipal elections for representation in those governments). Under the 5 percent rule, smaller parties have tended to fade, with most of their members absorbed by the three major parties. However, the Green Party in the early 1980s and the former Communist Party of East Germany, reformed as the Party of Democratic Socialism, in the 1990s, now *die Linke* (the Left Party), surpassed the threshold and appear likely to remain in the *Bundestag*. No extreme right-wing parties, however, have ever achieved 5 percent of the national vote to attain seats in the *Bundestag* (although three have won seats in *Länder* governments in the past ten years).

The *Bundestag* has achieved working majorities for several other reasons. Because the interval between elections is set at four years (except under unusual circumstances), and does not have easy provisions for "snap" elections as in Weimar, governments have a fair opportunity to implement their programs and take responsibility for success or failure. The electoral system was also changed from a pure proportional representation system under the Weimar government to a combination of proportional representation and single-member electoral districts. New constitutional provisions limited the possibility for the *Bundestag* to vote a government from office. Under the Weimar constitution, majorities of disparate forces could be mustered to unseat the chancellor but were unable to agree on the choice of a replacement. To overcome the weakness of the cabinet governments of Weimar, the Federal Republic's founders added a twist to the practice familiar in most other parliamentary systems, in which a prime minister is brought down by a vote of no confidence. In the Federal Republic, a no-confidence vote must be "constructive," meaning that a chancellor cannot be removed unless the *Bundestag simultaneously* elects a new chancellor (usually from an opposition party).

This constitutional provision, called the **constructive vote of no confidence,** strengthens the chancellor's power in two ways. First, it means that chancellors can more easily reconcile disputes among cabinet officials because the dispute does not threaten the chancellor's position. Second, it forces the opposition to come up with concrete and specific alternatives to the existing government and prevents them from fostering opposition for its own sake. In other words, to vote out one chancellor, the *Bundestag* must simultaneously vote in another.

The one time a constructive vote of no confidence occurred was in 1982, when Helmut Kohl replaced Helmut Schmidt. However, in 2005 Gerhard Schröder called for a new election a year ahead of schedule when his SPD party lost a major *Land* election. In a maneuver subsequently ruled legal by the federal president and the Constitutional Court, Schröder intentionally lost a vote of confidence in order to hold an early election. He argued that the loss in the *Land* election, thereby changing the balance of power in the *Bundesrat*, or upper house (see below for details), required a new election to clarify his coalition's mandate.

Another element that strengthens political stability involves increasing the chancellor's powers. As the leader of the dominant party or coalition of parties, the chancellor now has control over the composition of the cabinet, so that the federal president is merely the ceremonial head of state. Under the Weimar Constitution, the president could wield emergency powers, but FRG presidents have been stripped of such broad power.

The principles of the Federal Republic's government contained in the Basic Law give the nation a solid foundation, one that appeared capable of assimilating the five *Länder* of the former GDR when unification occurred in 1990. After surviving for over a half-century, the Federal Republic has clearly attained its most important goals. It has permitted successful alternations in power and has encouraged the Left Party (i.e., the former Communist Party in the east) to democratize. In addition, undemocratic right-wing parties have received only miniscule support, despite occasional neo-Nazi threats and some incidents of racist violence.

Government Institutions

Germany is organized as a federal system, with sixteen *Länder* (states), each with considerable powers (see Figure 4.2). As a parliamentary democracy, the

FIGURE 4.2

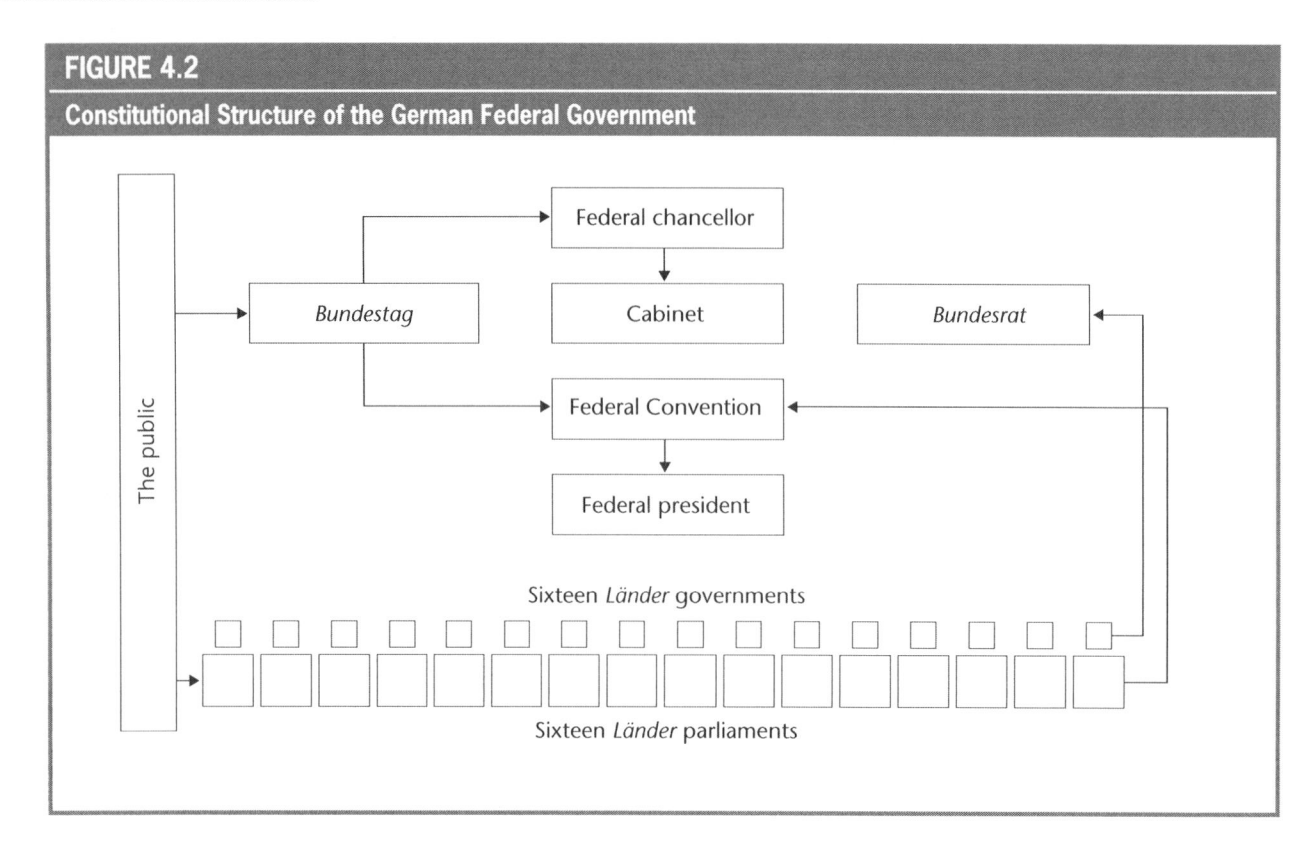

Constitutional Structure of the German Federal Government

German government resembles the parliamentary systems of Britain and Japan: there is a fusion of powers in that the chancellor, the executive or head of government, is also the leader of the leading party (or coalition) in the *Bundestag*. This contrasts with the separation of powers in the United States, in which the president and cabinet officials cannot simultaneously serve in the Congress. Generally, the executive dominates the legislature in the Federal Republic. Most members of the governing parties support the chancellor at all times, since their own positions depend on a successful government.

The Executive

The division between the head of government (the chancellor) and the head of state (the president) is firmly established in the Federal Republic, with major political powers delegated to the chancellor. Responsibilities and obligations are clearly distinguished between the two offices. For example, the chancellor can be criticized for the government's policies without the criticism being perceived as an attack against the state itself. This division of power in the executive branch was essential to establish respect for the new West German state after Hitler assumed both offices as the *Führer*.

The President

The German president is the head of state, a much weaker position than that of the chancellor. Like constitutional monarchs in Britain, for example, German presidents stand above the political fray, which means that their role is more ceremonial than political. Among the most common functions are signing treaties, presiding at formal state functions, and overseeing *Bundestag* protocols. German presidents are almost always senior politicians who are moderates within their respective parties and thus broadly acceptable to the electorate. However, if there were a political crisis affecting the chancellor, the president would remain as a caretaker of the political process, thus providing continuity in a time of national uncertainty.

For example, should a parliamentary crisis arise and no candidate could command the support of an absolute majority of *Bundestag* members, the president could provide stability. He or she could decide whether the country is to be governed by a minority administration under a chancellor elected by a plurality of deputies or whether new elections should be called.[10]

The Federal Convention (*Bundesversammlung*), an assembly of all *Bundestag* members and an equal number of delegates elected by the state legislatures (the equivalent of an electoral college), chooses the president according to the principle of proportional representation. Horst Köhler, sponsored by the opposition CDU/CSU and FDP, defeated Gesine Schwann, sponsored by the governing SPD/Green coalition, in a narrow vote of 604 to 598 in 2004. Schwann would have been the first female Federal president. The term of office is five years and, since 1969, only one president has served a second term. But in May 2008, Köhler announced that he wanted to run for a second term beginning in 2009.

The Chancellor

The chancellor is elected by a majority of the members of the *Bundestag*. In practice, this means that the chancellor's ability to be a strong party leader (or leader of a coalition of parties) is essential to the government's success. A government is formed after a national election or, if the chancellor leaves office between elections, after a majority of the *Bundestag* has nominated a chancellor in a constructive vote of no confidence. The new leader consults with other party (and coalition) officials to make up the cabinet. These party leaders have considerable influence in determining which individuals receive ministries. In the event of a coalition government, party leaders often designate during the election campaign who will receive certain ministries. Negotiations on which policies a coalition will pursue can often become heated, and the choice of ministers for particular ministries is made on policy as well as personal grounds.

The most significant cabinet ministries are those of finance, economics, justice, interior, and foreign policy (the Foreign Ministry). Decision-making within the cabinet meetings is often pro forma, since many of the important deliberations are conducted beforehand. In many cases, chancellors rely on strong ministers in key posts, but some chancellors have taken ministerial responsibility themselves in key areas such as economics and foreign policy. The economics and finance ministries always work closely with the European Central Bank (ECB).

Once the cabinet is formed, the chancellor has considerable authority to govern, thanks to the power of the Federal Chancellery (*Bundeskanzleramt*). This office is a kind of super ministry with wide-ranging powers in many areas. It enables the chancellor to oversee the entire government as well as to mediate conflicts among the other ministries.

The office of the chancellor has played a pivotal role in the Federal Republic. Perhaps the most significant source of the chancellor's powers is the constructive vote of no confidence, mentioned above, along with the fact that he or she is usually the leader of the largest party in parliament. Chancellors also face significant limits on their power. As discussed in Section 4, the *Bundesrat* (upper house) must ratify all legislation passed in the *Bundestag* (lower house) unless overridden by a two-thirds vote. In addition, since the *Bundesrat* generally implements most legislation, chancellors have to consider the position of the upper house on most issues. Although Germany did not get its first female president in 2004, more significantly it got its first chancellor in Angela Merkel in 2005. She had a generally successful first few years despite dealing with a difficult coalition government.

The Bureaucracy

An essential component of the executive is the national bureaucracy. In Germany, it is very powerful and protected by long-standing civil service provisions. Firing or otherwise removing a bureaucrat is very difficult. **Civil servants** strongly believe that their work is a profession, not just a job.

Surprisingly, the federal government employs only about 10 percent of civil servants, with the remainder employed by state and local governments. Today, most civil servants either are graduates from major German universities or come from positions within the political parties. The federal bureaucrats are primarily policy-makers who work closely with their ministries and the legislature. The bureaucrats at the state and local levels are the predominant agents of policy implementation because the states must administer most policies determined at the national level. This overlapping and coordinating of national, regional, and local bureaucracies is supported by the importance that Germans give to the provision of public services. The ongoing institutionalized relationship among the various levels of the bureaucracy has produced more consistent and effective public policies than are found in most other countries, where federal and state governments are often at odds with one another. **Overlapping responsibilities** on policy issues make it difficult to demarcate specifically the responsibility of federal institutions from the national to the regional level and from the regional to the local level.

During the Second and Third Reichs, German civil servants had a reputation for inflexibility and rigidity. The modern German bureaucracy has won high, if grudging, respect from the population. It is generally seen as efficient, although sometimes arcane. German bureaucrats enjoy a well-deserved reputation for competence. Some bureaucrats, mostly top federal officials, are appointed on the basis of party affiliation, following the traditional German pattern of proportionality, namely, allowing all major political groupings to be represented in the society's institutions, in this case the bureaucracy. However, in the 1970s, the Social Democratic Brandt government attempted to purge the bureaucracy of suspected left-wing radicals by issuing the so-called Radicals Decree, a move that tarnished its reputation for impartiality and fairness. The majority of civil servants are chosen on the basis of merit, with elaborate licensing and testing for those in the highest positions.

Semipublic Institutions

In the late 1940s, the idea of a strong central state in Germany was discredited for two reasons: the excesses of Nazism and the American occupation authorities' preference for the private sector. West German authorities faced a dilemma. How could they rebuild society if a strong public sector role were prohibited? The answer was to create modern, democratic versions of those nineteenth-century institutions that blurred the differences between the public and private sectors. These semipublic institutions have played a crucial role in the German political economy, one that has long been unrecognized.

Semipublic institutions (called quasigovernmental institutions in the U.S.) are powerful, efficient, and responsible for much national policy-making. The most influential include the *Bundesbank* (until some powers were usurped by the European Central Bank—ECB), the health insurance funds that administer the national health care system, and the vocational education system (which encompasses the apprenticeship training system). These are part of the integrated system of **democratic corporatism** in which national (and state) governments delegate certain policy-making authority to these institutions, which engage in continuous dialogue with all relevant participants in the policy community to develop appropriate policies.

In countries that had a guild system in the Middle Ages, such as Germany, an inclusionary, democratic corporatist form of representation is common. Here, various professions or organized groups represent the interests of their members. In return for access to deliberation and power, these groups are expected to aggregate the interests of their members and act responsibly. Semipublic institutions, with their democratic corporatist membership, combine aspects of both representation and implementation. German semipublic institutions differ greatly from pluralist representation in countries such as the United States, where interest groups petition public authority for redress of grievances while keeping at arm's length from the implementation process. The democratic corporatist interest groups are also closely intertwined with the Federal Republic's semipublic agencies. For example, implementation of the health care system requires an intricate set of negotiations among many semipublic institutions. These institutions are an apparent seamless web that shapes, directs, implements, and diffuses German public policy.

The political scientist Peter Katzenstein has described semipublic agencies as *detached institutions*.[11] He sees them as primarily mediating entities that reduce the influence of the central state. Katzenstein finds that they have tended to work best in areas of social and economic policy. Among the most important semipublic agencies are the Chambers of Industry, the Council of Economic Advisors (known colloquially as the Five Wise Men), and the institutions of worker participation (co-determination and the works councils). Even areas of the welfare system are semipublic because welfare benefits are often distributed by organizations not officially part of the state bureaucracy. The most significant examples of this are the **health insurance funds** (*Krankenkassen*), which bring all major health interests together to allocate costs and benefits through an elaborate system of consultation and group participation.

Another important set of semipublic institutions is the unions, which participate in industrial relations through the system known as co-determination (*Mitbestimmung*) (see "Citizen Action: Co-Determination"). This group of institutions is discussed here because **co-determination** legally gives workers opportunities to shape public policy.

Another German institution, the works councils (*Betriebsräte*), gives German workers access to the policy implementation process. In contrast to codetermination, which gives trade unions a voice outside the plant (that is, on the board), the works councils represent workers inside the workplace and address shop-floor and plant-level affairs. The trade unions have historically addressed collective bargaining issues, whereas the works councils have concentrated on social and personnel matters. With the trend to more flexible workplaces since the late 1980s, these lines of demarcation have blurred.

The unions are a countrywide, multi-industry organization representing 6.41 million diverse workers. The works councils, on the other hand, owe their primary allegiance to their local plants and firms. Despite an 85 percent overlap in personnel between unions

Citizen Action

Co-Determination

Co-determination is a government-sanctioned institutional relationship between organized labor and business that gives labor movements the right to participate in major decisions that affect their firms and industries. Often seen as a specific organizational form of **democratic corporatism**, co-determination is found in northern Europe, including the Netherlands and Scandinavia, but best known in the Federal Republic of Germany. Co-determination (*Mitbestimmung*) allows representatives of workers and trade unions to obtain voting seats on the supervisory boards of directors of firms with 2,000 or more employees.

German co-determination has two official forms: one for the coal and steel industries and one for all other industries. The former provides full parity for worker representatives in all decisions on the supervisory board, whereas the latter provides a representative of management with the tie-breaking vote. Post–World War II roots of co-determination sprang from the anger of German workers toward the complicity of German industrialists with the Nazi war machine. This was especially true of the coal and steel barons; hence, the full parity in those industries. The idea of placing workers and union representatives on the boards of directors of these firms was seen by many as a way to ensure accountability from German capitalism.

The laws governing co-determination, first passed in the early 1950s and expanded in the 1970s, reflect the powerful role of the trade unions in the politics of the Federal Republic. They give the workers—and indirectly their unions for those firms so organized—a form of institutionalized participation through membership on the supervisory boards of German firms. Rather than making German firms uncompetitive, this system actually has had the opposite effect. Workers and unions can comprehend, if not unilaterally determine, corporate decisions regarding investment and the introduction of new technologies. Co-determination has allowed German workers a broader and deeper knowledge of the goals and strategies of the firms for which they work. In addition, it has boosted worker-management cooperation. The most pressing challenge for co-determination in the future will be whether these German-specific institutional patterns will spread to other European countries or whether they will be overtaken by European-wide labor relations policies that are more deregulatory and market oriented.

and works councils and despite a structural entanglement between these two major pillars of labor representation in the Federal Republic, these divisions can produce tensions among organized labor. A period of general flux and plant-related, management-imposed flexibility beginning in the mid- and late 1980s and sporadically continuing since, particularly in eastern Germany, has exacerbated these tensions. Until the early twenty-first century the unions were usually able to avoid the proliferation of any serious plant-level divisions among workers that might have eroded their stature in the German economy. However, in the wake of the Hartz IV reforms during Schröder's second term that merged the unemployment and welfare systems reforms and required the unemployed to take jobs either outside their home region or outside their chosen profession, the unions' privileged position in Germany had begun to erode.

Other State Institutions

In addition to the institutions discussed so far, the military, the judiciary, and subnational governments are essential institutions for governance and policy-making.

The Military and Police

From the eighteenth century (when Prussian and other military forces in German-speaking regions dominated pre-unified Germany) through World War II, the German military was powerful and aggressive. After World War II, the military was placed completely under civilian control and tightly circumscribed by law and treaty. The end of the cold war produced two other important changes in German military policy: the reduction in U.S. armed forces stationed in Germany and payments made to Russia for removal of soldiers and materiel from the former East Germany.

Germany has a universal service arrangement requiring all citizens over the age of eighteen to perform one year of military or civilian service. In 1990, Germany had about 600,000 men and women in the military, but in 1994 after unification and the end of the Cold War, the Federal Government fixed the figure at approximately 340,000 as the costs of unification rose. Germany spends approximately 1.5 percent of its GDP on the military. Germany's armed forces have been legally proscribed from extra-national activity, first by the Allied occupation and later by the German Basic Law. Under the provisions of the Basic Law, the German military is to be used only for defensive purposes within Europe, and then in coordination with NATO authorities. Only very limited military activity under tightly circumscribed approval (via NATO) has altered the general prohibition. German participation in the UN peacekeeping mission in Bosnia was one example. Agreeing to participate in opposition to Serbian aggression in Kosovo in 1999, a decision made by the Red-Green government, was another, and sending troops to Afghanistan—even forming a joint Franco-German brigade—was a third. Thus, the post–World War II opposition to deployment of the German army is gradually eroding.

Discussion of the German police involves focusing on three areas. The first is the postwar experience in the FRG, where police powers have been organized on a *Land* basis and, after the excesses of the Third Reich, have been constitutionally circumscribed to ensure that human and civil rights remain inviolate. To be sure, there have been exceptions. For example, during the dragnets for the Red Army *Faktion* terrorists in the late 1970s, many critics argued that German police forces were compromising civil liberties in their desire to capture the terrorists.

The second area is that of the GDR's notorious secret police, the *Stasi*. The Ministry for State Security (the *Stasi*'s formal name) included some 91,000 official employees; moreover, in 1989, more than 180,000 East Germans and perhaps 4,000 West Germans worked as informants for the *Stasi*.[12] In proportion to the 16 million GDR citizens, the *Stasi* was more encompassing than was the Gestapo during Nazi rule. The *Stasi* spied on virtually the entire society and arbitrarily arrested and persecuted thousands of citizens. Since unification, *Stasi* archives have been open to all because the East Germans and later the FRG believed that full and open disclosure of *Stasi* excesses was essential in a democratic state. In so doing, however, names of informants were made public, which created bitter confrontations among former friends and neighbors.

The third area is the heightened concern for security in Germany in the wake of 9/11. Germany is particularly concerned about terrorism since numerous members of the Al Qaeda terrorist organization, including several of the 9/11 bombers, lived for years in Hamburg and other German cities. Germany will need to balance the pressing demand for terrorist surveillance with the preservation of civil liberties.

The Judiciary

The judiciary has always played a major role in German government because of the state's deep involvement in political and economic matters. During the Nazi regime, the judiciary was induced to issue a wide range of antidemocratic, repressive, and even criminal decisions, including banning non-Nazi parties, allowing the seizure of Jewish property, and sanctioning the deaths of millions.

The Federal Republic's founders were determined that the new judicial system would avoid these abuses. One of the first requirements was that the judiciary explicitly safeguard the democratic rights of individuals, groups, and political parties. In fact, the Basic Law contains a more elaborate and explicit statement of individual rights than exists in either the U.S. Constitution or in British common law.

However, the Federal Republic's legal system differs from the common law tradition of Britain and its former colonies (including the United States). The common law precedent-based system is characterized by adversarial relationships between contending parties, in which the judge (or the court itself) merely provides the arena for the struggle. In continental Europe, including France and Germany, the legal system is based on a codified legal system with roots in Roman law and the Napoleonic code.

In the Federal Republic, the judiciary is an active administrator of the law rather than solely an arbiter. While the task of the state is to create the laws to attain specified goals, the judiciary should safeguard their implementation. In both defining the meaning of complex laws and in implementing their administration, German courts go considerably beyond those in the United States and Britain, which supposedly have avoided political decisions. The German judiciary is an independent institution. In 2001, there were over 21,000 judges in Germany, with approximately 25 percent of them female. The German judiciary remains outside the political fray on most issues. However, a ruling in 1993 that limited access to abortion for many women, in direct opposition to a more liberal law in East Germany, was a clear exception to the general pattern. The judiciary was also criticized in the 1990s for showing too much leniency toward perpetrators of racist violence.

The court system in the Federal Republic is three-pronged. One branch consists of the criminal-civil system, which has as its apex the Federal High Court. It is a unified rather than a federal system and tries to apply a consistent set of criteria to cases in the sixteen states. The Federal High Court reviews cases that have been appealed from the lower courts, including criminal and civil cases, disputes among the states, and matters that would be viewed in some countries as political, such as the abortion ruling.

The Special Constitutional Court deals with matters directly affecting the Basic Law. A postwar creation, it was founded to safeguard the new democratic order. Precisely because of the Nazis' abuses of the judiciary, the founders of West Germany added a layer to the judiciary, basically involving judicial review, to ensure that the democratic order was maintained. However, several subsequent rulings have caused concern about the judiciary's commitment to protecting civil liberties from arbitrary executive actions.

The **Administrative Court** system is the third branch of the judiciary. Consisting of the Labor Court, the Social Security Court, and the Finance Court, the Administrative Court system has a much narrower jurisdiction than the other two branches. Because the state and its bureaucracy have such a prominent place in the lives of German citizens, this level of the court system acts as a check on the arbitrary power of the bureaucracy. Compared to Britain, where much public policy is determined by legislation, German public policy is more often determined by the administrative actions of the bureaucracy. Citizens can use these three courts to challenge bureaucratic decisions, for example, with respect to labor, welfare, or tax policies.

In the 1990s, the courts came under great pressure to resolve the intractable policy issues that unification and European integration brought about. As they were drawn deeper into the political thicket, their decisions came under increased scrutiny. Clandestine searches for terrorists in the late 1970s left many observers believing that the rights of citizens were compromised. Many critics wish that today's courts would show the same diligence and zeal in addressing the crimes of neo-Nazism, not to mention potential Al Qaeda terrorists, as the courts did in the 1970s, when Germany was confronted with violence from small ultra-leftist groups. The judicial system as a whole now must walk a fine line between maintaining civil rights in a democratic society and providing security from various sources of extremist violence.

Subnational Government

There are sixteen *Länder* (states) in the Federal Republic; eleven constituted the old West Germany and five the former East Germany. Unlike the weakly developed regional governments of Britain and France, German state governments enjoy considerable autonomy and independent powers. Each state has a regional assembly (*Landtag*), which functions much as the *Bundestag* does at the federal level. The governor (*Minister-Präsident*) of each *Land* is the leader of the largest party (or coalition of parties) in the *Landtag* and forms a government in the *Landtag* in much the same way as does the chancellor in the *Bundestag*. Elections for each of the sixteen states are held on independent, staggered four-year cycles, which generally do not coincide with federal elections and only occasionally coincide with elections in other *Länder*. Like the semipublic institutions, subnational governments in Germany are powerful, important, and responsible for much national policy implementation.

Particularly significant is Germany's "marble-cake" federalism—the interaction among state and federal governments that sees the former implement many of the laws passed by the latter. In fact, from its hybrid beginnings, German federalism has become one of the most imitated systems in the world among newly democratized countries. A good way to show how German federalism works in a specific policy arena is to cite the example of **industrial policy** (*Ordnungspolitik*). Regional governments are much more active than the national government in planning and targeting economic policy and therefore have greater autonomy in administering industrial and environmental policies. Since the *Länder* are constituent states, they are able to develop their own regional versions of public policies. Because the different regions have different economic needs and industrial foundations, most voters see these powers as legitimate and appropriate.

The state governments encourage banks to make direct investment and loans to stimulate industrial development. They also encourage cooperation among regional firms, many in the same industry, to spur international competition. State governments also invest heavily in vocational education to provide the skills needed for manufacturing high-quality goods, the core of the German economy. Organized business and organized labor have a direct role in shaping curricula to improve worker skills through the vocational education system. These *Land* governments have improved industrial adaptation by shaping the state's competitive framework rather than by adopting a heavy-handed regulatory posture. The states do not pursue identical economic policies, and there are various models of government involvement in economic policy.

In the Federal Republic, state politics is organized on the same political party basis as the national parties. This does not mean that national politics dominates local politics. However, the common party names and platforms at all levels let voters see the connection among local, regional, and national issues. Because parties adopt platforms for state and city elections, voters can see the ideological differences among parties and not be swayed solely by personalities. This does not mean that personalities do not play a role in German regional politics. Rather, the German party system encourages national political figures to begin their careers at the local and state levels. Regional and local party members' careers are tied closely to the national, regional, and local levels of the party. Thus, ideological and policy continuity across levels is rewarded. Some observers suggest that this connection in the Federal Republic among national, regional, and local politics may be one reason that voter turnout in German state elections far exceeds that of equivalent U.S. elections.

Local governments in the Federal Republic can raise revenues by owning enterprises, and many do. This has partly resulted from the historical patterns of public sector involvement in the economy but also from the assumption that these levels of government are the stewards of a collective public good. By operating art museums, theater companies, television and radio networks, recreational facilities, and housing complexes and by providing various direct and indirect subsidies to citizens, local governments promote the quality of life in modern society. Even during the various recessions since the early 1980s, there have been relatively few cutbacks in ownership of public enterprises or in social spending.

The Policy-Making Process

The chancellor and the cabinet have the principal responsibility for policy-making, but their power cannot be wielded in an arbitrary fashion. The policy-making process in Germany is largely consensus-based, with contentious issues usually extensively debated within various public, semipublic, and private institutions. Although the legislature has a general role in policy-making, the primary driving forces are the respective cabinet departments and the experts on whom they call.

Policy implementation is similarly diffuse. Along with corporatist interest groups and various semipublic organizations, the *Bundesrat* (upper house) also plays a significant role. Among the areas of policy most likely to be shaped by multiple actors are vocational education, welfare, health care, and worker participation. Germany's status as a federal state, one populated by a broad range of democratic corporatist groups and parapublic institutions, means that policy implementation has many participants. Even in such areas as foreign and security policy, the federal cabinet departments sometimes rely on business interests in policy implementation. EU policy is shaped by both national and regional governments, as well as by private sector interests that use corporatist institutions to participate in the process.

Both unification issues and the increasing significance of the EU changes have put this informal style of policy-making under tremendous pressure. Among the issues that proved most intractable at the domestic level are those of political asylum, racist violence, and scandals that tarnished the reputations of major public figures in the political system and in major interest groups. At the European level, issues involving the euro and counterterrorism remain difficult. Moreover, for all of its system-maintaining advantages, the German consensual system contains a certain intolerance of dissent. Among examples are the structure of the party system that forces politicians to work slowly through the organization, the 5 percent threshold for party representation, and judicial banning of political parties. This intolerance helps to explain the protest from outside the parties that started in the 1960s and has continued on and off ever since.

SECTION 4 Representation and Participation

In the aftermath of unification and European integration, Germany continues to strive for democratic participation that is both inclusive and representative. The nation still struggles with issues surrounding collective identities. Incorporating disparate political cultures (east and west, for example) is a dilemma for any society. The key issue for Germany is how to develop a system of democratic participation that encompasses both extra-institutional groups and organized political institutions.

Legislature

The legislature occupies a prominent place in the political system, with both the lower house (*Bundestag*) and the upper house (*Bundesrat*) holding significant and wide-ranging powers. The Federal Republic is similar to other parliamentary regimes that have a fusion of power in which the executive branch derives directly from the legislative branch. In other words, there is not a sharply defined separation of powers between cabinet and legislature.

The process for choosing members of the two houses differs substantially. The *Bundestag* elects its members directly; voters choose both individual district representatives and the political parties that represent their interests. The *Bundesrat*'s members, on the other hand, are officials who are elected or appointed to the regional (*Länder*) governments. Both branches of the legislature are broadly representative of the major interests in German society, although some interests such as business and labor are somewhat overrepresented, whereas ecological and noneconomic interests are somewhat underrepresented.

Germany's two-ballot electoral system for the *Bundestag* has produced two significant outcomes. First, the proportional representation electoral system produces multiple parties. Second, the 5 percent hurdle ensures that only parties with significant support obtain seats in the *Bundestag*. This has helped Germany avoid the wild proliferation of parties that plagues some democracies, such as Italy and Israel, where coalitions are extremely difficult to form.

The German parliamentary system represents a synthesis between the British and U.S. traditions of a single legislator representing one district and the European tradition of proportional representation in which the percentage of the vote is equal to the percentage of the parliamentary seats (see "Institutional Intricacies: Proportional Representation and the Story of the German 'Double Ballot'"). The German hybrid system, known as **personalized proportional representation,** requires citizens to cast two votes on each ballot: the first for an individual candidate in the local district and the second for a list of national/regional candidates grouped by party affiliation (see Figure 4.3).

At the same time, however, seats in the *Bundestag* are allocated among parties by proportional representation. Specifically, the percentage of total seats won per party corresponds strongly with the party's percentage of the popular vote. For example, if a party's candidate wins a seat as an individual member, his or her party is allotted one less seat from the party's slate elected via list voting. In practice, the two large parties, the Social Democrats and the Christian Democrats, win most of the district seats because they are elected by a plurality system of winner-take-all in each district. The smaller parties' representatives are almost always elected through the party lists. Thus, the list system creates stronger, more coherent parties.

The *Bundestag*

The lower house of the legislature, the *Bundestag*, consists of 614 seats. *Bundestag* members almost always vote with their parties. This party unity contributes to consistency in the parties' positions over the course of a four-year legislative period and enables the electorate to identify each party's stance on

Institutional Intricacies: Proportional Representation and the Story of the German "Double Ballot"

Proportional representation is a method of electing legislative representatives in parliamentary democracies. In the more commonly used list form, proportional representation involves allocating seats in the legislature among political parties in the same proportion as the parties' share of the popular vote. For example, if a political party received 20 percent of the vote in an election, under proportional representation this party would receive 20 percent of the seats in the legislative body. Germany uses a combination of single-member districts and proportional representation (see the sample ballot in Figure 4.3), but the allocation of seats in the *Bundestag* still depends on the proportion of the vote that the parties obtain in the votes by party list. The advantage of this system is that every voter has his or her "own" local representative, yet the entire *Bundestag* comprises members who reflect the respective share of each party's total vote.

This system has the effect of personalizing list voting because voters have their own local representative, but they also can choose among several parties representing various ideologies. To ensure that only major parties are represented, only those that get 5 percent of the vote or that have three candidates who directly win individual seats can gain representation in the *Bundestag*.

Sources: The Oxford Companion to Politics of the World, edited by Joel Krieger. Copyright 2001 by Oxford University Press, Inc. Used by permission of Oxford Press, Inc.

FIGURE 4.3
Bundestag Election Ballot

With their "first vote," voters from the Bonn electoral district can choose a candidate by name from the lefthand column. The "second vote" in the righthand column is cast for a party list at the federal level.

a range of issues. Consequently, all representatives in the *Bundestag* can be held accountable, based on their support for their parties' positions. Party discipline, in turn, helps produce more stable governments.

The tradition of strong, unified parties in the *Bundestag* has some drawbacks. The hierarchy within parties relegates newer members to a comparatively long stint as backbenchers. Since party elders and the Federal Chancellery control the legislative agenda and key policy decisions, individual legislators have few opportunities to make an impact. Some of the most prominent national politicians preferred to serve their political apprenticeship in state or local government, where they would have more visibility. Chancellors Gerhard Schröder and Helmut Kohl took this route as governors of Lower Saxony and Rhineland Palatinate, respectively.

The executive branch introduces legislation in accordance with the Basic Law, which requires that the executive initiate the federal budget and tax legislation. Although most bills are initiated by the cabinet, this does not diminish the influence of *Bundestag* or *Bundesrat* members. In fact, because the chancellor is the leader of the major party or coalition of parties, no sharp division exists between the executive and legislative branches. There is generally strong consensus within parties and within coalitions about what legislation should be introduced. Parties and coalitions, which depend on party discipline to sustain majorities, place a high value on agreement regarding major legislation.[13]

When the chancellor and the cabinet propose a bill, it is sent to a relevant *Bundestag* committee. Most of the committee deliberations take place privately so that the individual committee members can have considerable latitude to shape details of the legislation. The committees will call on their own expertise as well as that of relevant government ministries and testimony from pertinent interest groups. This arrangement may appear to be a kind of insiders' club. However, the committees generally call on a wide range of groups, both pro and con, that are affected by the proposed legislation. By consulting the corporatist interest groups, a more consensus-oriented outcome is achieved. In contrast, legislative sessions in countries with a more pluralist (less inclusive) form of lobbying, such as Britain and the United States, tend to be contentious and less likely to produce agreement. Under pluralism, it is relatively easy for groups to articulate issues; however, without a coordinated institutional structure, policy-making is more haphazard.

After emerging from committee, the bill has three readings in the *Bundestag*. The debate in the *Bundestag* often produces considerable criticism from the opposition and sharp defense by the governing parties. The primary purpose of the debate is to educate the public about the major issues of the bill. Following passage in the *Bundestag*, the *Bundesrat* must approve the bill.

Most members of the national legislature are male, middle-class professionals, even in the supposedly working-class Social Democratic Party, which had a much greater proportion of blue-collar deputies in the 1950s. There were few women lawmakers until the 1980s and 1990s, when the Greens elected an increasing number of female *Bundestag* members, and women began to gain slots on the Social Democrats' electoral lists.[14] Fewer than 10 percent of *Bundestag* members were women through the 1983 election, but since 1987, the number of women has increased substantially, reaching 31.6 percent with the 2005 election (see Table 4.3). The addition of newer parties such as the worker-oriented ex-communist Left Party and the continued presence of the Greens with their counterculture lifestyles has increased the variety of backgrounds among *Bundestag* members. In fact, the proportional representation system used in Germany increases the number of women and minorities elected to the *Bundestag*. Many parties, particularly the Social Democrats, the Greens, and the Left, select candidates for their electoral lists based on gender and diversity.

The *Bundesrat*

The *Bundesrat* has a different role from the U.S. Senate or the British House of Lords. The *Bundesrat* is the mechanism that makes the federal system work. It is responsible for the distribution of powers between national and state governments and grants to the states the right to implement federal laws. It is the point of intersection for the national and the state governments and is made up of sixty-nine members from the sixteen state governments. Each state sends at least three representatives to the *Bundesrat,* depending on its population. States with more than 2 million residents have four votes, and states with more than 6 million people have five votes.

The political composition of the *Bundesrat* at any given time is determined by which parties are in power in the states. Each state delegation casts its votes on legislation in a bloc, reflecting the views of the majority party or coalition. Consequently, the party controlling the majority of state governments can have a significant effect on legislation passed in the *Bundestag*. And because state elections usually take place between *Bundestag* electoral periods, the *Bundesrat* majority can shift during the course of a *Bundestag* legislative period.

The *Bundesrat* must approve all amendments to the constitution as well as all laws that address the fundamental interests of the states, such as taxes, territorial integrity, and basic administrative functions. It exercises a **suspensive veto;** that is, if the *Bundesrat* votes against a bill, the *Bundestag* can override the *Bundesrat* by passing the measure again by a simple majority. If, however, a two-thirds majority of the *Bundesrat* votes against a bill, the *Bundestag* must pass it again by a two-thirds margin. In usual practice, the *Bundesrat* has not acted to obstruct. When the legislation is concurrent—that is, when the state and national governments share administrative responsibilities for implementing the particular policy—there is almost always easy agreement between the two houses. Also, a party or coalition that has achieved a stable majority in the *Bundestag* can overcome any possible obstruction by the *Bundesrat*.

The *Bundesrat* introduces comparatively little legislation, but its administrative responsibilities are considerable. Most of the members of the *Bundesrat* are also state government officials, well experienced in the implementation of particular laws. Their expertise is frequently called on in the committee hearings of the *Bundestag,* which are open to all *Bundesrat* members. This overlapping is a unique feature of the Federal Republic. Many U.S. observers make the mistake of equating German and U.S. federalism; however, Germany has a qualitatively different relationship between national and state governments.

Table 4.3
Percentage of Women Members of the *Bundestag*

Year	Percentage	Year	Percentage
1949	6.8	1980	8.5
1953	8.8	1983	9.8
1957	9.2	1987	15.4
1961	8.3	1990	20.5
1965	6.9	1994	26.3
1969	6.6	1998	30.2
1972	5.8	2002	32.2
1976	7.3	2005	31.8

Source: Bundeszentrale für Politische Bildung, 2005.

The *Bundesrat*'s strong administrative role is a key component of the government. For example, the *Bundesrat* administers a major television network (ARD) and coordinates the link between regional and national economic policies and vocational education systems. The *Bundesrat*'s structure positions it close to the concerns and needs of the entire country and provides a forum for understanding how national legislation will affect each of the states.

Although the *Bundesrat* was originally envisioned to be more technocratic and less politically contentious than the popularly elected *Bundestag*, debates in the *Bundesrat* became strongly politicized beginning in the 1970s. The most common occurrence was the conflict that emerged when regional elections caused a change in control of the *Bundesrat*, especially when this change gave more influence to the party, or group of parties, that was in opposition to the *Bundestag*. For example, part of Helmut Kohl's difficulty in his last term (1994–1998) resulted from the Social Democrats' controlling a majority of state governments, where they occasionally blocked national legislation. After Schröder's narrow victory in the 2002 federal elections and the CDU victory in several *Land* elections since then, similar conflict occurred in the remainder of the SPD-Green second term.

With the increasing significance of the European Union (EU), the *Bundesrat* has a role to play here as well. It promotes representation for the *Länder* in EU institutions, most notably in the Council of Regions. It also gained a veto power over certain German positions on EU decisions.

Political Parties and the Party System

Germany has often been called a **party democracy** because its parties are so important in shaping state policy. Its multiparty system has proved quite stable for most of the period since World War II. Until the early 1980s, Germany had a "two-and-a-half" party system, composed of a moderate-left Social Democratic Party (SPD), a moderate-right Christian Democratic grouping (CDU in all of West Germany except Bavaria, where it is called the CSU), and a small centrist Free Democratic Party (FDP). During their time as the only parties on the political landscape (1949–1983), these groups presided over a stable, growing economy and a broad public consensus on economic and social policies.

During the 1980s and 1990s, two new parties emerged to challenge the "two-and-a-half" major parties and to complicate Germany's comparatively tidy political landscape.[15] These were the Greens/*Bündnis* '90, generally of the left and favoring ecological, environmental, and peace issues; and the Party of Democratic Socialism (PDS), the former Communist Party of East Germany. In 2005, the latter merged with a group of former left-wing Social Democrats who believed Schröder's reforms undermined social democracy and formed *die Linke* (Left Party). Two other small right-wing parties, the National Democratic Party (*Nationaldemokratische Partei Duetschlands*, NPD) and the German People's Union (*Deutsche Volksunion*, DVU), also emerged. Much more conservative than the CDU/CSU, they emphasized nationalism and intolerance toward immigrants and ethnic minorities. Neither of these two right-wing parties has yet won seats in the *Bundestag* because of the 5 percent rule. Both have occasionally exceeded 5 percent in regional elections, however, and have won seats in those bodies.

The five main parties have clearly identifiable social bases. The traditional Christian Democratic bases are moderate conservative Protestants and Catholics, but in recent years religion has played a much less significant role in their policies. Social Democrats represented the traditional working class for the first half of the twentieth century, but since then have tried to catch more middle-class voters in the center. The Free Democrats are a secular party that favors small government and individual freedoms. The Greens focus on ecological issues, and the new Left Party's social bases are eastern Germans who feel left behind by unification and western German former Social Democrats who believe their former party has moved too far toward the center.

The Christian Democrats

The Christian Democrats combine the Christian Democratic Union (CDU, in all *Länder* except Bavaria) and the Christian Social Union (CSU, the affiliated Bavarian grouping). Unlike the older parties

FIGURE 4.4
Distribution of Seats

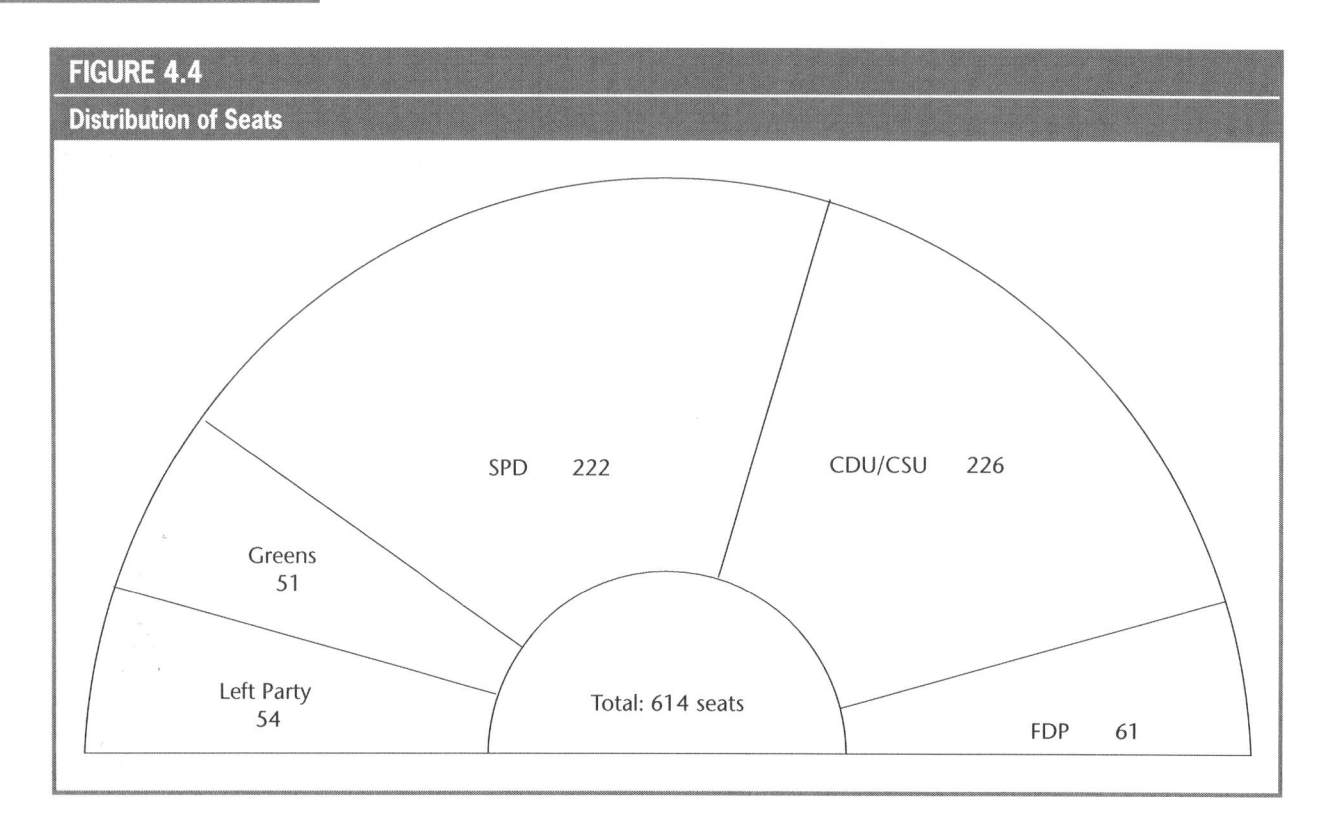

- SPD 222
- CDU/CSU 226
- Greens 51
- Left Party 54
- FDP 61
- Total: 614 seats

(SPD and FDP) of the Federal Republic, the CDU/CSU was founded immediately after World War II and united Catholics and Protestants in one confessional (Christian) party and served as a catchall party of the center-right. During Weimar, the two Christian denominations were divided politically with the former in the Catholic Center Party and the latter in several other parties.

Programmatically, the CDU/CSU stressed the social market economy, involving procapitalist elements as well as a paternalistic sense of social responsibility.[16] Under chancellors Adenauer and Erhard, the Christian Democrats held political power for almost twenty years. Its social policies during this period were paternalistic and moderately conservative. The CDU/CSU even explicitly codified this approach with the phrase *Kinder, Kirche, Kuche* (children, church, and kitchen), which defined the Christian Democrats' view of women's primary roles and was originally a motto of the last Kaiser's wife.

After the SPD and FDP established their center-left coalition in 1969, the CDU/CSU spent thirteen years as the opposition party. Returning to power in 1983 under the leadership of Helmut Kohl, the CDU/CSU with their FDP coalition partners retained power through four elections until 1998. The most significant and historic accomplishments—truly twin legacies—of the long Kohl regime are German unification and Germany's integration into the EU.

Although Angela Merkel became Germany's first female chancellor after the 2005 election, the circumstances of her victory were much less glorious than either she or her Christian Democratic colleagues originally expected. Instead of the preferred coalition with the FDP, their traditional coalition partner, the CDU/CSU was forced into a "Grand Coalition" with the SPD for only the second time in the Federal Republic's history. Merkel only emerged as chancellor three weeks after the election, after the CDU/CSU and SPD contentiously negotiated their agreement. It came at a heavy price for the Christian Democrats; in return for Gerhard Schröder stepping aside as the SPD's chancellor candidate, the Christian Democrats agreed to take only six of the fourteen cabinet seats, leaving the remaining eight to the SPD. Essentially the "Grand Coalition" is what Americans call "divided

Leaders

Angela Merkel

Angela Merkel, fifty-one years old when she became the first female chancellor in 2005, has had a remarkable road to the pinnacle of German politics. A minister's daughter, a physicist by profession, a latecomer to political life, an eastern German, a Protestant in a party dominated by Catholics, and a woman who has eschewed feminist positions, Merkel surprised many Germans when she finally became Germany's head of government after the most inconclusive election in the fifty-six-year history of the Federal Republic of Germany.

She was actually born in western Germany, but her family moved to eastern Germany when her father was offered the ministry of a Lutheran church in Brandenburg (eastern Germany). She showed no interested in politics in communist East Germany, preferring to study science. She earned a degree in physics and obtained a research position in East Berlin when Germany was still divided. Like many East Germans, she acquired her political awakening in 1989 when she took part in pro-democracy protests as the Berlin wall came down. When free political parties emerged, Merkel was drawn to the Christian Democrats, perhaps because of her father's professional religious background.

A quick political learner, Merkel rose through the ranks of the Christian Democrats, particularly since western parties that wanted to establish a presence in eastern Germany desired skilled and astute easterners who would help these parties establish a political foundation there. She held several regional Christian Democratic Party positions and soon caught the political eye of four-time CDU chancellor Helmut Kohl. She won a seat in the *Bundestag* and was named the environment minister in 1994. After the Christian Democrats were defeated in the 1998 election, Merkel rapidly moved into the political vacuum in the wake of Helmut Kohl's departure from the Christian Democratic leadership.

In the 2005 election, she failed to develop two potential advantages, namely her gender and her background in eastern Germany. She pointedly avoided feminist positions, perhaps necessary in the male-dominated CDU/CSU. However, she lost considerable political support from women when she chose to

Source: © Jens Buettner/epa/Corbis

support the much more restrictive West German abortion law instead of the more liberal law that had prevailed in East Germany. She also has not been effective in recruiting large numbers of women from her party to run for seats in the *Bundestag*. In fact, the three parties of the left (SPD, Greens, and Left) have 41.2 percent women among their deputies while the parties of the right (Christian Democrats and FDP) have only 20.9 percent women in the *Bundestag*. She also failed to use her background to alleviate the fears of eastern Germans, who suffer from much higher unemployment (20 to 25 percent) than do the states of the former West Germany (8 percent). In numerous campaign appearances in eastern Germany, she would address the crowds using the pronoun "you" instead of "we." The CDU finished third in the five eastern German states behind the SPD and the Left parties. Merkel's achievement in becoming the first female chancellor was most impressive, but she faced formidable obstacles as she began her historic political journey.

In her first several years leading the "Grand Coalition" she did well in managing international issues and the economy began to rebound in 2007. But because the Christian Democrats and Social Democrats disagree on fundamental issues (immigration, the nature of structural economic reform, and foreign policy), they were unable to achieve significant progress.

government." When things go well, both take credit; when they don't, each blames the other. This can impede political accountability, which can sometimes result in lower support for both parties in subsequent elections since there are now three other options besides the CDU/CSU and the SPD.

The Social Democratic Party

As the leading party of the left in Germany, the *Sozialdemokratische Partei Deutschlands* (SPD) has had a long and durable history. The SPD was founded in 1875 in response to rapid industrialization and Bismarck's authoritarian role. After surviving Bismarck's attempts in the 1880s to outlaw it, it grew to be the largest party in the *Reichstag* by 1912.[17] Following World War I, it became the leading party—but without a majority—of the Weimar Republic during its early years.

Despite being the second-largest party in postwar Germany from 1945 to 1948, the SPD was able to obtain only about 30 percent of the popular vote from 1949 until the early 1960s. In an attempt to broaden its constituency, it altered its party program at a 1959 party conference in Bad Godesberg. Deemphasizing its primary reliance on Marxism and its working-class base, its new goal was to broaden its appeal to recruit voters from throughout the social structure and become what the political scientist Otto Kirchheimer has called a "catchall party."[18] The Bad Godesberg conference transformed the SPD into a party similar to other western European social democratic parties.

In 1969, the SPD was finally elected to office as the leading member of a majority coalition, with the FDP. It remained in power for thirteen years under chancellors Willy Brandt and Helmut Schmidt. The SPD brought to the coalition a concern for increased welfare and social spending.[19] This was due partly to pressure by left-wing extra-parliamentary opposition groups and student demonstrations in 1968. The FDP brought support for increased individual freedom of expression at a time when youths in all industrialized societies were seeking a greater voice. The principal factor cementing these two dissimilar parties for such a long time was the strong performance of the economy. The coalition finally broke up in the early 1980s, when an economic recession prevented the increased social spending demanded by the SPD left wing.

During the 1980s and 1990s when it was out of power, the SPD failed to formulate clear alternative policies to make itself attractive to its members, supporters, and voters. In 1998, the Kohl regime was exhausted and the SPD was able to form an unexpected coalition with the Greens and formed a government that lasted until 2005. The seven years

Image removed due to copyright restrictions

of the second SPD-led regime were initially successful, but divisions within the party about the nature of structural reform—and the direction of Social Democracy in Germany—brought the second term of the SPD-Green government to an early end.

The Greens

The Greens entered the political scene in 1979 and have won seats at national and regional levels ever since. It is a heterogeneous party that first drew support from several different constituencies in the early 1980s: urban-based **Citizens Action Groups,** environmental activists, farmers, anti–nuclear power activists, the remnants of the peace movement, and small bands of Marxist-Leninists. After overcoming the 5 percent hurdle in the 1983 *Bundestag* elections, the Green Party went on to win seats in most subsequent state elections by stressing noneconomic quality-of-life issues. The electoral successes of this "antiparty party" generated a serious division within the party. The *realos* (realists) believed that it was important to moderate the party's positions in order to enter political institutions and gain access to power; the *fundis* (fundamentalists) opposed any collaboration with existing parties, even if this meant sacrificing some of their goals and damaging their chances of gaining power.

Although the realists gained the upper hand, the party failed to benefit because all the other parties began to include environmental and quality-of-life issues in their party programs. Until merging with the eastern German Bündnis '90 in 1993, the Greens' position looked bleak. The squabbling between *fundis* and *realos* undercut the party's credibility. The Greens' failure to motivate its own core constituency during the early 1990s greatly hampered the party. The unexpected death of a popular former party leader—the American-born Petra Kelly, a *fundi*—and the moderation of a former party leader (and former foreign minister), Joschka Fischer, signaled the transformation of the Greens into a dependable, innovative coalition partner.

The persistent ecological problems of the former East German states have presented the Greens with a tremendous opportunity. After several years in which the party's fortunes were uncertain, it increased its share of the vote to 8.6 percent in 2002 by pressing anti-nuclear, anti-genetic modification and climate change issues and now appears to be a permanent fixture in the *Bundestag*. Following the 2005 election, the Greens returned to the opposition benches in the *Bundestag* when its share of the vote dropped to 8.1 percent after briefly flirting with the idea of entering a coalition with the Christian Democrats and FDP. However, Green party members rebelled against the idea of coalition with pro-business parties. Yet in 2008 in Hamburg following its *Land* election, the Greens agreed to join the CDU in the regional government. This is yet another sign of possible increased party volatility in Germany.

The Free Democratic Party

The FDP's major influence is its role as a swing party because it has allied with each of the two major parties (SPD and CDU/CSU) at different periods since 1949. Regularly holding the foreign and economics ministries in coalition with the Christian Democrats, the FDP's most notable leaders were Walter Scheel, Count Otto Lambsdorff, and Hans-Dietrich Genscher.

The FDP's perspective encompasses two ideologies, broadly characterized here as economic liberalism (*liberal* in the European sense of *laissez-faire* individualism) and social liberalism (namely individual personal freedoms). During the postwar period, the FDP relied on two philosophies to align itself with the two major political groupings, the CDU/CSU and the SPD. The party was a member of almost all governing coalitions from 1949 to 1998, but with its strategy of cogoverning with first one major party and then the other, the FDP has occasionally been accused of lacking strong political convictions.

During the years of the SPD-Green governments (1998–2005), the FDP became much more explicitly a free-market party, emphasizing deregulation and privatization. After winning 9.8 percent of the vote in 2005, it hoped to join the Christian Democrats in a right-wing coalition, but the latter's poor showing prevented it from forming a majority. The growth of both the Green and the Left Parties has diminished the former fifty-year "kingmaker" status of the FDP and its role with the two large parties. There are more options for all of the parties now.

The Left Party (*die Linke*)

In June 2005, the former eastern German Communist Party (Party of Democratic Socialism) merged with a breakaway faction of the SPD that called itself the *Wahlalternative Arbeit und Soziale Gerechtigkeit* (WASG, or "electoral alternative for labor and social justice") to form the Left Party. The PDS was concentrated in the five states of the former East Germany, and although it received as much as 25 percent of the vote in some regional and local elections, it always drew well under the 5 percent mark in elections in the *Länder* of the former West Germany. While it was officially a new party concentrated in the former East Germany, it has had a long and volatile history. It formed from the Communist Party of Germany (*Kommunistische Partei Deutschlands,* KPD), which was founded after World War I. In the late 1940s, the Communist Party flourished in the Soviet zone and was renamed the Socialist Unity Party (*Sozialistische Einheits Partei,* SED). It dominated all aspects of life in East Germany and was considered the most Stalinist and repressive regime in eastern Europe.

After unification in 1990, the SED demonstrated considerable tactical agility by changing its name and program, and it received considerable support in the five *Länder* of the former East Germany. Throughout the 1990s, the difficulties of unification helped boost the strength of the PDS. It gained over 20 percent of the vote in the five new German states in the *Bundestag* elections of 1994, 1998, and 2002 and won seats in the *Bundestag* in four consecutive elections.

The WASG, composed of left-wing dissident former SPD members and led by former finance minister Oskar Lafontaine, offered an attractive option for the PDS. Based primarily in western Germany, the WASG provided electoral support for the PDS precisely where the latter was weakest. Polling as high as 12 percent nationwide prior to the election, it obtained 8.7 percent of the vote in September 2005 and represented an intriguing complication for the other parties.

In fact, the Left Party's strong showing, largely due to its opposition against budget cuts, is the main reason why neither the SPD and Greens, nor the CDU/CSU and FDP, were able to form either a left-wing or right-wing coalition. With a growing base in the west (4.9 percent) and traditional eastern support (nearly 25 percent) it seems solidly entrenched as the fifth party. However, all other parties have ruled out dealing with the Left—including the SPD and Greens—even though the three left-of-center parties won 51.1 percent of the votes and had a potential 21 seat majority. Since its breakthrough in the 2005 *Bundestag* election, the Left Party has won seats in four western *Länder* parliaments (now ten of the sixteen German *Länder*) and had regularly attained between 12 to 14 percent in opinion polls by mid-2008.

While the Left Party is still finding its way as a parliamentary party on the opposition benches, it is performing an important task in eastern Germany. The FRG is one of the few countries in western Europe that has not had a far-right and/or neo-fascist party gain seats in its national legislature. Because the primary support for the Left Party in the east comes from marginalized and/or unemployed people in German society, it has provided a left-wing alternative to those who, under other circumstances, might turn to the far right.

The Far Right

There have been various splinter-group right-wing parties throughout the Federal Republic's history, but with the exception of the neo-Nazi National Democratic Party of Germany (*Nationaldemokratische Partei Deutschland,* NPD), which received 4.3 percent of the vote in 1969, they had never seriously threatened to win seats in the *Bundestag*. There are two far-right political parties[20] that have won seats in regional parliaments since 2000: the German People's Union (*Deutsche Volksunion*, DVU), and the NPD. None, however, have come close to winning seats in the *Bundestag*. The latter two parties have won *Land* government seats in 2006.

Elections

For nearly fifty years in the Federal Republic, voting participation rates averaging 80 to 90 percent at the federal level matched or exceeded those in all other western European countries There have been five major periods of party dominance (plus the 1966–69 Grand Coalition) between 1949 and the present:

1. CDU/CSU-FDP coalition (1949–1966; CDU/CSU majority, 1957–1961)

2. Grand Coalition (CDU/CSU–SPD) interregnum (1966–1969)
3. SPD–FDP coalition (1969–1982)
4. CDU/CSU–FDP coalition (1982–1998)
5. SPD-Green coalition (1998–2005)
6. Grand Coalition (CDU/CSU–SPD) (2005–)

As Table 4.4 suggests, Germany has enjoyed relatively stable electoral allegiance, despite unification, European integration, and the introduction of two new parties in the *Bundestag* during the decade of the 1990s. The electorate appears to be divided into relatively stable party followings, but as recent support for the two large parties has waned, to the benefit of the three smaller parties, voter volatility is increasing.

Political Culture, Citizenship, and Identity

With political parties representing such a broad ideological spectrum, there is wide-ranging political debate in Germany. This diversity is reflected in the media, where newspapers appeal to a broad range of political opinion. There is a wide variety of private TV cable and satellite channels, but the three main public channels (two national, one a series of regionals) provide a balance of major party positions. Until the late 1990s, most public channels prohibited paid TV campaign commercials during the two-month electoral campaigns.

There is a strong participatory ethic among the democratic left, fostered by the many opportunities for participation at the workplace through co-determination and the works councils. Moreover, one of the primary appeals of the Greens has been their emphasis on **grass-roots democracy**—that is, rank-and-file participation. The strength of the Greens, and now the Left Party, has forced the traditional parties to focus on mobilizing their supporters and potential supporters. The presence of the Greens and the Left Party has also helped dispel some of the old stereotypes about the country's legendary preference for consensus, order, and stability.

Germany's educational system has also changed since the Federal Republic was created, particularly in terms of the socialization of German citizens. The catalyst was the student movement of the 1960s. At that time, the university system was elitist and restrictive and did not offer sufficient critical analysis of Germany's bloody twentieth-century history. Not only did the student mobilizations of the 1960s open up the educational system to a wider socioeconomic spectrum, they also caused many of the so-called '68 Generation (1968 was the year of the most significant student demonstrations) to challenge their parents about attitudes shaped by the Nazi period and before.

However, anti-ethnic and anti-immigrant violence in the late 1980s, mid-1990s, and early 2000s raised questions among some observers regarding the genuineness of German toleration. Given Germany's persecution of Jews, homosexuals, and political opponents during the first half of the twentieth century and the unimaginable horrors of the Holocaust, such concerns must be taken extremely seriously. Although Germany is not alone among industrialized nations in racist violence, its history imposes a special burden to overcome any display of intolerance if it is to gain the world's respect.

The Schröder Red-Green government began to change the rules on citizenship, democracy, and participation in Germany. Until 1998, German citizenship was based on blood, that is, German ethnicity. Unlike many European nations, Germany made it difficult for residents without native ethnicity to be naturalized, and it denied citizenship even to the children of noncitizens who were born and brought up in Germany. Ethnic Germans whose ancestors had not lived in Germany for centuries were allowed to enter Germany legally and to become citizens immediately. One of the first acts of the Schröder government was to allow expedited citizenship for long-time foreign residents.

Perhaps the most contentious citizenship/identity problem has surrounded the political asylum question. Following World War II, Germany passed one of the world's most liberal political asylum laws, in part to help atone for the Nazis' political repression of millions. With the end of the cold war and the opening up of east European borders, the trickle of asylum seekers turned into a flood. This influx drove the Kohl government to curtail drastically the right of political asylum. Germany's commitment to democratic rights appeared to contain some new conditions, and many

Table 4.4
FRG Election Results, 1949–2005

Year	Party	Percentage of Vote	Government	Year	Party	Percentage of Vote	Government
1949	Voter turnout	78.5	CDU/CSU–FDP	1983	Voter Turnout	89.1	CDU/CSU
	CDU/CSU	31.0			CDU/CSU	48.8	
	SPD	29.2			SPD	38.2	
	FDP	11.9			FDP	7.0	
	Others	27.8			Greens	5.6	
1953	Voter turnout	86.0	CDU/CSU–FDP		Others	0.5	
	CDU/CSU	45.2		1987	Voter turnout	84.3	CDU/CSU
	SPD	28.8			CDU/CSU	44.3	
	FDP	9.5			SPD	37.0	
	Others	16.7			FDP	9.1	
1957	Voter turnout	87.8	CDU/CSU		Greens	8.3	
	CDU/CSU	50.2			Others	1.3	
	SPD	31.8		1990	Voter turnout	78.0	CDU/CSU
	FDP	7.7			CDU/CSU	43.8	
	Others	10.3			SPD	33.5	
1961	Voter turnout	87.8	CDU/CSU–FDP		FDP	11.0	
	CDU/CSU	45.3			Greens	3.8	
	SPD	36.2			PDS	2.4	
	FDP	12.8			Bündnis '90	1.2	
	Others	5.7			Others	3.5	
1965	Voter turnout	86.8	CDU/CSU–SPD	1994	Voter turnout	79.0	CDU/CSU
	CDU/CSU	47.6	Grand		CDU/CSU	41.5	
	SPD	39.3	Coalition		SPD	36.4	
	FDP	9.5			FDP	6.9	
	Others	3.6			Greens	7.3	
1969	Voter turnout	86.7	SPD–FDP		PDS	4.4	
	CDU/CSU	46.1			Others	3.5	
	SPD	42.7		1998	Voter turnout	82.3	SPD-Greens
	FDP	5.8			CDU/CSU	35.1	
	Others	5.4			SPD	40.9	
1972	Voter turnout	86.0	SPD–FDP		FDP	6.2	
	CDU/CSU	44.9			Greens	6.7	
	SPD	45.8			PDS	5.1	
	FDP	9.5			Others	6.0	
	Others	16.7		2002	Voter turnout	79.1	SPD-Greens
1976	Voter turnout	90.7	SDP–FDP		SPD	38.5	
	CDU/CSU	48.2			CDU/CSU	38.5	
	SPD	42.6			Greens	8.6	
	FDP	7.9			FDP	7.4	
	Others	0.9			PDS	4.0	
1980	Voter Turnout	88.6	SPD–FDP		Others	3.0	
	CDU/CSU	44.5		2005	Voter turnout	77.7	
	SPD	42.9			CDU/CSU	35.2	
	FDP	10.6			SPD	34.2	
	Others	0.5			FDP	9.8	
					Left Party	8.7	
					Greens	8.1	

Source: German Information Center, 2005.

Current Challenges

The Complicated Politics of Immigration

Germany, like virtually all other western European nations, has discovered that it has become an immigrant country. To be sure, a nation-state that did not achieve unity until 1871 faced calamitous questions of immigration and nationality. In fact, the nationalism unleashed in the late nineteenth century in the wake of economic and political upheaval caused catastrophe for nonethnic Germans. Because of that late-nineteenth- and early-to-mid-twentieth-century oppression of racial and ethnic minorities, the Federal Republic realized in the postwar period that it had a special obligation to both Jews and other ethnic minorities whom the Nazis had persecuted and killed. It was this history that caused the new FRG government to pass generous asylum laws, allowing those who faced political persecution to obtain residency, if not citizenship, in a democratic Germany.

Citizenship was a more difficult proposition for immigrants to Germany. The 1913 Immigration Law (until liberalized by the SPD/Green Schröder government in 1999) stipulated that citizenship was based on blood (*jus sanguis*) and not naturalization (*jus solis*). This meant that German citizenship was easy to obtain for "ethnic" Germans who had lived in Russia or eastern Europe for generations and did not speak German, but difficult for the *Gastarbeiter* (guest workers) who had lived in Germany since the 1960s.

In fact, the tension between cultural conceptions of citizenship and the economic demands of both Germany and the EU lie at the heart of the complicated politics of immigration. On the one hand, some Germans and Europeans are fearful of what immigration will do to traditional conceptions of what being a "German" actually is. Racist violence is an extreme manifestation of this sentiment. On the other hand, globalization and Europeanization have opened up the Continent to increasing migration, which, to some, is the very point of the process. Adding to the economic pressures on European countries to increase immigration is the demographic time-bomb that affects almost all western European countries: a population decrease of the "native" or "ethnic" portions of their population, fueling the fears of some among this population. Yet this aging population is also relying on a welfare and pension system that demands that there be a young work force to pay for it. Western European policy-makers now realize that a partial solution to the fiscal obligations that an aging population represents is new, young, immigrant workers who will both revitalize economic growth and help fund the pension and welfare obligations. To do so, however, requires that Germany—and many of its neighbors—fundamentally reconsider what it means to be a citizen.

---

involved a definition of identity that looked remarkably insular in a Europe that was becoming more international and global.

Gender did not appear to be a politically significant cleavage in Germany until the 1960s, since women had remained politically marginalized for most of the first half of the Federal Republic's history. Taking to heart the admonition *Kinder, Kirche, Küche* (children, church, and kitchen), many German women were socialized into believing that their status as second-class citizens was appropriate. Until the social explosions of the 1960s, very few women held positions in society outside the home.

Even with the spread of feminism since the 1970s, German women have generally lagged slightly behind their American counterparts in business and in civil society. However, as the data in Table 4.3 show, German women have quadrupled their representation in the *Bundestag* from approximately 8 percent in 1980 to almost 32 percent in 2005; and of course Angela Merkel is the first female chancellor.

The differences between East and West Germany on social policy affecting women provoked great controversy after unification. Women in the former East Germany had far more presence and influence in public life and in the workplace than did their counterparts in West Germany. In the former East Germany, women had made far greater social and economic progress (relatively speaking) and enjoyed greater government provision for such services as childcare and family leave. In fact, one of the hottest items of contention in Germany during the early 1990s was whether to reduce East German–style benefits to women (including abortion) in favor of the more conservative and restrictive ones of the Federal Republic. The West German law prevailed after unification, to the consternation of many.

Interests, Social Movements, and Protest

Germany remains a country of organized collectivities: major economic producer groups such as the BDI (Federal Association of German Industry), BDA (Federal Association of German Employers), and DGB (German Trade Union Confederation); political parties (in which authentic participatory membership remains higher than in most other countries); and social groups.

From the descriptions of organized business and organized labor in Section 3, it is clear that interest groups in Germany operate differently than they do in the United States and Britain. In the Federal Republic, interest groups are seen as having a societal role and responsibility that transcend the immediate interests of their members. Germany's codified legal system specifically allows private interests to perform public functions, albeit within a clearly specified general framework. Thus, interest groups are seen as part of the fabric of society and are virtually permanent institutions. This view places a social premium on their adaptation and response to new issues.

Strikes and demonstrations do occur on a wide range of economic and noneconomic issues. Political institutions sometimes are mistakenly seen as fixed structures that are supposed to prevent or repress dissent. A more positive way to analyze strikes and other conflicts is to interpret them as mechanisms pressuring institutions and policies to be responsive.[21] Rather than being detrimental to democratic participation, such bottom-up protests embody its essence.

Such a system does not encourage fractious competition; instead, it creates a framework within which interest groups can battle yet eventually come to an agreement on policy. Moreover, because they aggregate the interests of all members of their group, they often take a broader, less parochial view of problems and policy solutions. How does the German state mediate the relationship among interest groups? Peter Katzenstein observes that in the Federal Republic, "the state is not an actor but a series of relationships," and these relationships are solidified in what he has called "parapublic institutions."[22] The parapublics encompass a wide variety of organizations, among which the most important are the *Bundesbank* (although many of its powers now reside with the European Central Bank, ECB), the institutions of codetermination, the labor courts, the social insurance funds, and the employment office. Katzenstein notes that the parapublics have been assigned the role of "independent governance by the representatives of social sectors at the behest of or under the general supervision of the state."[23] In other words, organizations that would be regarded as mere interest groups in other countries work with certain quasigovernment agencies to fill a parapublic role in the Federal Republic. These organizations assume a degree of social responsibility, through their roles in policy implementation that go beyond what political scientist Arnold Heidenheimer has called the "freewheeling competition of 'selfish' interest groups."[24] For example, through the state, the churches collect a church tax on all citizens born into either the Protestant or Roman Catholic churches. This provides the churches with a steady stream of income, ensuring them institutional permanence while compelling them to play a major role in the provision of social welfare and aid to the families of foreign workers.

Interest groups and parapublic agencies limit social conflict by regular meetings and close coordination. However, this system is subject to the same problems that have plagued corporatism in more centralized industrial societies such as Sweden and France. If the system fails and conflicts are allowed to go unresolved, the effectiveness of the institutions is questioned, and some elements of society may go unrepresented. A partial failure of certain interest groups and institutions led to a series of social movements during the 1960s and 1970s, particularly around university reform, wage negotiations, and foreign policy. The rise of the Green Party in the 1980s and 1990s is a prime example of a movement that responded to the inability of existing institutions to address, mediate, and solve certain contentious issues. Likewise the growth of the Left Party to represent some 25 to 30 percent of the voters in eastern Germany who did not feel represented by the traditional western parties is another.

Until recently, most conflicts and policy responses were encompassed within this system. Yet not all individuals found organizations to represent their interests. Those who are outside the organized groups fall into several categories. Political groups that fail to meet the 5 percent electoral threshold, such as the NPD and the German People's Union (DVU), belong in this category, along with smaller right-wing groups. The substantial Turkish population, comprising 2.3 percent of Germany's inhabitants, might be included here. Many Turks have resided in Germany for decades, but unlike workers from EU countries like Italy and Spain, Turkish residents have few rights in Germany. Finally, the once-active leftist community of revolutionary Marxists still retains a small presence, mostly in large cities and university towns. Some of these left-wing parties contest elections, but they never get more than 1 percent of the vote.

Since the student mobilizations of the late 1960s, Germany has witnessed considerable protest and mobilization of social forces outside established channels. Among the most significant have been feminists, the peace movement, the antinuclear movement, and the peaceful church-linked protests in East Germany in 1989 that were a catalyst for the breakdown of the communist regime. All four groups, in different ways, challenged fundamental assumptions about German politics and highlighted the inability of the institutional structure to respond to their needs and issues. Opposition to a restrictive abortion law in the 1970s, demonstrations against the stationing of nuclear missiles on German soil in the 1980s, regular protests against nuclear power plants since the 1970s, and courageous challenges to communism have shown the vibrancy of German protest.

Since the 1990s, there has been less protest from the left than from the right. Illegal neo-Nazi groups were responsible for racist attacks. Significantly, all of these attacks by the right-wing fringe provoked spontaneous, peaceful marches of 200,000 to 500,000 people in various cities. This reaction suggests that social protest, as a part of an active democratic political discourse, has matured. In the early twenty-first century, the issue of the Iraq war has produced an increase in social protest, largely among forces on the left of the governing SPD-Green coalition. There have also been smaller right-wing protests against continued immigration, such as the May Day Hamburg riot in 2008, but these have not approached the violent episodes of the 1990s.

SECTION 5 German Politics in Transition

Political Challenges and Changing Agendas

The announcement by Federal President Horst Kölher in May 2008 that he wanted to serve a second term would normally not be surprising. He was a popular figure in this largely ceremonial office and had performed the head of state function well. However, this announcement complicated further the increasingly uneasy relationship between the Grand Coalition partners, the CDU/CSU and SPD. Köhler won in 2004 by narrowly defeating the SPD candidate Gesine Schwann. After Köhler's announcement, the SPD promptly announced that it would nominate Schwann again for this presidential contest to be decided by the *Bundestag* and *Bundesrat* in May 2009.

This decision by Köhler and the CDU/CSU has exacerbated the tensions among the German parties in several ways. First, the two Grand Coalition partners are running competing candidates for head of state. Second, the SPD's backing down to Köhler and the Christian Democrats by not running their own candidate would cause even more Social Democratic voters to desert the SPD and vote for the Left Party in the *Bundestag* election in September 2009. Third, the only way that Schwann could win would be with the support of the

SPD, Greens, and the Left Party, which the SPD was fearful of doing (the FDP supports Köhler). Fourth, the Left Party would be forced to take on a "kingmaker" status for which neither the party nor the country may be ready.

By mid-2008 there were both encouraging and discouraging political developments in Germany. Despite predictions to the contrary, Germany's economy had avoided the most severe effects of the credit crisis that had hit countries like the U.S. and U.K. with their emphasis on deregulation and unconstrained markets. Germany, with some degree of pride, could look to its more organized economic policy model with improved economic growth and a drop in unemployment to 8.5 percent, the lowest in half a decade, and be thankful that it had—for the most part—avoided deregulatory, housing, and financial crises.

On the other hand, Angela Merkel's chancellorship seemed to signify a refreshing change from the strife-ridden second Schröder term. Three years after her narrow election, Merkel was personally popular and seemed ahead of the curve by stressing climate change and human rights as major international issues. But the reality of contemporary German politics is more complicated. The five-party system, with the three smaller parties representing 35 percent of the electorate, does not auger well. Merkel would either have to form a complicated three-party coalition with two of the small parties, or organize another Grand Coalition with the SPD—which would only increase the strength of the three smaller parties over the longer term. And the strains of disagreement with her SPD coalition partner on economic and foreign policy did not bode well with an election looming in a year. Moreover, Merkel still faces the challenges that bedeviled Schröder: (1) the still-formidable uncompleted tasks in eastern Germany associated with unification; (2) the rapid expansion of the European Union (EU) and its free-market–style policy focus that is at odds with the institutionally based, organized-capitalist German economy; and (3) the intense pace of globalization that threatens Germany's competitive edge. Even more alarming was a May 2008 government report that showed that 25 percent of Germans were classified as poor or relied on welfare benefits. The 64,000-euro question is whether Germany can deploy the institutional and political skills to recover its formerly strong position.

The path taken by German politics will be determined by the resolution of the four core themes identified in Section 1. The more hopeful outcome would be for Merkel to negotiate a genuine compromise with the SPD and bridge the formidable gaps between these two large parties. Only with a sound and effective foundation of domestic policy will Germany be able to successfully address the larger issue of European integration and the challenge of globalization and a more volatile international climate in the wake of the Iraq war. By finding common ground to address such problems as economic competitiveness, unemployment, and the still gaping East–West divide, among many others, the Grand Coalition could develop the patience and sound institutional foundation to accomplish a great deal. To her credit, Merkel has been very good at fostering incremental change.

The more pessimistic outcome would see unresolved major issues as dividing the coalition partners and producing a continued stalemate. One result would be an increased share of the vote going to the three opposition parties. Democracies need both a government and an opposition, but if the Grand Coalition has major fissures, finding stable new coalitions may be difficult. Can Germany's organized society and institutional political structure muster the increased cooperation necessary to maintain a vibrant democracy? And what of Germany's high-wage economy and welfare structure in the face of increased economic competition from lower-wage countries in East Asia and elsewhere? Will using the euro enable Germany to thrive, or will it undermine the previous strengths of the German economy? And what is the state of the German economy in the face of domestic structural challenges, as well as globalization of the international economy? It remains to be seen whether the Grand Coalition can implement significant economic and political reforms such as Schröder's policy that merged the unemployment and welfare systems reforms and required the unemployed to take jobs outside their home region or outside their chosen profession.

For many years, Germany was held up as a model for other industrialized societies to emulate. But there have been significant changes in Germany since unification. The expansion of the EU since the 1990s has enabled more European citizens to live and work outside their home countries. What will happen to

German collective identity given this fluidity and the change in German citizenship laws by the SPD-Green government, and the subsequent criticism by some far-right forces? Can the elaborate and long-effective institutional structure that balances private and public interests be maintained? Will the EU augment or challenge Germany's position in Europe? Will these challenges threaten Germany's enviable position in the face of increased globalization of the world economy?

The future of German politics depends on how the country addresses the four primary themes identified in this analysis of the Federal Republic. For much of the period after World War II, Germany enjoyed a spiral of success that enabled it to confront these issues with confidence and resolve. For example, problems of collective identities were handled in a much less exclusionary way as women, nonnative ethnic groups, and newer political parties and movements began to contribute to a stable and healthy diversity in German politics. Democratic institutions effectively balanced participation and dissent, offsetting the country's turbulent and often racist past by almost fifty years of a stable multiparty democracy. Germany's economic success has been significant and unique. The country is a stronghold of advanced capitalism yet supports an extensive state welfare program and mandates worker/trade union/works councils' participation in managerial decision-making. These successes have helped Germany participate more effectively on the international scene. Since the late 1980s, Germany has confidently, and with the support of its neighbors and allies, taken a leading role in European integration. It is firmly anchored in western Europe but is uniquely positioned to assist in the transition of the former communist central and eastern European states toward economic and political modernization and EU membership.

However, close examination of the four themes reveals that Germany's path is not yet certain. In the area of collective identities, Germany faces many unresolved challenges. Turkish and other non-German guest workers remain essential to Germany's economy, and some will now be able to obtain German citizenship. Their long-term acceptance by the CDU/CSU, not to mention the smaller ultra-right parties, will likely be the key to a fundamental change in the concept of who is a German. The influx of refugees and asylum seekers has placed great strains on German taxpayers and increased ethnic tensions. German nationalism, suppressed since the end of World War II, has shown some signs of resurgence. Two generations after the end of World War II, some younger Germans are asking what being German actually means. The change in citizenship laws will complicate this issue, for although this search for identity can be healthy, various extremist groups still preach exaggerated nationalism and hatred of foreigners and minorities. Such tendencies are fundamentally incompatible with Germany's playing a leading role in a unifying Europe.

Democracy in Germany appears well established after almost sixty years of the Federal Republic. It features high voter turnout, a stable and responsible multiparty political system, and a healthy civic culture. Despite the inconclusive election, German politicians have negotiated an interim solution, and they have done so via constitutional principles common to all multiparty parliamentary systems.[25]

Many observers believe that broad-based participation is part of the fabric of German political life. The overriding challenge for Germany's political institutions is the assimilation of the five eastern states. Can eastern Germans who have lost jobs and benefits in the transition to capitalism understand that ethnic minorities are not the cause of their plight? Can tolerance and understanding offset a right-wing fringe that preaches hatred and targets scapegoats to blame for the costs of unification? Also, what is the legacy of a bureaucratic state that as recently as the 1970s, under a Social Democratic-led government, purged individuals alleged to have radical tendencies? In other words, if social tensions continue to grow, how will the German state respond?

There is reason for optimism. Eastern Germans have shown that they understand and practice democracy amazingly well. After years of authoritarian communist rule, many East Germans initially regarded dissent not as political participation but as treason. However, the evolution of the Left Party into an effective political force that articulates the interests of its voters—now in the West as well as the East—offers considerable promise. In the recent elections, the Left Party has been considered unsuitable as a potential coalition partner because of its communist origins. However, when the Greens first obtained seats in the *Bundestag* in 1983, it was often viewed as an irresponsible party and not appropriate as a coalition partner. Yet fifteen years later, the Greens joined the SPD in the first left-wing majority government in German history. The lesson to be learned from the Greens' transformation from a motley crew of *alternativen* (counterculture) to a governing coalition partner is that continued participation in democratic institutions can have positive results for both the party and the institutions.

Germany's approach to governing the economy also faces challenges in the early twenty-first century. For many years, the German economy was characterized as "high everything," in that it combined high-quality manufacturing with high wages, high fringe benefits, high worker participation, and high levels of vacation time.[26] Critics insisted that such a system could not last in a competitive world economy. Nevertheless, the German economy has remained among the world's leaders. But the huge costs of unification, the globalization of the world economy, and the strong emphasis on laissez-faire principles in many neighboring countries challenge the German model anew.[27]

German Politics in Comparative Perspective

Germany offers important insights for comparative politics. First, how successfully has Germany remade its political culture and institutions in the wake of a fascist past? Countries such as Japan, Italy, and Spain, among developed states, also bear watching on this point. To what extent has Germany's impressive democratic experience during the first fifty years of the Federal Republic exorcised the ghosts of the Third Reich? To what extent have the educational system, civil service, and the media addressed the Nazi past? To what extent do these institutions bear some responsibility for the recent rise of right-wing violence? Have the reforms in the educational system since the 1960s provided a spirit of critical discourse in the broad mainstream of society that can withstand right-wing rhetoric? Can judges effectively sentence those who abuse the civil rights of ethnic minorities? Will the news media continue to express a wide range of opinion and contribute to a healthy civic discourse? Or will strident, tabloid-style journalism stifle the more reasoned debate that any democracy must have to survive and flourish?

Second, Germany's historical development provides important material for comparative analysis. It was late to achieve political unity and late to industrialize. These two factors, combined with an unfavorable institutional mix, eventually helped produce a catastrophic first half of the twentieth century for Germany and the whole world. Yet the country's transition to a successful, developed economy with an apparently solid democratic political system would seem to provide more positive lessons for other countries. Those that might derive the most benefit may be industrializing nations as they also attempt to achieve economic growth and develop stable democracies.

Third is the role of organized capitalism. Germany offers a distinctive model for combining state and market. Germany's organized capitalism, together with its social market economy, has blurred the distinction between the public and private sectors. The German state pursues development plans based on its cooperative interaction with a dense network of key social and economic participants, particularly in such areas as climate change. Despite Germany's prominence as a powerful, advanced, industrialized economy, this model remains surprisingly understudied.

Germany offers a fourth insight, one that relates to the issues of tolerance and respect for civil rights for ethnic minorities. The Schröder government modified Germany's immigration policies to provide a path for long-time foreign workers to gain citizenship. Can residual ethnic tensions be resolved in a way that enhances democracy? Clearly, the issue of collective identities offers both powerful obstacles and rich opportunities to address one of the most crucial issues that Germany faces in the new century.

Finally, what is the role of a middle-rank power as the potential leader of a regional world bloc of some 450 million people? Germany is facing intense pressures from within its borders, such as conflict among ethnic groups, and from a complex mix of external influences. Its role as both a western and an eastern European power pulls it in opposite directions. Should the country emphasize the western-oriented EU and build a solid foundation with its NATO allies? Or should it turn eastward to step into the vacuum created by the demise and fragmentation of the former USSR? Can Germany's twentieth-century history permit it to play a leading geopolitical role? What an ironic but inspiring twist if Germany, the country whose virulent nationalism caused the most widespread destruction and destabilization in the twentieth century, took the lead at the head of the supranational EU in promoting democracy, creativity, and stability in the twenty-first century.

Key Terms

Gastarbeiter (guest workers)
federal state
Junkers
liberal
chancellor
Kulturkampf
procedural democracy
Nazi
Zollverein
framework regulations
social market economy
works councils
Basic Law
5 percent rule
constructive vote of no confidence
civil servants
overlapping responsibilities
democratic corporatism
health insurance funds
co-determination
Administrative Court
industrial policy
personalized proportional representation
suspensive veto
party democracy
Citizens Action Groups
grass-roots democracy

Suggested Readings

Allen, Christopher S., ed. *Transformation of the German Political Party System: Institutional Crisis or Democratic Renewal?* New York: Berghahn, 2001.

———, "Ideas, Institutions and the Exhaustion of *Modell Deutschland?*" *German Law Journal* 5, no. 9 (September 2004): 1133–1154.

Braunthal, Gerard. *The Federation of German Industry in Politics.* Ithaca: Cornell University Press, 1965.

———. *Parties and Politics in Modern Germany.* Boulder: Westview Press, 1996.

Craig, Gordon. *The Politics of the Prussian Army.* Oxford: Oxford University Press, 1955.

Dahrendorf, Ralf. *Society and Democracy in Germany.* Garden City: Anchor, 1969.

Deeg, Richard. *Finance Capital Unveiled: Banks and Economic Adjustment in Germany.* Ann Arbor: University of Michigan Press, 1998.

Eley, Geoff. *Reshaping the German Right: Radical Nationalism and Political Change After Bismarck.* New Haven: Yale University Press, 1980.

Esping-Anderson, Gøsta. *Three Worlds of Welfare Capitalism.* Princeton: Princeton University Press, 1990.

Gerschenkron, Alexander. *Bread and Democracy in Germany.* 2d ed. Ithaca: Cornell University Press, 1989.

Hirschman, Albert O. *Exit, Loyalty, and Voice: Responses to Decline in Firms, Organizations, and States.* Cambridge: Harvard University Press, 1970.

Inglehart, Ronald. *Culture Shift in Advanced Industrial Society.* Princeton: Princeton University Press, 1990.

Jacoby, Wade. *Imitation and Politics: Redesigning Modern Germany.* Ithaca: Cornell University Press, 2001.

Katzenstein, Peter, ed., *Industry and Politics in West Germany: Toward the Third Republic.* Ithaca: Cornell University Press, 1989.

Katzenstein, Peter. *Policy and Politics in West Germany: The Growth of a Semi-Sovereign State.* Philadelphia: Temple University Press, 1987.

———. *Tamed Power: Germany in Europe.* Ithaca: Cornell University Press, 1997.

Kemp, Tom. *Industrialization in Nineteenth Century Europe.* 2d ed. London: Longman, 1985.

Markovits, Andrei S., and Reich, Simon. *The German Predicament: Memory and Power of the New Europe.* Ithaca: Cornell University Press, 1997.

Moore, Barrington. *Social Origins of Dictatorship and Democracy.* Boston: Beacon Press, 1965.

Piore, Michael, and Sabel, Charles. *The Second Industrial Divide.* New York: Basic Books, 1984.

Rein, Taagepera, and Shugart, Matthew Soberg. *Seats and Votes: The Effects and Determinants of Electoral Systems.* New Haven: Yale University Press, 1989.

Richter, Michaela. "Continuity or *Politikwechsel*? The First Federal Red-Green Coalition." *German Politics and Society* 20:1 (Spring 2002), 1–48.

Röpke, Wilhelm. "The Guiding Principle of the Liberal Programme." In H. F. Wünche, ed., *Standard Texts on the Social Market Economy.* New York: Gustav Fischer Verlag, 1982.

Rueschemeyer, Dietrich, Stephens, Evelyne Huber, and Stephens, John D. *Capitalist Development and Democracy.* Chicago: University of Chicago Press, 1992.

Schmitter, Philippe C., and Lembruch, Gerhard, eds. *Trends Toward Corporatist Intermediation.* Beverly Hills: Sage, 1979.

Shirer, William. *The Rise and Fall of the Third Reich.* New York: Simon & Schuster, 1960.

Steinmo, Sven, Thelen, Kathleen, and Longstreth, Frank, eds. *Structuring Politics: Historical Institutionalism in Historical Perspective.* New York: Cambridge University Press, 1992.

Streeck, Wolfgang. "Introduction: Explorations into the Origins of Nonliberal Capitalism in Germany and Japan." In Wolfgang Streeck and Kozo Yamamura, eds., *The Origins of Non-Liberal Capitalism* (Ithaca: Cornell University Press, 2002), pp. 1–38.

Thelen, Kathleen. *How Institutions Evolve: The Political Economy of Skills in Germany, Britain, the United States and Japan.* Cambridge: Cambridge University Press, 2004.

Tilly, Charles, ed. *The Formation of National States in Western Europe.* Princeton: Princeton University Press, 1975.

Turner, Lowell, ed. *Negotiating the New Germany: Can Social Partnership Survive?* Ithaca: Cornell University Press, 1997.

Yamamura, Kozo, and Streeck, Wolfgang. *The End of Diversity? Prospects for German and Japanese Capitalism.* Ithaca: Cornell University Press, 2003.

Suggested Websites

American Institute for Contemporary German Studies, Johns Hopkins University
www.aicgs.org/
German Embassy, German Information Center
www.germany-info.org/relaunch/index.html
German News (in English) 1995–Present
www.germnews.de/dn/

German Studies Web, Western European Studies Section
www.dartmouth.edu/~wess/
Max Planck Institute for the Study of Societies, Cologne
www.mpi-fg-koeln.mpg.de/index_en.html
WZB, Social Science Research Center, Berlin
www.wz-berlin.de/default.en.asp

Endnotes

[1] Charles Tilly, ed., *The Formation of National States in Western Europe* (Princeton: Princeton University Press, 1975).

[2] Barrington Moore, *Social Origins of Dictatorship and Democracy* (Boston: Beacon Press, 1965).

[3] Tom Kemp, *Industrialization in Nineteenth Century Europe*, 2d ed. (London: Longman, 1985).

[4] Richard Deeg, "The Comeback of *Modell Deutschland*? The New German Political Economy in the EU," *German Politics* 14 (2005): 332–353.

[5] Ralf Dahrendorf, *Society and Democracy in Germany* (Garden City: Anchor, 1969).

[6] Alexander Gerschenkron, *Bread and Democracy in Germany*, 2d ed. (Ithaca: Cornell University Press, 1989).

[7] Richard Deeg, *Finance Capital Unveiled: Banks and Economic Adjustment in Germany* (Ann Arbor: University of Michigan Press, 1998).

[8] Joyce Mushaben, "Challenging the Maternalist Presumption: Gender and Welfare Reform in Germany and the United States," in Ulrike Liebert and Nancy Hirschman, eds., *Women and Welfare: Theory and Practice in the U.S. and Europe* (Rutgers: Rutgers University Press, 2001).

[9] For an excellent understanding of the dynamics of institutional adaptation, see: Albert O. Hirschman, *Exit, Voice, and Loyalty: Responses to Decline in Firms, Organizations, and States* (Cambridge: Harvard University Press, 1970).

[10] http://eng.bundespraesident.de/en/-,11167/The-role-of-the-Federal-Presid.htm.

[11] Peter Katzenstein, *Policy and Politics in West Germany: The Growth of a Semi-Sovereign State* (Philadelphia: Temple University Press, 1987).

[12] John O. Koehler, *Stasi: The Untold Story of the East German Secret Police* (Boulder: Westview Press, 1999).

[13] Michaela Richter, "Continuity or Politikwechsel? The First Federal Red-Green Coalition." *German Politics & Society* 20, no. 1 (Spring 2002): 1–48.

[14] Frank Louis Rusciano, "Rethinking the Gender Gap: The Case of West German Elections," *Comparative Politics* 24, no. 3 (April 1992): 335–358.

[15] Christopher S. Allen, ed., *Transformation of the German Political Party System: Institutional Crisis or Democratic Renewal?* (New York: Berghahn, 2001).

[16] Aline Kuntz, "The Bavarian CSU: A Case Study in Conservative Modernization" (Ph.D. diss., Cornell University, 1987).

[17] Carl E. Schorske, *German Social Democracy, 1905–1917: The Development of the Great Schism* (Cambridge: Harvard University Press, 1983).

[18] Otto Kirchheimer, "The Transformation of Western European Party Systems," *Political Parties and Political Development* (Princeton: Princeton University Press, 1966), pp. 177–200.

[19] Gerard Braunthal, *The German Social Democrats Since 1969: A Party in Power and Opposition*, 2nd ed. (Boulder: Westview Press, 1994).

[20] Hans-Georg Betz, *Radical Right-Wing Populism in Western Europe* (New York: St. Martin's Press, 1994).

[21] Wolfgang Streeck and Kathleen Thelen, eds., *Beyond Continuity: Institutional Change in Advanced Political Economies* (New York: Oxford University Press, 2005).

[22] Katzenstein, *Policy and Politics in West Germany*.

[23] Peter J. Katzenstein, ed., *Industry and Politics in West Germany: Toward the Third Republic* (Ithaca: Cornell University Press, 1989), p. 333.

[24] Arnold J. Heidenheimer, *Comparative Public Policy: The Politics of Social Choice in America, Europe and Japan*, 3d ed. (New York: St. Martin's Press, 1990).

[25] Gabriel A. Almond and Sidney Verba, eds., *The Civic Culture Revisited* (Newbury Park: Sage, 1989).

[26] Lowell Turner, ed., *Negotiating the New Germany: Can Social Partnership Survive?* (Ithaca: Cornell University Press, 1997).

[27] Gary Herrigel, "The Crisis in German Decentralized Production," *European Urban and Regional Studies* 3, no. 1 (1996): 33–52.

Official Name:	Russian Federation (*Rossiyskaya Federatsiya*)
Location:	Eastern Europe/Northern Asia
Capital City:	Moscow
Population (2007):	141.4 million
Size:	17,075,200 sq. km.; approximately 1.8 times the size of the United States

CHAPTER 3 Russia

■ Joan DeBardeleben

SECTION 1 | The Making of the Modern Russian State
SECTION 2 | Political Economy and Development
SECTION 3 | Governance and Policy-Making
SECTION 4 | Representation and Participation
SECTION 5 | Russian Politics in Transition

Chronology of Soviet and Russian Political Development

1917	1918–1921	1921–1928	1929	1929–1953	1929–1938
The Bolshevik seizure of power	Civil War and war communism	New Economic Policy	Stalin consolidates power	Stalin in power	Collectivization and purges

1985–1991	1991	1992	1993	1995–1996
The Gorbachev era and *perestroika*	Popular election of Boris Yeltsin as president of Russia (July); collapse of the USSR and formation of fifteen independent states (December); establishment of the Russian Federation as an independent state	Market reforms launched in Russia (January)	Adoption of the new Russian constitution by referendum; first (multiparty) parliamentary elections in the Russian Federation (December)	Second parliamentary elections in the Russian Federation (December 1995) with the Communists winning the most seats; first presidential elections under the new Russian constitution (June–July 1996), with Yeltsin reelected in two rounds of voting.

SECTION 1

The Making of the Modern Russian State

FOCUS QUESTION

In what ways may terrorism present challenges to Russia's democratization processes?

Politics in Action

For children of Middle School No. 1 in Beslan (population about 34,000) in southern Russia, the first day of school in 2004 was marked by tragedy. As parents accompanied children to school, terrorist forces herded 1,000 children and family members into the gymnasium. Not permitting the victims food or water, the hostage takers made demands that were unacceptable to the Russian government: the removal of Russian troops from the neighboring secessionist region, the Republic of Chechnya, and the release of Chechen rebels held by the government. On Friday, September 3—fifty-two hours later—Russian special forces heard an explosion inside. They stormed the building in an effort to release the victims. Over 300 hostages, the majority children, were dead.

The Beslan massacre followed numerous other terrorist attacks since 1995. The previous month, two Russian passenger planes crashed simultaneously, killing at least eighty-nine passengers. In May 2004, a bomb killed Chechen president Akhmad Kadyrov. He had been installed by elections some claimed were unfairly controlled by Moscow. Two years earlier, bomb-laden terrorists took over 700 hostages in a Moscow theater; at least 120 died. Other attacks targeted theaters, apartment buildings, and public transport.

1941–1945	1953	1953–1955	1956–1964	1965–1982	1982–1985
Nazi Germany invades Soviet Union; "Great Patriotic War"	Death of Stalin	Leadership change after Stalin's death	The Khrushchev era and de-Stalinization	The Brezhnev era and bureaucratic consolidation	Leadership change after Brezhnev's death
			1962 Cuban Missile Crisis	1972 Initiation of détente (easing of tension between the USSR and the United States)	

1998	1999	2000	2003	2004	2007–2008
Financial crisis and devaluation of the ruble	Third parliamentary elections in the Russian Federation; Unity Party gains strong support, as does Communist Party; resignation of Yeltsin as president (December)	Election of Vladimir Putin as president of Russia	Third parliamentary elections in the Russian Federation; strong win for United Russia Party (December)	Reelection of Vladimir Putin as president of Russia (March); September hostage taking of school children and bloody conflict to free hostages in Beslan, southern Russia; Putin announces new centralizing measures	Most recent Russian election cycle, with parliamentary elections in December 2007 and presidential elections in March 2008, the latter marking the end of Vladimir Putin's two terms in office.

Although Chechen terrorists have links to international networks, including Al Qaeda, the context of the Russian problem is local. Terrorism responds to an extended war in the Russian republic of Chechnya resulting from Russia's efforts to control rebel secessionist forces. An increasingly prominent role for Chechen women among the suicide bombers suggests the depth of the social alienation that underlies the terrorist wave.

Following the Beslan tragedy, Russian president Putin announced reforms to increase central control over selection of regional governors. A counterterrorism law was proposed making it easier to restrict press freedom and civil liberties in the face of alleged terrorist threats. Just as economic revived beginning in 1999, worries about security increased. Russians wondered whether the state could ensure their well-being and security. While Western experts were debating whether Putin's centralizing reforms would undermine democratization, many Russians were just hoping that they would give the government the authority it needs to ensure a secure and stable way of life.

FOCUS QUESTION

In what ways does geography make Russia a difficult country to govern?

Geographic Setting

After the Soviet Union broke up in 1991, fifteen newly independent states emerged on its territory. This section focuses on the Russian Federation, the largest successor state and the largest European country in population (between

Chapter 3: Russia

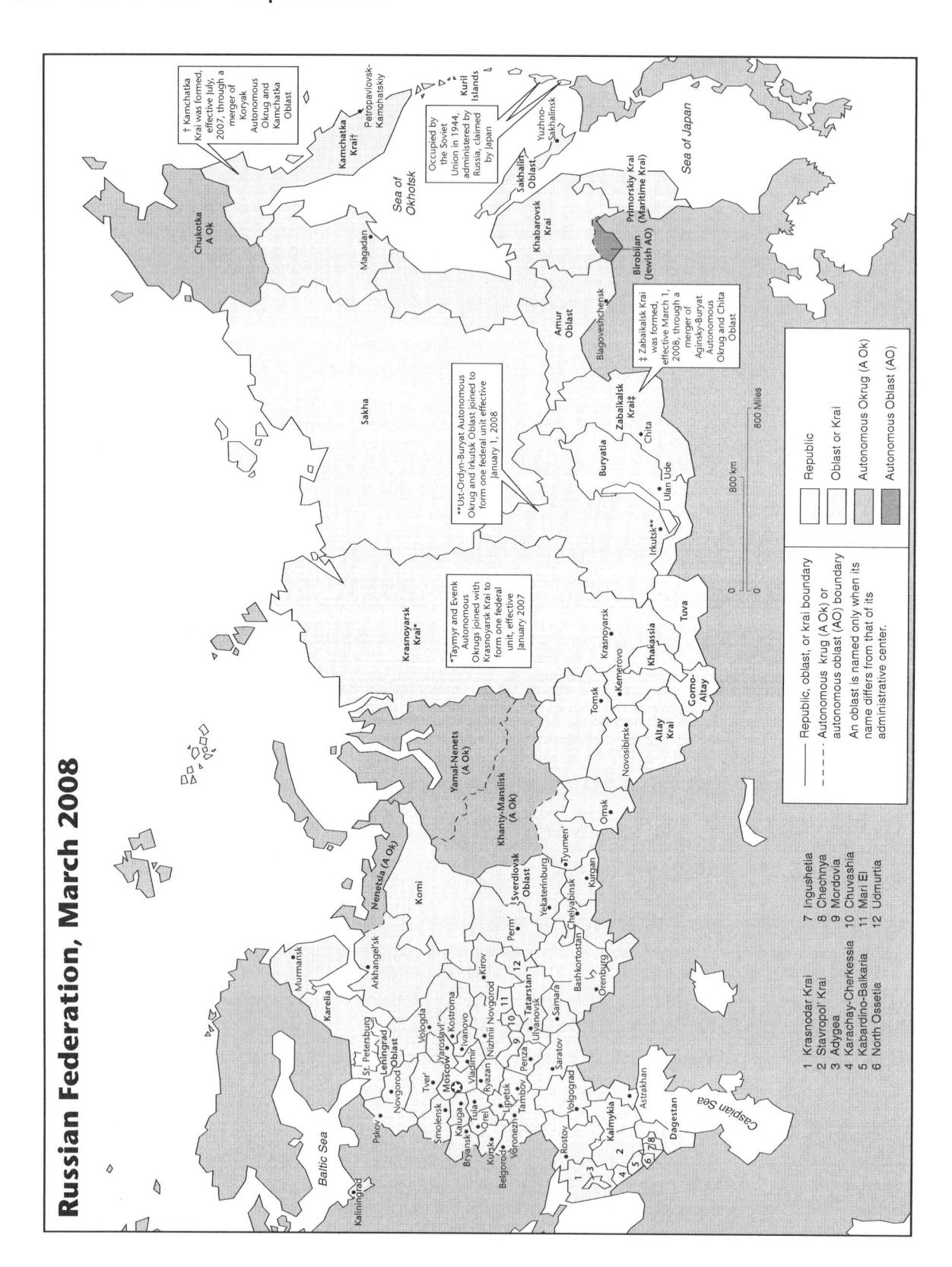

Russian Federation, March 2008

† Kamchatka Krai was formed, effective July, 2007, through a merger of Koryak Autonomous Okrug and Kamchatka Oblast

Occupied by the Soviet Union in 1944, administered by Russia, claimed by Japan

‡ Zabaikalsk Krai was formed, effective March 1, 2008, through a merger of Aginsky-Buryat Autonomous Okrug and Chita Oblast

**Ust-Ordyn-Buryat Autonomous Okrug and Irkutsk Oblast joined to form one federal unit effective January 1, 2008

*Taymyr and Evenk Autonomous Okrugs joined with Krasnoyarsk Krai to form one federal unit, effective January 2007

Legend:
- Republic
- Oblast or Krai
- Autonomous Okrug (A Ok)
- Autonomous Oblast (AO)
- Republic, oblast, or krai boundary
- Autonomous krug (A Ok) or autonomous oblast (AO) boundary
- An oblast is named only when its name differs from that of its administrative center.

1. Krasnodar Krai
2. Stavropol Krai
3. Adygea
4. Karachay-Cherkessia
5. Kabardino-Balkaria
6. North Ossetia
7. Ingushetia
8. Chechnya
9. Mordovia
10. Chuvashia
11. Mari El
12. Udmurtia

The Making of the Modern Russian State

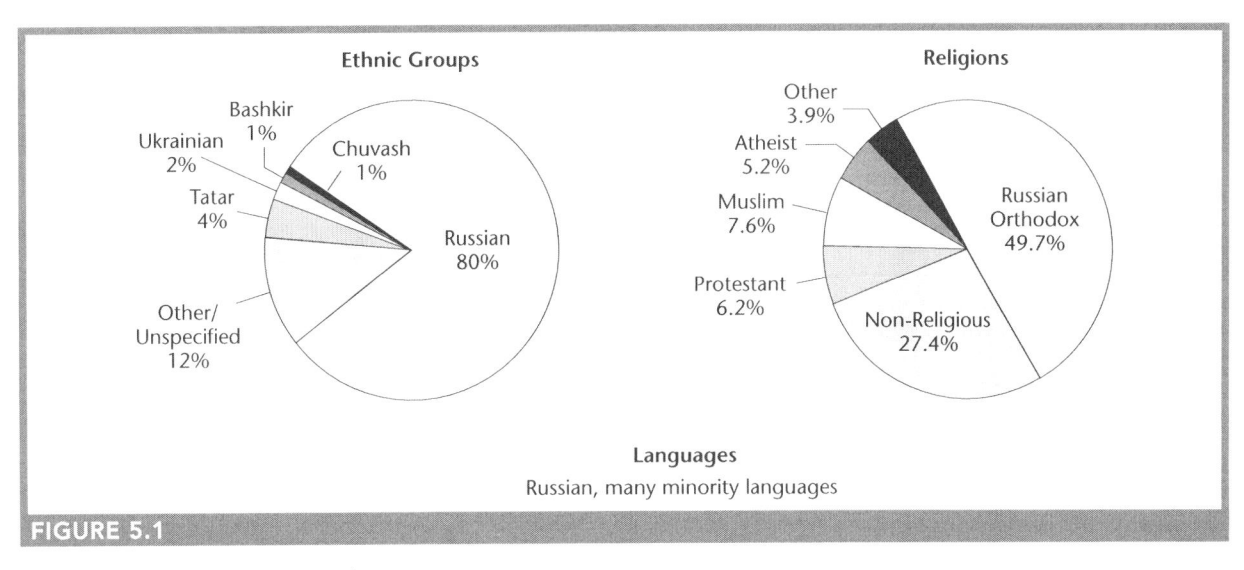

Ethnic Groups
- Russian 80%
- Other/Unspecified 12%
- Tatar 4%
- Ukrainian 2%
- Bashkir 1%
- Chuvash 1%

Religions
- Russian Orthodox 49.7%
- Non-Religious 27.4%
- Muslim 7.6%
- Protestant 6.2%
- Atheist 5.2%
- Other 3.9%

Languages
Russian, many minority languages

FIGURE 5.1

The Russian Nation at a Glance

TABLE 5.1

Political Organization

Political System	Constitutionally a federal state, semipresidential system.
Regime History	Re-formed as an independent state with the collapse of communist rule in December 1991; current constitution since December 1993.
Administrative Structure	Federal system, originally with eighty-nine subnational governments including twenty-one republics, fifty-five provinces (*oblast, krai*), eleven autonomous districts or regions (*okrugs* or autonomous *oblast*), and two cities of federal status. As of July 2007 the number of subnational governments was reduced to eighty-five, through a merger of regions.
Executive	Dual executive (president and prime minister). Direct election of president; prime minister appointed by the president with the approval of the lower house of the parliament (State *Duma*).
Legislature	Bicameral. Upper house (Federation Council) appointed by heads of regional executive and representative organs. Lower house (State *Duma*) chosen by direct election, with half of the 450 deputies chosen through a proportional representation system and half from single-member constituencies until 2007, when a full proportional representation system was introduced for all 450 deputies. Powers include proposal and approval of legislation, approval of presidential appointees.
Judiciary	Independent constitutional court with nineteen justices, nominated by the president and approved by the Federation Council, holding twelve-year terms with possible renewal.
Party System	Multiparty system with a dominant party (United Russia).

141 and 142 million in 2007) and, in area, the largest country in the world, spanning eleven time zones.

Russia underwent rapid industrialization and urbanization under Soviet rule. Only 18 percent of Russians lived in urban areas in 1917; 73 percent do now. Less than 8 percent of Russia's land is arable, while 45 percent is forested. Russia is rich in natural resources, concentrated in western Siberia and northern Russia. These include minerals (even gold and diamonds), timber, oil and natural gas exports, which now form the basis of Russia's economic wealth.

The czarist empire extended east to the Pacific, south to the Caucasus Mountains and the Muslim areas of Central Asia, north to the Arctic Circle, and west into present-day Ukraine, eastern Poland, and the Baltic states. In the USSR the Russian Republic formed the core of a multiethnic state. Russia's ethnic diversity and geographic scope have made it a hard country to govern. Currently Russia faces pockets of instability on several of its borders, most notably in Tajikistan and Afghanistan in Central Asia, and in Georgia and Azerbaijan on the southern border. Russia's western neighbors include Ukraine, Belarus, and several EU member states (Finland, Estonia, Latvia, Lithuania, and Poland). Located at a critical juncture between Europe, the Islamic world, and Asia, Russia's regional sphere of influence is now disputed.

Critical Junctures

The Decline of the Russian Tsarist State

> **FOCUS QUESTION**
>
> Consider three crucial junctures in Russian history. In what ways was each juncture a reaction to a recurring problem in Russian history?

Until 1917, an autocratic system headed by the tsar ruled Russia. Richard Pipes explains that before 1917, Russia had a **patrimonial state** that not only ruled the country but also owned the land.[1] The majority of the peasant population was tied to the nobles the state, or the church (through serfdom). The serfs were emancipated in 1861 as a part of the tsar's effort to modernize Russia and to make it militarily competitive with the West.

patrimonial state
A system of governance in which the ruler treats the state as personal property (patrimony).

The key impetus for industrialization came from the state and from foreign capital. Despite some reforms workers became increasingly discontented, as did liberal intellectuals, students, and, later, peasants, in the face of Russia's defeat in the Russo-Japanese war and continued tsarist repression. Revolution broke out in 1905. The regime, however maintained control through repression and economic reforms, until its collapse in 1917.

The Bolshevik Revolution and the Establishment of Soviet Power (1917–1929)

In March 1917, during the height of World War I, a revolution threw out Tsar Nicholas II and installed a moderate provisional government. In November, the Bolsheviks, led by Vladimir Lenin, overthrew that government. Instead of imitating Western European patterns, the Bolsheviks applied a dramatically different blueprint for economic, social, and political development.

The Bolsheviks were Marxists who believed their revolution reflected the political interests of a particular social class, the proletariat (working class). Most of the revolutionary leaders, however, were not themselves workers, but came from a more educated and privileged stratum, the intelligentsia. Nonetheless, their slogan, "Land, Peace, and Bread," appealed to both the working class and the discontented peasantry, which made up over 80 percent of Russia's population.

The Bolsheviks formed a tightly organized political party. Their strategy was based on two key ideas: democratic centralism and vanguardism. **Democratic centralism** mandated a hierarchical party structure in which leaders were elected from below, but strict discipline was required in implementing party decisions once they were made. The centralizing elements of democratic centralism took precedence over the democratic elements, as the party tried to insulate itself first from informers of the tsarist forces and later from real and imagined threats to the new regime. The concept of a **vanguard party** governed the Bolsheviks' relations with broader social forces. Party leaders claimed that they understood the interests of the working people better than the people did themselves. Over time, this philosophy was used to justify virtually all actions of the party and the state it dominated. Neither democratic centralism nor vanguardism emphasized bottom-up democratic procedures or accountability of the leaders to the public. Rather, these concepts focused on achieving a "correct" political outcome that would reflect the "true" interests of the working class, as defined by the leaders of the party.

In 1922 the Bolsheviks formed the Union of Soviet Socialist Republics (USSR). The Bolsheviks took extraordinary measures to ensure the survival of the regime. The initial challenge was an extended civil war (1918–1921) for control of the countryside and outlying regions. The Bolsheviks introduced war communism to ensure materials necessary for the war effort. The state took control of key economic sectors and forcibly requisitioned grain from the peasants. The *Cheka*, the security arm of the regime, was strengthened, and restrictions were placed on other political groups, including other socialist parties. By 1921, the leadership had recognized the political costs of war communism. In an effort to accommodate the peasantry, the New Economic Policy (NEP) was introduced in 1921 and lasted until 1928. State control over the economy was loosened so that private enterprise and trade were revived. The state, however, retained control of large-scale industry.

Gradually, throughout the 1920s, the authoritarian strains of Bolshevik thinking eclipsed the democratic elements. Lacking a democratic tradition and bolstered by the vanguard ideology of the party, the Bolshevik leaders were plagued by internal struggles following Lenin's death in 1924. By 1929, however, all open opposition, even within the party itself, had been silenced.

The Bolshevik revolution also initiated a period of international isolation; to fulfill their promise of peace, the new rulers had had to cede important chunks of territory to Germany under the Brest-Litovsk Treaty (1918), which were returned to Russia's only after Germany was defeated by Russia's allies (the United States, France, and Britain). However these countries were hardly pleased with Russia's revolution, which led to expropriation of foreign holdings and which represented the first successful challenge to the capitalist order. The former allies sent material aid and troops to oppose the new Bolshevik government during the civil war.

---

democratic centralism a system of political organization developed by V. I. Lenin and practiced, with modifications, by all communist party–states. Its principles include a hierarchical party structure.

vanguard party a political party that claims to operate in the "true" interests of the group or class it purports to represent, even if this understanding doesn't correspond to the expressed interests of the group itself.

The Stalin Revolution (1929–1953)

From 1929 until his death in 1953, Stalin consolidated his power as Soviet leader. Stalin brought changes to virtually every aspect of Soviet life. The state became the engine for rapid economic development, with state ownership of virtually all economic assets. By 1935, over 90 percent of agricultural land had been taken from the peasants and made into state or collective farms. This **collectivization** campaign was justified as a means of preventing the emergence of a new capitalist class in the countryside. But it actually targeted the peasantry as a whole, leading to widespread famine and the death of millions. A program of rapid industrialization favored heavy industries, and consumer goods were neglected. Economic control operated through a complex but inefficient system of central economic planning, in which the state planning committee (Gosplan) set production targets for every enterprise in the country. Under the influence of rapid industrialization, people were uprooted from their traditional lives in the countryside and catapulted into the rhythm of urban industrial life. Media censorship and state control of the arts strangled creativity as well as political opposition. The party/state became the authoritative source of truth; anyone deviating from the authorized interpretation could be charged with treason.

Gradually, the party became subject to the personal whims of Stalin and his secret police. Overall, an estimated 5 percent of the Soviet population was arrested at one point or another under the Stalinist system, usually for no apparent cause. Only among trusted friends and family members did people dare to express their true views. Forms of resistance were evasive rather than active. Peasants killed livestock to avoid giving it over to collective farms. Laborers worked inefficiently. Absenteeism was high.

Isolation from the outside world was a key tool of Stalinist control. This policy did shield Soviet society from the Great Depression of the 1930s. But it also allowed an inefficient system of production to survive. Without foreign competition, the economy failed to keep up with the rapid economic and technological transformation in the West.

In 1941, Nazi Germany invaded the Soviet Union, and Stalin had little choice but to join the Allied powers. Casualties in the war were staggering, about 27 million people, including 19 million civilians. War sacrifices and heroism have remained powerful symbols of pride and unity for Russians up through the present day. After the war, the other Allied powers allowed the Soviet Union to absorb new territories into the USSR itself (these became the Soviet republics of Latvia, Lithuania, Estonia, Moldavia, and portions of western Ukraine). The allies implicitly granted the USSR free rein to shape the postwar governments and economies in East Germany, Poland, Hungary, Czechoslovakia, Yugoslavia, Bulgaria, and Romania. Western offers to include parts of the region in the Marshall Plan were rejected under pressure from the USSR. Local Communist parties gained control of all of these countries. Only in Yugoslavia were indigenous Communist forces sufficiently strong to hold power largely on their own and thus later to assert their independence from Moscow.

In the post-war period, the USSR emerged as a global superpower as the Soviet sphere of influence encompassed large parts of Central and Eastern Europe.

---

collectivization a process undertaken in the Soviet Union under Stalin from 1929 into the early 1930s and in China under Mao in the 1950s, by which agricultural land was removed from private ownership and organized into large state and collective farms.

In 1947, in the face of crises in Greece and Turkey, the American president Harry Truman proclaimed a policy to contain further Soviet expansion (subsequently referred to as the Truman Doctrine). In 1949 a defensive military alliance, the North Atlantic Treaty Organization (NATO), was formed involving several West European countries, the United States, and Canada, to protect against potential Soviet aggression, and in 1955 the Soviet Union initiated the Warsaw Pact in response. These events marked the beginning of the Cold War, characterized by tension and military competition between the two superpowers (the United States and USSR), leading to an escalating arms race that was particularly costly to the Soviet Union. Tensions reached a high point during the Cuban Missile Crisis of 1962. In 1972, the initiation of détente brought some relaxation of relations between the two superpowers.

The Soviet Union isolated its satellite countries in Central and Eastern Europe from the West and tightened their economic and political integration with the USSR. Some countries within the Soviet bloc, however, had strong historic links to Western Europe (especially Czechoslovakia, Poland, and Hungary). Over time, these countries served not only as geographic buffers to direct Western influence but also as conduits for such influence.

Attempts at De-Stalinization (1953–1985)

Stalin's death in 1953 triggered another critical juncture in Soviet politics. Even the Soviet elite realized that Stalin's terror could be sustained only at great cost. The terror destroyed initiative and participation, and the unpredictability of Stalinist rule inhibited the rational formulation of policy. From Stalin's death until the mid-1980s Soviet politics became more regular and stable. Terror abated, but political controls remained in place, and efforts to isolate Soviet citizens from foreign influences continued.

Nikita Khrushchev, who eventually followed Stalin as party leader, embarked on a bold policy of de-Stalinization, rejecting terror as an instrument of political control. The secret police (KGB) was subordinated to party authority, and party meetings resumed on a regular basis. However, internal party structures remained highly centralized, and elections were uncontested. Khrushchev's successor, Leonid Brezhnev (party head 1964–1982) partially reversed Khrushchev's de-Stalinization efforts. Controls tightened again in the cultural sphere. Individuals who expressed dissenting views through underground publishing or publication abroad were harassed, arrested, or exiled. However, unlike in the Stalinist period, the political repression was predictable. People knew when they were transgressing permitted limits of criticism.

From the late 1970s onward, an aging political leadership was increasingly ineffective at addressing the mounting problems facing Soviet society. Economic growth rates declined, living standards improved only minimally, and opportunities for upward career mobility declined. To maintain the Soviet Union's superpower status, resources were diverted to the military sector, gutting the consumer and agricultural spheres. An inefficient economic structure meant that costs of exploiting new natural resource deposits soared. High pollution levels affected health through higher morbidity rates and declining life expectancy. At the same time, liberalization in some Eastern European states and the telecommunications revolution made it increasingly difficult to shield the population from exposure to Western lifestyles and ideas. Among a certain critical portion of the population, aspirations were rising just as the capacity of the system to fulfill them was declining.

Perestroika and Glasnost (1985–1991)

Mikhail Gorbachev took office as a Communist Party leader in March 1985. He endorsed a reform program that centered around four important concepts intended to spur economic growth and bring political renewal. These were *perestroika, glasnost, demokratizatsiia*, and "New Thinking." **Perestroika** (restructuring) involved decentralization and rationalization of economic structures to enable individual enterprises to increase efficiency and take initiative. **Glasnost** (openness) involved relaxing controls on public debate and allowing diverse viewpoints to be aired. **Demokratizatsiia** was an effort to increase the responsiveness of political organs to public sentiment. Finally, "New Thinking" referred to a foreign policy approach involving integration of the USSR into the global economy and emphasizing common challenges facing East and West, such as the cost and hazards of the arms race and environmental degradation.[2] Gorbachev's reform program was designed to adapt the communist system to new conditions rather than to usher in its demise.

The most divisive issues were economic policy and demands for republic autonomy. Only 50.8 percent of the Soviet population was ethnically Russian in 1989. Soon, demands for national autonomy arose in some of the USSR's union republics. This occurred first in the three Baltic republics (Latvia, Lithuania, and Estonia), then in Ukraine, Georgia, Armenia, and Moldova, and finally in the Russian Republic itself. Gorbachev's efforts failed to bring consensus on a new federal system.

Gorbachev's economic policies failed as well. Half-measures sent contradictory messages to enterprise directors, producing a drop in output and undermining established patterns that had kept the Soviet economy functioning, although inefficiently. To protect themselves, regions and union republics began to restrict exports to other regions, despite planning mandates. In "the war of laws," regional officials openly defied central directives.

Just as his domestic support was plummeting, Gorbachev was awarded the Nobel Peace Prize, in 1991. Under his New Thinking, the military buildup in the USSR was halted, important arms control agreements were ratified, and many controls on international contacts were lifted. In 1989, Gorbachev refused to prop up unpopular communist governments in the East European countries. First in Hungary and Poland, then in the German Democratic Republic (East Germany) and Czechoslovakia, pressure from below pushed the communist parties out of power. To Gorbachev's dismay, the liberation of Eastern Europe fed the process of disintegration in the Soviet Union itself.

---

perestroika the policy of restructuring embarked on by Gorbachev when he became head of the Communist Party of the Soviet Union in 1985.

glasnost Gorbachev's policy of "openness" or "publicity," which involved an easing of controls on the media, arts, and public discussion.

demokratizatsiia the policy of democratization identified by former Soviet leader Mikhail Gorbachev in 1987 as an essential component of *perestroika*.

Collapse of the USSR and the Emergence of the Russian Federation (1991 to the Present)

In 1985 Mikhail Gorbachev had drafted Boris Yeltsin into the leadership team as a nonvoting member of the USSR's top party organ, the Politburo. Little did he know the pivotal role that Yeltsin would play in bringing about the final demise of the Soviet Union. In December 1991, Yeltsin joined the leaders of Ukraine and Belorussia (later renamed Belarus) to declare the formation of a loosely structured entity, called the Commonwealth of Independent States, to replace the Soviet Union. The Russian Federation now stepped out as an independent country in the world of states.

As leader of the newly independent Russian Federation, Yeltsin took a more radical approach to reform than Gorbachev had done. He quickly proclaimed his commitment to Western-style democracy and market economic reform. However, that program was controversial and proved hard to implement. Russians faced an increasingly uncertain future, declining real wages, high inflation, and rising crime. A major financial crisis in August and September 1998 triggered a political one. Plagued by poor health and failed policies, Yeltsin could hope only to serve out his second presidential term and groom a successor.

In 1999, Yeltsin appointed Vladimir Putin to the post of prime minister of Russia. Putin, a little-known figure from St. Petersburg, was a former KGB operative in East Germany. His political advance was swift, and the rise in his popularity was equally meteoric. In December 1999, Yeltsin resigned as president of the Russian Federation. In the March 2000 elections Putin won a resounding

The White House, seat of the Russian parliament, burns while under assault from troops loyal to President Yeltsin during the confrontation in October 1993. *(Source: AP Images)*

Profile

Boris Nikolaevich Yeltsin

Like so many men of his generation who later rose to top Communist Party posts, Yeltsin's education was technical. His early jobs were as foreman, engineer, supervisor, and finally director of a large construction combine. Yeltsin joined the Communist Party of the Soviet Union (CPSU) in 1961. He made his career in the party, taking on full-time work in the regional party organization in 1968. In 1981, Yeltsin moved on to the national stage, as a member of the Central Committee of the CPSU, and was appointed to the top leadership group in 1985.

Yeltsin soon gained a reputation as an outspoken critic of party privilege. He became a popular figure in Moscow as he mingled with average Russians on city streets and public transport. In 1987, party conservatives launched an attack on Yeltsin for his outspoken positions. Yeltsin was removed from the Politburo and from his post as Moscow party leader in 1988. At the party conference in June 1988, Yeltsin defended his position in proceedings that were televised across the USSR; Russian citizens were mesmerized by this open display of elite conflict. Yeltsin's popular support soared as he single-handedly took on the party establishment.

Yeltsin articulated a radical reform path, in contrast to Gorbachev's gradualism. His political base was in the Russian Republic, one of the fifteen republics of the USSR. Under Yeltsin's leadership on June 8, 1990, the Russian Republic declared sovereignty (not a declaration of independence, but an assertion of the right of the Russian Republic to set its own policy). One month later, Yeltsin resigned his party membership. On June 12, 1991, Yeltsin became president of the Russian Republic through direct popular vote, establishing his democratic credentials. (Gorbachev never faced direct popular election.)

During an attempted coup d'état by party conservatives in August 1991, Yeltsin took a firm stand against the plotters while Gorbachev remained captive at his *dacha* in the Crimea. Yeltsin's defiance gave him a decisive advantage in the competition with Gorbachev and laid the groundwork for the December 1991 dissolution of the USSR engineered by Yeltsin (representing Russia) and the leaders of Ukraine and Belorussia.

In 1992, Yeltsin began implementing his radical reform policy in the newly independent Russian Federation. Unfortunately, economic crisis, rising corruption and crime, and a decline of state authority ensued. His reputation as a democratic reformer was marred by his use of force against the Russian parliament in 1993 and in the Chechnya war in 1994–1996. In December 1999, in the face of plummeting popularity, failing health, and an increasingly evident alcohol problem, Yeltsin resigned, appointing Vladimir Putin as acting president. However, by 2004 Yeltsin was expressing disillusionment with the direction of Putin's political reforms: "The stifling of freedoms and the rolling back of democratic rights will mean, among other things, that the terrorists will have won."* Mixed reviews of Yeltsin's achievements followed his death on April 23, 2007. Although some hailed his contribution to the development of Russian democracy, others decried his ineffectiveness in realizing those values. ❖

*"Yeltsin fears for Russia freedoms," *BBC News*, September 17, 2004, http://news.bbc.co.uk/2/hi/europe/3663788.stm (accessed May 12, 2005).

victory, with an even stronger show of support in elections that followed for the *Duma* in December 2003 and for the presidency in March 2004. Putin benefited from auspicious conditions, as high international gas and oil prices fed tax dollars into the state's coffers; in 1999, the economy began a period of sustained economic growth, the first in over a decade.

After September 11, 2001

After September 11, 2001, President Putin expressed solidarity with the American people in their struggle against terrorism. Terrorist attacks in Russia reinforced a sense of common purpose between the two world powers, but Russia withheld its support for the American incursion into Iraq, opening a period of renewed tension between the two countries. Still an outsider as more and more neighboring states joined NATO and the European Union (EU), Russia faced the issue of how to balance its global, European, and Eurasian roles.

Themes and Implications

Historical Junctures and Political Themes

In the 1990s Russia's status as a world power waned, and the expansion of Western organizations (NATO, EU) to Russia's western border undermined its sphere of influence in Central and Eastern Europe. Russia's western neighbors, except Belarus, looked more to Europe than to Russia as a guidepost for the future. But Russia's economic recovery, the rise of energy prices and Europe's dependence on imports of Russian natural gas and oil provided an important basis for Russia's renewed international influence. No longer simply a supplicant in its relationship to the West, Russia reasserted itself as a major European power in 2005 under Putin's leadership. September 11, however, provided a new impetus for Russia's claim to be a key link in the antiterrorist chain, alongside the United States. Ironically, however, the war on terrorism expanded American influence into Russia's traditional sphere of influence as U.S. bases were established in post-Soviet Central Asia (as well as neighboring Afghanistan), creating the potential for new tensions between Russian and the United States.

By the late 1990s, the Russian public was disillusioned and distrustful of its leaders, and resentment remained over the disappointing results of the Western-inspired reform program. In recent years, however, the population has shown a marked increase in economic confidence and senses a return to some degree of normalcy in everyday life. Nonetheless problems remain. Wide disparities in wealth and income, as well as important regional inequalities, continue to plague the system. Reforms that weakened the social welfare system in 2005 fed fears that the state would not assure fulfillment of basic needs for those at the bottom of the social ladder.

The relationship between President George W. Bush and Russian President Vladimir Putin reflects moments of tension in the light of Russian objections to the U.S.-led invasion of Iraq and U.S. criticism of Russian political developments. *(Source: AP Images)*

FOCUS QUESTIONS

How has Russia had to redefine its place in the world since the breakup of the Soviet Union? What were its principal challenges in the earlier period? What are they now?

On the positive side, the constitution adopted in 1993 has gained a surprising level of public acceptance, even as observers express intensifying concern about the democratic credentials of the Russian system. Key reforms after 2000 have seemed to undermine prospects for real political competition, accompanied by increased controls on the electronic media (especially TV). United Russia, favored by Putin, emerged as the dominant political party in the lead up to elections in December 2007 for the State *Duma* (the upper house of the legislature). Despite speculation, in 2008 Putin could not run for office again due to a constitutional provision prohibiting a third consecutive term as president. However, Putin identified a preferred successor, Dmitry Medvedev (since 2005 first deputy prime minister), who stood as the "establishment" candidate in the March 2008 presidential race. There was widespread speculation that Putin might be appointed prime minister after leaving the presidency.

The loss of superpower status, the dominance of Western economic and political models, and the absence of a widely accepted ideology have all contributed to uncertainty about what it means to be Russian and where Russia fits into the world as a whole. Meanwhile, Russia itself suffers from internal divisions. Overt separatism has been limited to the Republic of Chechnya, but differing visions of collective identity have emerged in some of Russia's ethnic republics, particularly in Muslim areas. Social class, a linchpin of Soviet ideology, may take on increasing importance in defining group solidarity, as working people seek new organizational forms to assert their rights. Changing gender roles have challenged both men and women to reconsider not only their relationships to one another, but also the impact of these changes on children and community values.

Summary

Russian history has been characterized by a series of upheavals and changes that have often made life unpredictable and difficult for the citizen. The revolutions of 1917 replaced tsarist rule with a political system dominated by the Communist Party. In the Stalinist period Communist rule involved a process of rapid industrialization, collectivization of agriculture, and purges of the party, followed by large losses of population associated with World War II. With the death of Stalin came another important transition, as politics was transformed into a more predictable system of bureaucratic authoritarianism, characterized by relative stability but without political competition or democratic control. The most recent transition, ushered in by the collapse of Communist Party rule in 1991, resulted in the emergence of the Russian Federation as an independent state. The new Russia experienced an almost immediate period of economic decline and halting efforts to democratize the system in the 1990s. However, since 1999, the economy has taken a turn for the better, at the same time that limits on political competition seem to be reversing some of the democratic gains of the 1990s. Throughout its entire history, Russian leaders have struggled to maintain control over a large expanse of territory with an ethnically diverse population, in part the legacy of Russia's imperial past.

SECTION 2: Political Economy and Development

Market reforms introduced after 1991 brought a dramatic decline in economic performance and fundamental changes in social relationships. The Russian government struggled to create tools to regulate the new market forces. Since 1999, after an unprecedented period of economic depression, Russia experienced renewed economic growth (see Table 5.2). Rising energy prices and the 1998 ruble devaluations were important factors in this economic revival; experts disagreed about the role of the Russian government's economic policies. Developing a more balanced economic structure that could weather global shocks or falling oil or natural gas prices remains an important challenge.

State and Economy

The Soviet Economy

FOCUS QUESTION
Describe Russia's principal problems in moving from a command economy toward a market economy. What are the principal advantages and disadvantages of each form of economy?

In the Soviet period, land, factories, and all other important economic assets belonged to the state. Short- and long-term economic plans defined production goals, but these were frequently too ambitious to be fulfilled. Except in the illegal black market and peasant market, prices were controlled by the state. Firms and individuals were not permitted to develop direct links to foreign partners; these were all channeled through the central economic bureaucracy.

The Soviet economic model registered some remarkable achievements: rapid industrialization, provision of social welfare and mass education, relatively low levels of inequality, and advances in key economic sectors such as the military and space industries. Nonetheless, over time, the top-heavy nature of Soviet planning could no longer deliver increased prosperity at home and competitive products for export. Furthermore, the Soviet economy legacy complicated economic reform efforts due to a sagging infrastructure, outdated equipment, and inefficient production practices.

State and Economy in the Russian Federation

market reform a strategy of economic transformation that involves reducing the role of the state in managing the economy and increasing the role of market forces.

shock therapy a variant of market reform that involves the state simultaneously imposing a wide range of radical economic changes, with the purpose of "shocking" the economy into a new mode of operation.

In 1992, Boris Yeltsin endorsed radical **market reform**, sometimes referred to as **shock therapy**. The changes were to be rapid and thorough. Although shock therapy would inevitably throw large parts of the economy into an initial downward spin, reformers hoped that the initial jolt would be followed by a quick recovery.

Four main pillars of reform were (1) lifting price controls, (2) encouraging small private businesses and entrepreneurs, (3) privatizing most state-owned enterprises, and (4) opening the economy to international influences. The immediate impact of the reforms on the Russian public was dramatic. In January 1992, price controls on most goods were loosened or removed entirely. The consumer price index increased by about 2,500 percent between December 1991 and December 1992. Real wages declined by 50 percent.

TABLE 5.2

Economic Indicators for the Russian Federation (percent change from the previous year unless otherwise indicated)

	1991	1992	1993	1994	1995	1996	1997	1998	1999	2000	2001	2002	2003	2004	2005
Economic growth	−5.0	−14.5	−8.7	−12.6	−4.0	−3.5	0.9	−5.3	6.4	10.0	5.1	4.7	7.3	7.1	6.4
Industrial production	−8.0	−18.8	−16.2	−22.6	4.7	−6.5	0.3	−5.2	11.0	11.9	4.9	3.7	7.0	7.3	4.0
Consumer price inflation	93	1526	875	307	197	48	15	28	86	21	22	16	14	12	11
Unemployment rate	n.a.	4.8	5.5	7.5	8.8	9.3	10.7	12.3	12.6	9.8	8.9	8.6	8.4	8.0	7.6
Rubles per one USD[a]	169	415	1247	3550	4640	5560	5960	20.7	26.8	28.2	30.1	31.8	29.5	28.5	28.3
Population (in millions, Jan. 1)[b]	148.3	148.9	148.7	148.4	148.3	148.0	147.1	146.5	146.0	145.2	144.5	144.0	145.0	144.2	143.2

[a]At year end; figures for 1998 and after are in new redenominated rubles, where one new ruble = 1,000 old rubles. The redenomination occurred in January 1998.
[b]January 21, 2005—143.5.

Sources:

Data from 1991–2001 are reprinted from *Introduction to Comparative Politics* (Houghton Mifflin, 2004), 361; updates for 2002–2004 and some adjustments to previous data are from *EBRD Transition Report* 2004, and World Bank, *Russian Economic Report* (April 2005) (www.worldbank.org.ru); population figures are from State Statistical Agency of the Russian Federation, http://194.84.38.65/mdb/upload/RERIO.eng.pdf.

joint-stock company a business firm whose capital is divided into shares that can be held by individuals, groups of individuals, or governmental units.

insider privatization the transformation of formerly state-owned enterprises into joint-stock companies or private enterprises in which majority control is in the hands of employees and/or managers.

privatization voucher a certificate worth 10,000 rubles issued by the government to each Russian citizen in 1992 to be used to purchase shares in state enterprises undergoing privatization.

Privatization was rapid compared to other postcommunist countries. By early 1994, 80 percent of medium-sized and large state enterprises in designated sectors of the economy had been transformed into **joint-stock companies**. The most widely adopted method for privatizing state enterprises, called **insider privatization**, gave managers and workers of the enterprise (jointly) the right to acquire a controlling packet (51 percent) of enterprise shares at virtually symbolic prices. Each citizen of Russia was issued a **privatization voucher** with a nominal value of 10,000 rubles (about ten U.S. dollars).

Many analysts believe that insider privatization hampered reform of business operations and reduced the expected gains of privatization. Managers, many of whom did not have the skills needed to operate in a market environment, were reluctant to lay off excess labor or resisted overtures by outside investors who might gain control of the enterprise. Some managers extracted personal profit from enterprise operations rather than investing available funds to improve production. Productivity and efficiency did not increase significantly; unprofitable firms continued to operate; investment was weak; and the benefits of ownership were not widely or fairly distributed. The government continued to subsidize ineffective operations, leaving most Russian firms uncompetitive.

In 1995, a second stage of privatization was launched; firms could sell remaining shares for cash or investment guarantees. However, many firms were unattractive to potential Russian and foreign investors because their backward technology would require massive infusions of capital for restructuring. Some of the more attractive enterprises fell into the hands of developing financial-industrial conglomerates that had acquired their wealth through positions of power or connections in the government. At the same time, new ventures, which were generally more efficient than former state firms, faced obstacles: confusing regulations, high taxes, lack of capital, and poor infrastructure (transport, banking, communications).

Reform of agriculture was even less satisfactory. Large joint-stock companies and associations of individual households were created on the basis of former state and collective farms. These privatized companies operated inefficiently, and agricultural output declined. Foreign food imports also undercut domestic producers, contributing to a downward spiral in agricultural investment and production.

By the late 1990s, it appeared that the government's reform program had failed (see Figure 5.2). Russia was in the grip of a severe depression. Industrial production was less than half the 1990 level. The depression fed on itself, as declining capacity in one sector deprived

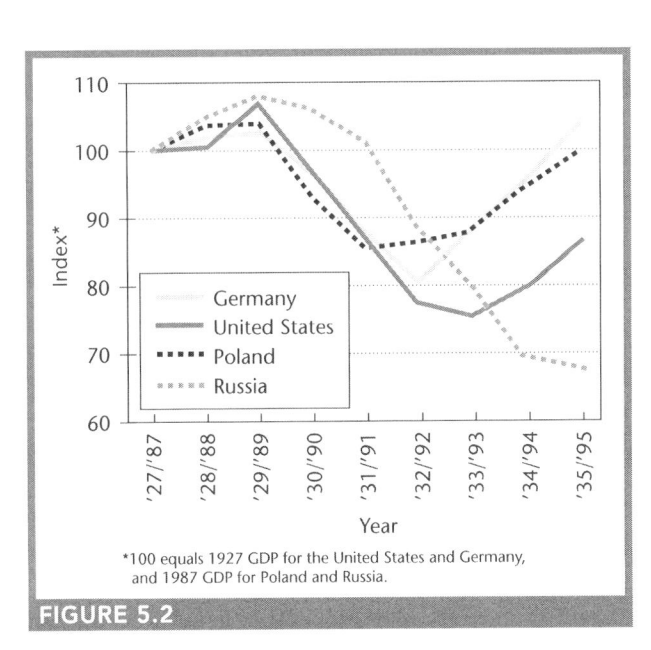

FIGURE 5.2

Downturn of the Russian Economy

Source: Copyright © 2002 by the National Bureau of Asian Research. Reprinted from Millar, James, R. "Normalization of the Russian Economy: Obstacles and Opportunities for Reform and Sustainable Growth," *NBR Analysis* 13, no. 2, April 2002, by permission of the National Bureau of Asian Research.

other sectors of buyers or suppliers. Even the state was behind in its wage, social benefit, and pension payments.

A key obstacle to the success of the market reform agenda was the weakness of state institutions. Without an effective tax collection system, for instance, the government cannot acquire revenues needed to pay its own bills on time, to provide essential services to the population, and to ensure a well-functioning economic infrastructure (such as transportation, energy, public utilities). State action is also needed to regulate the banking sector and to enforce, health, safety, and labor standards. If the state fails to carry out these functions, businesses may take matters into their own hands, for example, by hiring private security services, turning to the mafia for protection, or by paying bribes. Weak government feeds corruption and criminality, producing risks both to business and to the population at large.

The central state in Moscow also had difficulty exerting its authority in relation to regional authorities and in the face of increasing power of business **oligarchs**. These oligarchs, wealthy individuals who benefited from the privatization process, often held significant political influence as well.[3] Diverse methods of laundering money to avoid taxes became widespread. Corruption involving government officials, the police, and operators abroad fed a rising crime rate. Rich foreigners, Russian bankers, and outspoken journalists became targets of the Russian **mafia**. Policies of the Russian government itself had contributed to the creation of this new group of financial and business oligarchs.

A financial crisis in August 1998 brought the situation to a head. The government successively took on new loans at progressively higher rates of interest in order to pay off existing debts, creating a structure of **pyramid debt**. Following a sharp upturn in 1996–1997, in August 1998 the Russian stock market lost

oligarchs a small group of powerful and wealthy individuals who gained ownership and control of important sectors of Russia's economy in the context of the privatization of state assets in the 1990s.

mafia a term borrowed from Italy and widely used in Russia to describe networks of organized criminal activity.

pyramid debt a situation when a government or organization takes on debt obligations at progressively higher rates of interest in order to pay off existing debt.

Russian oil oligarch Mikhail Khodorkovsky, shown under arrest, displayed in a cage. (Source: © Alexander Natruskin/ Reuters/Corbis)

over 90 percent of its value. The government defaulted on its bonds. Many Russian banks, holders of the Russian government's short-term bonds, faced imminent bankruptcy. The government began to print more of the increasingly valueless rubles, threatening to undermine the ruble's value further and thus intensify the underlying financial crisis.

The government finally allowed a radical devaluation of the ruble. Within a two-week period, the ruble lost two-thirds of its value against the U.S. dollar, banks closed or allowed only limited withdrawals, supplies of imported goods decreased, and business accounts were frozen—forcing some firms to lay off employees and others to close their doors. Despite its immediate disastrous effects, the 1998 financial crisis ushered in positive changes. First, the devalued ruble made Russian products more competitive with foreign imports. Firms were able to improve their products, put underused labor back to work, and thus increase productivity. The state budget benefited from improved tax revenues. Barter declined, as did payment arrears.[4] Economic growth revived, beginning in 1999.[5] See Figure 5.3.

Experts have continued to debate the contribution of government policy to Russia's economic recovery. After a sluggish first year, an active legislative program emerged under President Putin. A 13 percent flat income tax, deemed easier to enforce, was one very visible aspect of the package. Other developments fueled optimism about Russia's economic future. A budget surplus replaced a deficit. The foreign debt load declined from 90 percent of GDP in 1998 to 28 percent in 2004.[6] By 2005 Russia had accumulated foreign reserves (including gold) of over $182 billion. Prospects for Russia's membership in the World Trade Organization also fueled optimism about Russia's trade growth.

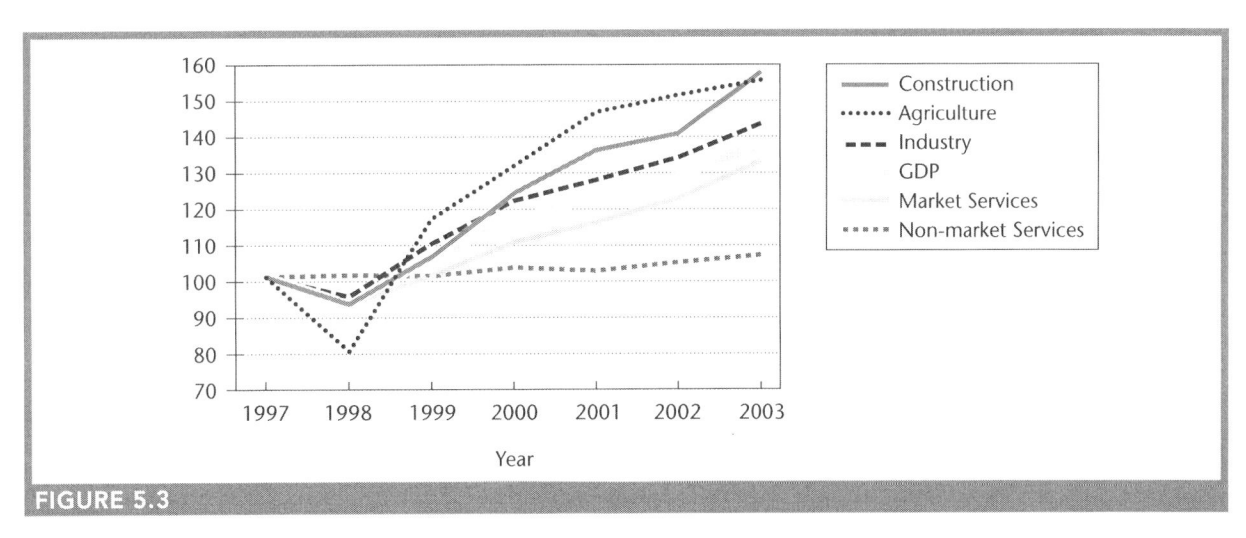

FIGURE 5.3

Economic Recovery Since 1998

Source: Data from the World Bank; http://194.84.38.65/mdb/upload/PAR_020805_eng.pdf.

Meanwhile, Putin made clear that economic oligarchs who used their financial positions to affect political outcomes would suffer sanctions. Charges of tax evasion and fraud were brought again media moguls, presented as part of the government's campaign to assure proper business practices. However, critics felt that enforcement efforts were selectively directed at critics of the government. One media magnate who had publicly criticized the Kremlin, Boris Berezovsky, fled to self-imposed exile in the United Kingdom. A particularly prominent case involved Mikhail Khodorkovsky, the chief executive officer and major shareholder of the giant Russian oil company Yukos. In October 2003 Khodorkovsky was placed under arrest for fraud and tax evasion, and in May 2005, he was sentenced by a Russian court to nine years in prison. Critics of the government charged that the process was motivated by political considerations because Khodorkovsky had provided financial support to opposition parties. The attack on Yukos undermined investor confidence with fears that political pretexts might justify future government economic takeovers.

Society and Economy

Soviet Social Policy

> **FOCUS QUESTIONS**
> In what ways did Soviet social policies accommodate or violate Russian social values?
> Have recent Russian policies done a better or worse job of accommodating these values?

The Soviet leadership established priorities with little input from society. One was military production, but the regime's social goals also produced some of the most marked achievements of the Soviet system. Benefits to the population included free health care, low-cost access to essential goods and services, maternity leave (partially paid), child benefits, disability pensions, and mass education. Universal access to primary and secondary schooling led to nearly universal literacy in a short period of time. Postsecondary education was free of charge, with state stipends provided to university students.

Guaranteed employment and job security were other priorities. Almost all able-bodied adults worked outside the home. Citizens received many social benefits through the workplace, making it a social as well as an economic institution. The full-employment policy made unemployment compensation unnecessary. Modest pensions were guaranteed by the state, ensuring a stable but minimal standard of living for retirement.

Although basic social needs were met, the Soviet system was plagued by shortages and low-quality service. For example, advanced medical equipment was in limited supply; sometimes under-the-table payments were required to prompt better-quality service. Many goods and services, although economically in the reach of every citizen, were in short supply. Queues were a pervasive part of everyday life. Housing shortages restricted mobility and forced young families to share small apartments with parents. Labor in many sectors was in constant short supply, reflecting the inefficient use of the work force. Productivity was low by international standards, and work discipline weak; drunkenness, and absenteeism were not unusual. A Soviet saying illustrated the problem: "We pretend to work, they pretend to pay us."

As a matter of state policy, wage differentials between the best- and worst-paid were lower than in Western countries. Although reflecting cultural values, this approach reduced the incentive for outstanding achievements and innovation. Due to state ownership, individuals could not accumulate wealth in real estate, stocks, or businesses. Privileges that did exist were modest by Western standards. Although political elites had access to scarce goods, higher-quality health care, travel, and vacation homes, these privileges were hidden from public view.

Economic Reform and Russian Society

The Soviet experience led Russians to expect the state to assure a social welfare network, but in the 1990s, budget constraints necessitated cutbacks, just when social needs were greatest. In line with the new market ideology, tuition fees for postsecondary education were introduced in many cases. Although universal health care remained, higher-quality care and access to medicine depended more obviously on ability to pay. Benefits provided through the workplace were cut back, as businesses faced pressures to reduce costs.

Some groups have benefited from the reform process, for example, those with foreign language skills and highly skilled employees in the natural resource sectors (such as oil and gas), in banking and finance. At the top of the scale are the super-wealthy, including people who took advantage of privatization to gain positions in lucrative sectors like banking, finance, oil, and gas.

But losers have been more numerous. Poverty is highest among rural residents, the unemployed, children, the less educated, pensioners, and the disabled. As a result of low wage levels, the majority of those in poverty are the working poor. Other groups suffered dramatic declines in income, including unskilled laborers in low-priority sectors of the economy and people working in the public service such as education. Consumer price inflation gradually declined over the 1990s but still had an important impact on incomes.[7] Unemployment has been lower than expected because many enterprises kept underemployed staff on their rolls, at low wages or with temporary layoffs. Official estimates are about 9.8 percent in 2000 and between 7 and 9 percent in 2004 and 2005, but actual rates are probably higher.[8] Social impacts of economic stress have included higher rates of crime, suicide, and mortality; alcoholism has continued to be a significant problem, particularly for males. All of these factors have increased the likelihood of dysfunctional family structures, producing a particularly marked impact on children.

With the economic upturn following 1999, large differentials in income and wealth remain, but the portion of the population living below the subsistence level has declined noticeably (from 27.3 percent of the population in 2001 to 15.8 percent in 2005). In addition average real disposable income has increased. Since 2000, levels of personal consumption have grown following years of decline, but many individuals (particularly men) have two to three jobs just to make ends meet. Public opinion surveys indicate that between 2003 and 2006 most Russians expected little change in the economic situation of their families

Moscow protest against cuts in social benefits in 2005. *(Source: © Smolsky Sergei/ITAR-TASS/Corbis)*

in the near future.[9] Social indicators of economic stress have begun to decline only slowly.

A particularly contentious issue led to massive street demonstrations in several Russian cities in early 2005 over changes to social welfare policy. Called "monetarization of social benefits," the reforms involved replacing certain services (such as public transport) that were provided free to disadvantaged groups (pensioners, veterans, the disabled) with a modest monetary payment to the individual. Subsidies for public utilities and housing were also reduced. Many Russians viewed the measures as direct reductions in social welfare benefits for the neediest in society. After large-scale demonstrations, the government agreed to accompany the reforms by a modest increase in pensions and to restore subsidized transport. Although Putin's popularity suffered a temporary decline, it rebounded quickly.

In the post-Soviet period, women continue to carry the bulk of domestic responsibilities while still working outside the home to boost family income. Many women take advantage of the permitted three-year maternity leave, which is only partially paid. Fathers play a relatively small role in child rearing; many families rely on grandparents to help out. Some data suggest, however, that while women are more likely to register with unemployment offices, levels of actual unemployment are about equal for men and women.[10]

Russia has seen a steady decline in population since 1992, as the birthrate fell from 16.6 births per 1,000 people in 1985 to about 10 in 2004.[11] Life expectancy for Soviet men fell from sixty-six years in 1966–1967 to fifty-nine in 2007 (from seventy-four to seventy-three for women).[12] The decline in population has been tempered by the immigration of ethnic Russians from other former Soviet republics (see Figure 5.4). Although declining birth rates often accompany economic modernization, in the 1990s many couples were especially reluctant to have children because of daily hardships, future uncertainty, a declining standard of living, and continuing housing shortages. To boost the birthrate, in May 2006 Putin announced a doubling of monthly child support payments and a large monetary bonus for women having a second child.

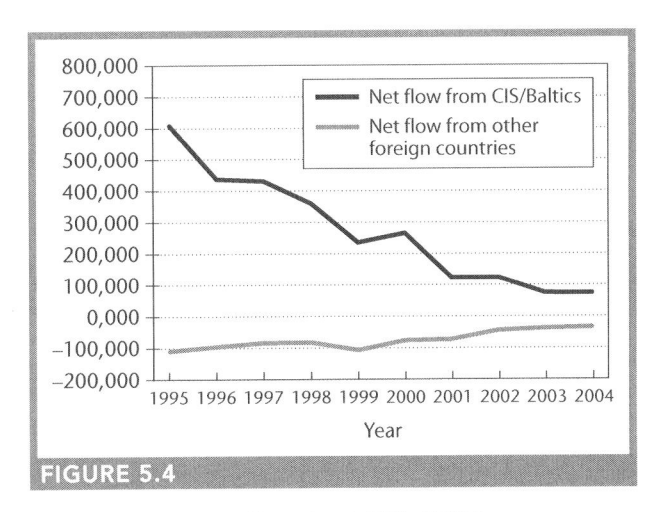

FIGURE 5.4

Immigration into Russia, 1995–2004

Source: Russian Annual Statistical Report 2003; Current Statistical Survey, no. 1 (48) 2004; and website of the Federal Statistical Agency of the Russian Federation, www.gks.ru.

Russian Political Culture and Economic Change

Alongside more objective factors, culture affects economic change. Several aspects of Russian culture may have inhibited adaptation to a market economy: a weak tradition of individual entrepreneurship, widespread commitment to egalitarian values, and reliance on personal trust rather than written contracts. Profit is less important to many Russians than support for friends and coworkers; thus, firing redundant workers may be unpalatable. Business partners or personnel may be selected by personal contacts and relationships rather than by merit. Incentive structures of the Soviet period also have been internalized by older population groups, including features that encourage risk avoidance, low productivity, poor punctuality, absenteeism, lack of personal responsibility and initiative, and a preference for security over achievement.[13]

However, young people in Russia are adapting to a new work environment. Younger Russians are not only more flexible due to their age, but they also have different expectations from their elders. Consequently, they are more supportive of the market transition and are more oriented toward maximizing self-interest and demonstrating initiative. Nevertheless, many Russians of all age groups still question values underlying market reform, preferring an economy that is less profit driven and more oriented to equality and the collective good.

FOCUS QUESTION

As Russia has become more closely tied to the world economy, what are the principal economic adjustments that Russia has had to make?

Russia in the Global Economy

Right up to the end of the Soviet period, the economy remained relatively isolated from outside influences. Foreign trade was channeled through central state organs, so individual enterprises had neither the possibility nor the incentive to seek external markets. Over time, restrictions on foreign investment have been lifted, the ruble has been allowed to respond to market conditions, and firms are allowed to conclude agreements directly with foreign partners. In response, in the 1990s, Western governments (especially Germany) made fairly generous commitments of technical and humanitarian assistance. The World Bank, the IMF, and the EU also contributed substantial amounts of economic assistance, often in the form of repayable credits. In the past, release of IMF credit, issued to stabilize the ruble, was made contingent on Russia's pursuing a strict policy of fiscal and monetary control and lifting remaining price controls. The Russian government had difficulties in meeting these conditions, and thus the funds were released intermittently. After the August 1998 crisis, the Russian government defaulted first on the ruble-denominated short-term debt and then on the former Soviet debt. Since then, debt repayments have been made on time. In 2001, the government decided to forgo additional IMF credits. By 2004, it had paid off its IMF debt and, bit by bit, has cut its remaining debt obligation.[14]

Russia has had problems attracting foreign investment. Levels still remain low compared to other East European countries, despite some improvements since 2004. An upward trajectory was interrupted by the 1998 financial crisis. Major sources of foreign direct investment since 2000 have been Germany, the United States, and Cyprus (mainly recycled Russian capital, exported earlier for tax reasons). The focus of Russia's foreign trade activity has shifted significantly since the Soviet period. In 2004, Russia's foreign trade with countries of the expanded EU (more than 50 percent of the total) far exceeded combined exports to countries of the Commonwealth of Independent States (CIS).[15] In 2004, the EU confirmed its support for Russian membership in the World Trade Organization (WTO) and in November 2006 the United States and Russia agreed on a trade pact that overcame another obstacle to Russia's admission.

With a highly skilled work force and an advanced technological base in some sectors, Russia has many of the ingredients necessary to become a competitive and powerful force in the global economy. However, excessive reliance on natural resource exports will leave Russia vulnerable to global economic fluctuations in supply and demand. At the same time, these resources give Russia advantages compared to its neighbors, since these expensive materials do not need to be imported. Ultimately, Russia's position in the global economy will depend on the ability of the country's leadership to fashion a viable approach to domestic economic challenges and to facilitate differentiation of the country's export base.

Summary

If the heavy hand of state control contributed to the inefficiency of the Soviet economy, in the postcommunist period the new Russian state has often been ineffective in providing the legal framework and institutional structures necessary for the new market economy. In the early 1990s, the government lifted price controls, privatized state enterprises, and opened the economy to international influences. The result was rapid inflation, a fall in the standard of living, and dramatic economic decline even more extreme than the Great Depression of the 1930s in the West. In postcommunist Russia a wider range of goods has been available to the consumer, but many people have difficulty making ends meet and inequality increased dramatically compared to the Soviet period. Under Soviet rule, Russians came to expect the government to provide a certain level of social welfare, including guaranteed employment, subsidized prices on basic necessities, easy access to recreational facilities, and universally free higher education. Market economic reform undermined many of these policies, and some Russians felt that Western economic models were not well suited to Russia. With the revival of economic growth since 1999, the situation has improved, but the Russian economy is highly dependent on exports of oil, gas, and other natural resources, making it susceptible to global economic influences.

SECTION 3 Governance and Policy-Making

When Russia became an independent country in December 1991, dramatic changes in state structure and governing processes followed. The new Russian leadership endorsed liberal democratic principles, and in April 2005 Putin declared, "[T]he development of Russia as a free and democratic state [is] the main political and ideological goal."[16] Over time, however, skeptics abound as Putin's measures to strengthen presidential power seem to many to have undermined some of the Russian Federation's founding democratic principles.

Organization of the State

FOCUS QUESTION
How is the federal system of the Russian Federation different from the Soviet federal system or the American federal system?

Ratification of a new Russian constitution in 1993 was a contested political process that followed a violent confrontation between the president and the parliament. Nonetheless, the new constitution has acquired broad-based popular legitimacy. The document affirms many established principles of liberal democratic governance—competitive multiparty elections, separation of powers, an independent judiciary, federalism, and protection of individual civil liberties. However, another key feature is the strength of the president's executive power. Nonetheless, in the 1990s the state demonstrated only a weak capacity to govern. During Putin's presidency (2000–2008), the power of the office was augmented in an effort to address the weakness of central state authority.

Between 1991 and 1993, negotiations between the central government and the various regions created a complicated federal structure with eighty-nine federal units (by mid-2008 reduced to eighty-three, through mergers). Some of these subnational governments demanded increased autonomy, even sovereignty, generating a process of negotiation and political conflict between the center and the regions that sometimes led to contradictions between regional and federal laws. The relationship between organs of the federal government itself also involved intense conflict. The constitution makes the executive dominant but still dependent on the agreement of the legislative branch to realize its programs. Tension between the two branches of government, which are selected in

The Chechnya Crisis

Despite its small size and population (estimated at 600,000 in 1994), the breakaway republic of Chechnya holds an important position on Russia's southern border. It is widely perceived as a safe haven for criminal elements that operate in Russia. In the early 1990s, the Russian leadership feared that Chechnya's attempted secession from the Russian Federation might embolden other republics to pursue a similar course and might lead to loss of control over Caspian Sea oil reserves. These concerns motivated Russia to send troops into Chechnya on December 11, 1994, fueling a regional civil war.

Before its incorporation into the Russian Empire in 1859 and again in 1917, local forces fought to maintain Chechnya's independence. In 1924, Chechnya was made part of the USSR, and in 1934 it was joined with an adjacent region, Ingushetia, to form a single autonomous republic within the Soviet Union.

In October 1991 the newly elected president of the republic, Dzhokar Dudaev, declared Chechnya's independence from Russia. In 1992, Checheno-Ingushetia was officially recognized by the Russian government as two separate republics. Intervention by Russian military forces in December 1994 evoked heated criticism within Russia. Some opposed the intervention completely, favoring a political solution; others were primarily critical of the ineffective manner in which the war effort was carried out. Civilians in Chechnya and the surrounding regions suffered at the hands of both sides, and the war imposed heavy economic costs on Russia and called into question the competence of the Russian military. The unpopular war became an important issue in the 1996 presidential campaign and threatened to undermine Yeltsin's already fragile support. In late May 1996, a cease-fire agreement was signed, and in June, Yeltsin decreed the beginning of troop withdrawals. In September 1996, an agreement with the rebels was again signed. The joint declaration put off a decision on Chechnya's status for five years, leaving the issue unresolved.

On January 27, 1997, an election was held for the president of the Republic of Chechnya. Observers generally considered the vote to be fair, with 79 percent of the eligible population participating. In a race involving thirteen candidates, Aslan Maskhadov received 59 percent of the vote. Relative to other leading candidates, Maskhadov was considered to be a moderate. However, he publicly supported Chechnya's independence, and later, after he was removed from power by Moscow, he became a rebel leader and was killed by Russian forces in March 2005.

In 1999, terrorist bombings, attributed to Chechen rebels, occurred in apartment buildings in Moscow and two other Russian cities, causing about 300 deaths. The second war in Chechnya was launched largely in response to these events. Allegations of human rights violations were made both against Russian troops and Chechen rebels; Western governments and international organizations such as Human Rights Watch demanded that the Russian government comply with international human rights standards. Russian authorities continue to resist external involvement in the situation, maintaining that the Chechnya crisis is a domestic political issue. President Putin has repeatedly emphasized links between Chechen rebels and international terrorist networks, including Al Qaeda, in an effort to gain Western acceptance for Russia's military actions.

The string of terrorist attacks by Chechen rebels since 1999, intensifying in 2004 with the Beslan tragedy, placed the problem clearly in the public mind. In March 2003, Russian authorities tried to set Chechnya on a track of normalization by holding a referendum on a new constitution in the republic that would confirm Chechnya's status within the Russian Federation. In October 2003, Akhmad Kadyrov was elected president of Chechnya with Russian support, only to be killed by Chechen rebels the next year. In July 2006 the radical insurgent Shamil Basayev, who claimed responsibility for the Beslan hostage taking, was killed, reportedly by Russian security forces. ❖

Source: Adapted from *Introduction to Comparative Politics*, 3rd ed. Copyright 2004 by Houghton Mifflin Company. Reprinted with permission.

nomenklatura a system of personnel selection in the Soviet period under which the Communist Party maintained control over the appointment of important officials in all spheres of social, economic, and political life.

republic one of 21 territorial units in the Russian federation defined by the constitution of 1993 to be among the 89 members of the federation and named after the indigenous non-Russian population group that inhabits the republic.

krai one of the six territorial units in the Russian Federation defined by the constitution of 1993 to be among the 89 members of the federation, with a status equal to that of the republics and oblasts.

oblast one of 49 territorial units in the Russian Federation defined by the constitution of 1993 to be among the 89 members of the federation, with a status equal to that of the republics and *krai*.

autonomous okrug one of originally 10 territorial units of the Russian Federation defined in the 1993 constitution to be among the 89 members of the federation, but reduced to 4 by 2008 as some of these ethnically-based units have been merged with the *oblast* or *krai* in which they are located.

separate electoral processes, was a persistent obstacle to effective governance under Yeltsin. The executive itself has two heads (the president and the prime minister), introducing another venue for intrastate tension. Establishing real judicial independence remained a significant political challenge. Finally, poor salaries and lack of professionalism in the civil service opened the door to corruption and political influence. Putin's centralizing measures tried to address all of these areas of contention, but, some would argue, in so doing may have undermined the very checks and balances that were supposed to offer protection against reestablishment of authoritarian control.

Many of the difficulties facing the new Russian state are, at least in part, legacies of the Soviet period. Following the collapse of the USSR, the new political leadership tried to wipe the slate clean and start anew. However, some observers see in Putin's reforms a reversion to practices and patterns reminiscent of the Soviet period, namely, centralization of power and obstacles to effective political competition. Other analysts interpret these measures as necessary to solidify rule of law and the state's capacity to govern.

The Soviet State

Before Gorbachev's reforms, top organs of the Communist Party of the Soviet Union (CPSU) dominated the state. The CPSU was hierarchical. Lower party bodies elected delegates to higher party organs, but elections were uncontested, and top organs determined candidates for lower party posts. The Politburo, the top party organ, was the real decision-making center. A larger body, the Central Committee, represented the broader political elite, including regional party leaders and representatives of various economic sectors. Alongside the CPSU were Soviet state structures that formally resembled Western parliamentary systems but had little decision-making authority. The state bureaucracy had day-to-day responsibility in both the economic and political spheres but followed the party's directives. People holding high state positions were appointed through a system (called the ***nomenklatura***) that allowed the CPSU to fill key posts with politically reliable individuals. The Supreme Soviet, the parliament, was a rubber-stamp body.

The Soviet constitution was of symbolic rather than operational importance since many of its principles were ignored. The constitution provided for legislative, executive, and judicial organs, but separation of powers was considered unnecessary because the CPSU claimed to represent the interests of society as a whole. When the constitution was violated (as it frequently was), the courts had no independent authority to protect its provisions.

The Soviet Union was also designated a federal system; but this was phony federalism, since all aspects of life were overseen by a highly centralized Communist Party. Nonetheless, the various subunits that existed within the Russian Republic (***autonomous republics, krais, oblasts,*** and ***okrugs***) were carried over into the Russian Federation in an altered form.

Gorbachev introduced competitive elections, increased political pluralism, reduced Communist Party dominance, revitalized the legislative branch of

The U.S. Connection
Federalism in the United States and Russia

Like the United States, Russia is, according to its constitution, a federal system. This means that powers are divided between the central government (located in Moscow in Russia, or Washington, D.C., in the United States) and the constituent units. When the Russian constitution was adopted in 1993 there were eighty-nine federal units; due to mergers, in mid-2008 there were eighty-three compared to the fifty U.S. states.

Federalism operates quite differently in the two countries. In comparison to the American system, the Russian structure seems complicated. Russia's multiethnic population underlies this complexity because diverse ethnic groups in Russia are regionally concentrated, forming the basis for some of the federal units. Although the United States has racial and ethnic diversity, this does not affect the way the states were formed.

Some of Russia's federal units are called republics, while others are called *oblasts* (regions), *krais* (another type of region), autonomous *okrugs* (districts), or cities of federal status (Moscow and St. Petersburg). The twenty-one "republics" and the smaller autonomous *okrugs* are named after non-Russian ethnic groups that reside there. If you think this is complicated, some federal units are located within other federal units, leading to the term "*matrushka* federalism," a name inspired by the Russian wooden dolls that are nested one inside another.

As in the United States, Russia's federal units are represented in the upper house of the national legislature (in the United States in the Senate, in Russia called the Federation Council). In the United States, two senators from each state are directly elected by the people. In Russia, each region also has two representatives, but their method of selection has been a point of contest. In 1993 they were elected directly by the population. From the mid-1990s, the elected governor (or chief executive) of each region and the head of the regional legislature themselves sat in the Federation Council. Since 2000 the system has again shifted so that these representatives are appointed, one by the region's governor and the other by the region's legislature. All of these changes have occurred in less than fifteen years, making it hard for Russian citizens to keep up.

In the 1990s Russia's federal government had difficulty controlling what happened in the regions; regional laws sometime deviated or even violated federal law. Bilateral treaties between the federal government and some of the republics and regions granted special privileges, producing what some called "asymmetrical federalism." Since 2000, President Putin put measures in place to ensure a greater degree of legal and political uniformity throughout the country. Seven federal districts were created to monitor implementation of federal policy in the regions. Beginning in 1996 regional governors were directly elected, but in 2004 this was replaced by a quasi-appointment procedure. These centralizing measures have led some observers to question whether Russian is really a federal system at all. Like the United States, Russia does have a constitutional court to resolve disputes over the jurisdictions of the federal government and the states (regions), but in Russia the constitution does not provide a strong basis for regional power, whereas in the United States, both through court cases and through legislative acts, states' rights have often been effectively defended. ❖

government, and renegotiated the terms of Soviet federalism. He also tried to bring the constitution into harmony with political reality. Many constitutional amendments were adopted that altered existing political institutions. These changes moved the political system haltingly and unevenly closer to the liberal democratic systems of the West. However, ultimately they led to the collapse of the Soviet system itself.

The New Russian State

Even before the collapse of the USSR, political institutions began to change in the Russian Republic, a constituent unit of the Soviet Union. A new post of president was created, and on June 12, 1991, Boris Yeltsin was elected by direct popular vote as its first incumbent. Once the Russian Federation became independent, a crucial turning point was the adoption by referendum of a new Russian constitution in December 1993. This constitution provides the legal foundation for current state institutions (see Figure 5.5). But political practice goes far beyond constitutional provisions and sometimes alters their interpretation.

The Executive

FOCUS QUESTIONS

In what ways has the executive branch of government become less centralized than it was in Soviet times? Are recent centralization measures changing this?

The constitution establishes a semipresidential system, formally resembling the French system but with stronger executive power. The president, who holds primary power, is the head of state, and the prime minister, appointed by the president but approved by the lower house of the parliament (the State *Duma*), is the head of government. This dual executive can introduce tensions within the executive branch, as well as between the president and the *Duma*. As a rule of thumb, the president has overseen foreign policy, relations with the regions, and the organs of state security, while the prime minister has focused his attention on the economy and related issues. However, with Yeltsin's continuing health problems in 1998 and 1999, operative power shifted in the direction of the prime minister. Following the election of Vladimir Putin in March 2000, however, the primary locus of power returned to the presidency.

In December 1999, Yeltsin resigned from office, making the prime minister, Vladimir Putin, acting president until the March 2000 elections, which he won handily. Putin's 2004 electoral victory was even more stunning (71 percent of the vote), but some international observers alleged that media bias raised questions about its genuine democratic character. Although the constitution excludes three consecutive terms as president, speculation is rife as to whether Putin might seek to return to the post after a break in his term of office beginning in 2008.

One of the president's most important powers is the authority to issue decrees, which Yeltsin used frequently to address contentious issues. Although presidential decrees may not violate the constitution or legislation passed by the bicameral legislature (the Federal Assembly), policy-making by decree can allow the president to ignore an uncooperative or divided parliament. Yeltsin's decision in 1994, and again in 1999, to launch the offensive in Chechnya was not approved by either house of parliament, despite strong objections from a broad range of political groups.

The president can also call a state of emergency, impose martial law, grant pardons, call referenda, and temporarily suspend actions of other state organs if he deems them to contradict the constitution or federal laws. Some of these actions must be confirmed by other state organs (such as the upper house of the

FIGURE 5.5

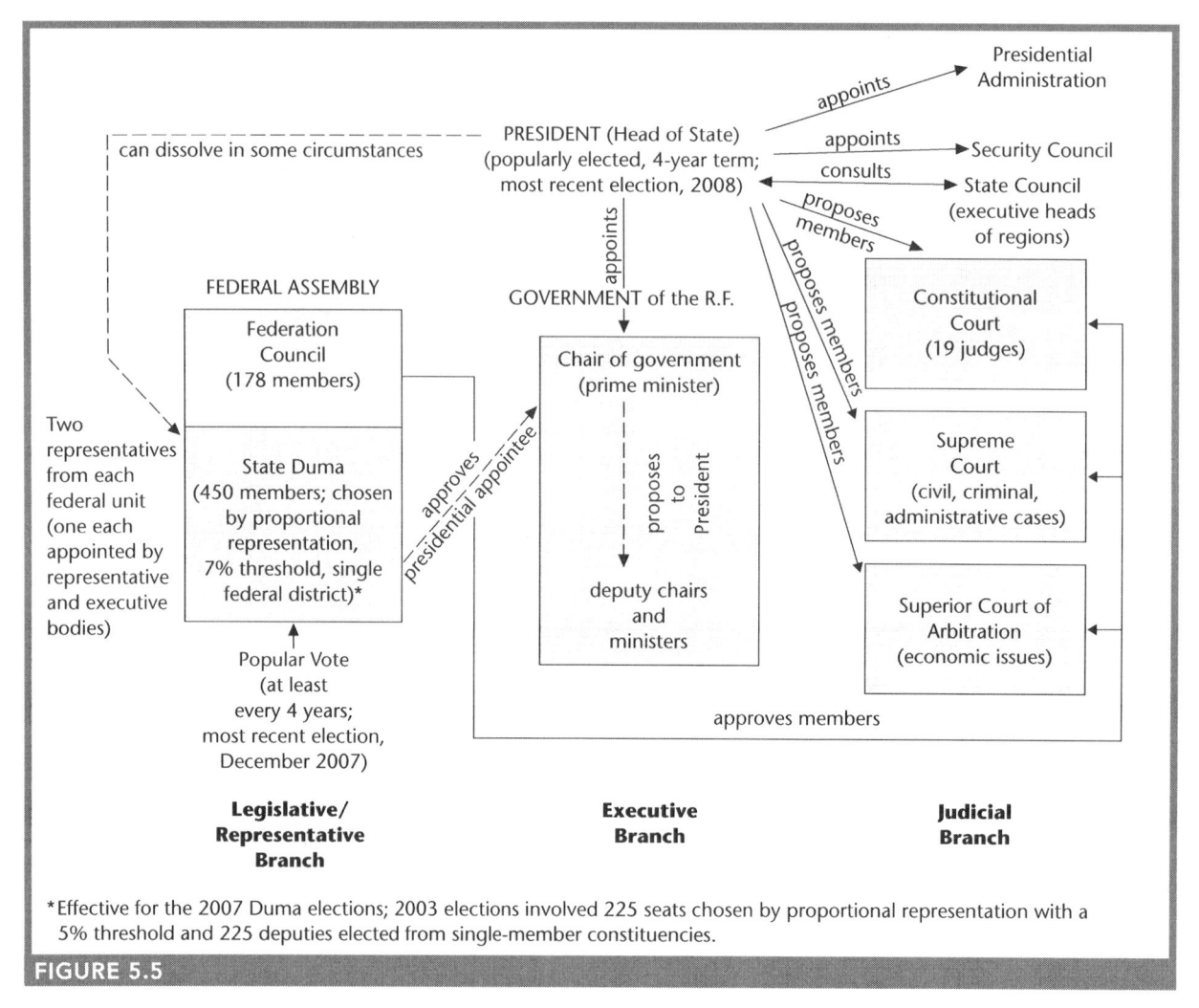

Political Institutions of the Russian Federation (R.F.), 2007

*Effective for the 2007 Duma elections; 2003 elections involved 225 seats chosen by proportional representation with a 5% threshold and 225 deputies elected from single-member constituencies.

parliament, the Federation Council). The president is commander in chief of the armed forces and conducts affairs of state with other nations. Impeachment of the president involves the *Duma*, the Federation Council, the Supreme Court, and the Constitutional Court. If the president dies in office or becomes incapacitated, the prime minister fills the post until new presidential elections can be held.

The Russian government is headed by the prime minister, flanked by varying numbers of deputy prime ministers. The president's choice of prime minister must be approved by the *Duma*. During Yeltsin's presidency, six prime ministers held office. Between 2000 and 2008, Putin had three prime ministers, Mikhail Kosyanov (until February 2004, later turned opposition figure), Mikhail Fradkov (March 2004–September 2007, following a brief period with an interim prime minister), and Viktor Zubkov (from September 2007).

The prime minister can be removed by the *Duma* through two repeat votes of no confidence passed within a three-month period. The *Duma* has ultimately been reluctant to consistently defy the president because rejection of the candidate three times can lead to dissolution of the *Duma* itself. The prime minister has never been the leader of the dominant party or coalition in the *Duma*. Principles of party accountability that apply in most Western parliamentary systems are not operative in Russia. Without disciplined parties and with no formal links between parties and the executive branch, the process of gaining *Duma* acceptance of government proposals depends on the authority of the president and on the particular configuration of power at the moment.

The National Bureaucracy

Efforts to downsize the executive bureaucracy have been only partially successful. Alongside the state bureaucracy is the presidential administration, which serves the president directly. Some government ministries (such as the Foreign Affairs Ministry, the Federal Security Service, and the Defense Ministry) report directly to the president.[17] The president has created various advisory bodies that solicit input from important political and economic actors and also co-opt them into support for government policies. The most important are the Security Council and the State Council. Formed in 1992, the Security Council advises the president in areas related to foreign policy and security (broadly conceived) and includes heads of appropriate government bodies (the so-called power ministries such as Defense and the Federal Security Service), the prime minister, and in recent years the heads of seven newly created federal districts. The State Council was formed in September 2000 as part of Putin's attempt to redefine the role of regional leaders in federal decision making (see below). A smaller presidium, made up of seven of the regional heads selected by the president, meets monthly.

The bureaucratic agencies include ministries, state committees, and other agencies. Ministers other than the prime minister do not require parliamentary approval. The prime minister makes recommendations to the president, who appoints these officials. Ministers and other agency heads are generally career bureaucrats who have risen through an appropriate ministry, although sometimes more clearly political appointments are made. Many agencies have been reorganized, often more than once. Top leaders also use restructuring to place their clients and allies in key positions. For example, Putin has drawn heavily on colleagues with whom he worked earlier in St. Petersburg or in the security establishment, referred to as **siloviki**, in staffing a variety of posts in his administration. In an effort to increase the role of merit and the professional character of the civil service, the president himself initiated a process of civil service reform in August 2002; legislation to begin the reform passed in 2004.

In Putin's restructuring of government agencies, a new Ministry for Economic Development and Trade took over functions of several previously existing ministries, as did a new Ministry of Industry, Science, and Technology. Observers question whether such reorganizations produce substantive benefits, and some are particularly controversial. Functions of the State Committee on Northern Affairs were transferred to the Ministry for Economic Development and Trade, viewed by some as a downgrading of northern concerns on the government's agenda.

siloviki derived from the Russian word *sil*, meaning "force." Russian politicians and government officials drawn from security and intelligence agencies, special forces, or the military, many of whom were recruited to important political posts under Vladimir Putin.

Other State Institutions

> **FOCUS QUESTIONS**
>
> How have the military, judiciary, and subnational governments evolved since the fall of the Soviet Union? Have they gained or lost importance?

The Military and Security Organs

Because of Vladimir Putin's career background in the KGB, he drew many of his staff from this arena. Thus, while the formal rank of the Federal Security Service has not changed, the actual impact of the security establishment took on increasing importance in the Putin era. This development preceded 9/11, and the important role placed on security concerns reflects the orientation of the Russian state under Putin's leadership. Because many Russians are alarmed by the crime rate and terrorist bombings in the country, restrictions on civil liberties have not elicited strong popular concern. At the same time, there is widespread public cynicism about the honesty of the ordinary police (*militsiia*). Such suspicions are likely often correct.[18]

The Russian government attributes repeated bombings since 1999 to Chechen terrorists and has claimed that the terrorists have international links to the Al Qaeda network. The year 2004 was particularly traumatic with the downing of two airliners and a suicide-bomb attack in Moscow in August, followed by the Beslan incident in September. Attacks on civilians by Russian forces in Chechnya have elicited Western human rights protests. Since the September 11 attacks, cooperation between Russian and Western security agencies has increased, as Russia has shared security information. However, closer NATO and American ties in neighboring Georgia have been an irritant to Russia, which sees this region as part of its sphere of influence.

The Soviet military once ranked as one of the largest and most powerful forces in the world, second only to that of the United States and justifying the country's designation as a superpower. The Communist Party controlled military appointments, and the military never usurped political power. During the August 1991 coup attempt, troops remained loyal to Yeltsin and Gorbachev, even though the Minister of Defense was among the coup plotters. In October 1993, despite some apparent hesitancy in military circles, military units defended the government's position, this time firing on civilian protesters and shocking the country.

In the postcommunist period, the political power and prestige of the military have suffered. Both Gorbachev and Yeltsin oversaw a reduction in military expenditures, bringing a decline in facilities and a reduction in conventional and nuclear forces. The military's failure to implement a successful strategy in the Chechnya war led the government to increase the role of the Federal Security Service there instead of relying on the army alone.[19] Reports of deteriorating conditions in some Russian nuclear arsenals have raised international concerns about nuclear security. In addition, the situation of military personnel, from the highest officers to rank-and-file soldiers, has worsened dramatically, producing a potential source of political discontent.

As of 2007, the Russian Federation still maintains a system of universal male conscription, but noncompliance and draftees rejected for health reasons have been persistent problems. A law to permit alternative military service for conscientious objectors took effect in 2004. Although critics of the military service law welcome the concept, they are critical of the restrictive conditions that the law imposes on alternative service. Government proposals to supplement the conscript army by a smaller professional military corps are on the agenda, but there are no definite plans to abolish the military draft,[20] although by 2008 the term of military service had been reduced from two years to one year.

The Judiciary

Concepts such as judicial independence and the rule of law were poorly understood in both pre–Revolutionary Russia and the Soviet era. These concepts have, however, been embedded in the new Russian constitution and are, in principle, accepted both by the public and political elites. However, their implementation has been difficult and not wholly successful.

In Russia, a Constitutional Court was formed in 1991. Its decisions were binding, and in several cases even the president had to bow to its authority. After several controversial decisions, Yeltsin suspended the operations of the court in late 1993. However, the Russian constitution now provides for a Constitutional Court again, with the power to adjudicate disputes on the constitutionality of federal and regional laws, as well as jurisdictional disputes between various political institutions. Justices are nominated by the president and approved by the Federation Council, a procedure that produced a stalemate after the new constitution was adopted, so that the court became functional only in 1995. Since 1995, the court has established itself as a vehicle for resolving conflicts involving the protection of individual rights and conformity of regional laws with constitutional requirements. The court has been cautious in confronting the executive branch, on which it depends to enforce its decisions.

Alongside the Constitutional Court is an extensive system of lower and appellate courts, with the Supreme Court at the pinnacle. These courts hear ordinary civil and criminal cases. In 1995, a system of commercial courts was also formed to hear cases dealing with issues related to privatization, taxes, and other commercial activities. The Federation Council must approve nominees for Supreme Court judgeships, and the constitution also grants the president power to appoint judges at other levels. Measures to shield judges from political pressures include criminal prosecution for attempting to influence a judge, protections from arbitrary dismissal, and improved salaries for judges. The Russian judicial system operates on a civil code system, similar to most of continental Europe. One innovation in the legal system has included introduction of jury trials for some types of criminal offenses.

Subnational Government

The collapse of the Soviet Union was precipitated by the demands of some union republics for more autonomy and, then, independence. After the Russian Federation became an independent state, the problem of constructing a viable federal structure within Russia resurfaced. Between 1991 and 1993, negotiations between the central government and the various regions led to the establishment of a federal structure including eighty-nine units, which have different historical origins and designations (such as republics, territories, and cities with federal status, namely Moscow and St. Petersburg). Mergers of federal units, such as those that occurred recently, are subject to approval by popular referendum.

One of the first issues to arise in the development of Russia's federal system was whether all of the federal units should have equal status. The twenty-one republics viewed themselves as a special category because of their different status in the Soviet period and the presence of significant minority groups within their borders. They have also been the most assertive in putting forth claims for autonomy or even sovereignty. The most extreme example is Chechnya, whose demand for independence has led to a protracted civil war. The ethnic dimension complicates political relations with some of the republics. The titular nationalities of several of the republics, including Tatarstan and Bashkortostan, which occupy relatively large territories in the center of the country, are of Islamic cultural background. Islamic fundamentalism has not, however, been a significant problem in Russia, since decades of Soviet socialization seems to have acculturated most parts of the Muslim population to secular, scientific values.

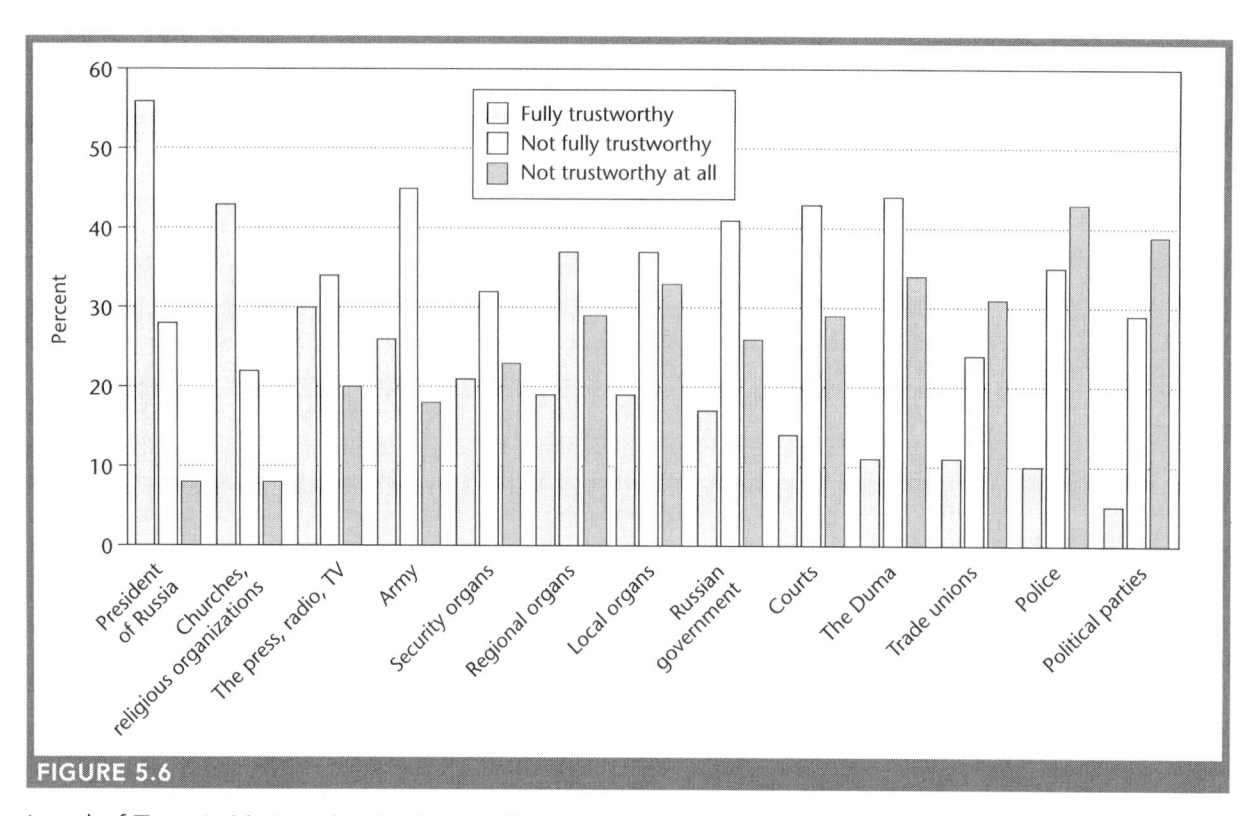

FIGURE 5.6

Level of Trust in Various Institutions in Russia

Source: Levada Center, http://www.levada.ru/press/2004092702.html (accessed April 28, 2005).

Following the March 2000 election Putin identified the establishment of a uniform system of federal-regional relations, governed by uniform legal principles, as an important priority. Steps to realize this objective included harmonization of regional laws and republic constitutions with federal legislation and constitutional provisions. Another measure gave the president the power, pending approval by a court, to remove a governor and disband a regional legislature if they engaged in anticonstitutional activity. In 2002, the Constitutional Court upheld the measure, but with many restrictions.[21]

Other reforms to the federal system introduced by Putin were even stronger measures to strengthen what Putin has called the "**power vertical**." This concept involves the strengthening of an integrated structure of executive power from the presidential level down through to the local level. Critics have questioned whether the idea is consistent with federal principles, and others see it as undermining Russia's fledgling democratic system. A first step in creating the power vertical was the creation of seven federal districts on top of the existing federal units. Although not designed to replace regional governments, the districts were intended to oversee the work of federal offices operating in these regions and to ensure compliance with federal laws and the constitution. Putin's appointees to head these new federal districts included several individuals (all male) with backgrounds in the security or military services, reinforcing concerns that the districts could become a powerful instrument of central control. In practice, the federal districts have been less intrusive in the affairs of the regions than many feared.

A second set of changes to create the power vertical has involved a weakening of the independence of governors (and republic presidents). Yeltsin agreed to their popular election, which gave them greater legitimacy and independence from Moscow. Beginning in 1996, the governors, along with the heads of each regional legislative body, also sat as members of the upper house of the Russian parliament, the Federation Council. This arrangement gave the regional executives a direct voice in national legislative discussions and a presence in Moscow. In 2001, Putin gained approval for a revision to the composition of the Federation Council. Regional executives were, as of January 2002, no longer members of the Federation Council. Rather, one regional representative is appointed by the regional executive and the other by the regional legislature. Some governors resisted this change, seeing it as an assault on their power (they also lost the legal immunity that goes along with being a member of parliament). Putin made concessions to make the change more palatable, for example, giving governors the right to recall their representatives. The State Council was formed to try to assure the regional executives that they would retain some role in the federal policy-making arena, although losing their seats in the Federation Council.

Following the Beslan massacre, Putin identified corruption and ineffective leadership at the regional level as culprits in allowing terrorists to carry out the devastating school hostage taking. Accordingly, he proposed an additional reform that created a decisive element of central control over regional politics. Approved by the State *Duma* in December 2004, the change eliminated popular election of governors. Governors are now nominated by the president and approved by

power vertical a term used by Russian president Vladimir Putin to describe a unified and hierarchical structure of executive power ranging from the federal level to the local level.

the regional legislature. As in the system for approving the prime minister, if the regional legislature refuses the nomination three times, the president may disband the body and call for new elections. With governors and republic presidents dependent on the goodwill of the president for appointment and reappointment, a self-perpetuating political process has taken on a formal character, leading some observers to declare the death of Russian federalism and the weakening of Russian democracy.

The Policy-Making Process

> **FOCUS QUESTIONS**
> What are the principal policy-making bodies in modern Russian?
> To what extent do these bodies really formulate policy, and to what extent do they simply rubberstamp policies that have really been made elsewhere?

Policy-making occurs both formally and informally. The federal government, the president and his administration, regional legislatures individual deputies, and some judicial bodies may, according to the constitution, propose legislation. In the Yeltsin era, conflict between the president and *Duma* made policy-making a contentious and fractious process; under Putin, the *Duma* generally went along with proposals made by the president and the government, and the proportion of legislation initiated by the executive branch increased significantly.

Sometimes, the government, deputies, or parliamentary factions offer competing drafts of laws, leading to protracted and complicated bargaining. In order for a bill to become law, it must be approved by both houses of the parliament in three readings and signed by the president. If the president vetoes the bill, it must be passed again in the same wording by a two-thirds majority of both houses of parliament in order to override the veto. Budgetary proposals can be put forth only by the government, and they have, in the past, elicited sharp controversy in the parliament since proposed budget reductions affect key interests and groups, such as regional and local governments, other state agencies, the military, trade unions, enterprise directors, state employees, and pensioners. Many policy proclamations are made through presidential or governmental decrees, without formal consultation with the legislative branch. This decision-making process is much less visible and may involve closed-door bargaining rather than an open process of debate and consultation.

Informal groupings also have an important indirect impact on policy-making. During the Yeltsin period, business magnates were able to exert behind-the-scenes influence to gain benefits in the privatization of lucrative firms in sectors such as oil, media, and transport. Putin has attempted to reduce the direct political influence of these powerful economic figures and to formalize business input through bodies such as the Entrepreneurship Council. Some observers see this development as an example of corporatism, a system in which the government identifies (or sometimes helps create) organizations that are consulted to represent designated societal interests (in this case, business interests) in the policy-making process. The emerging Russian corporatism seems to be a state corporatist variant, a top-down variety in which the government itself plays an active role in defining these vehicles of societal input.[22] One problem is that some interests, particularly those that are less powerful or well organized, may be excluded from the process. Another less formal linkage between the government and business is through continued government ownership of enterprise shares. This allows the government to influence leadership positions in key firms such as Gasprom, the main exporter of natural gas. Through such personal links, the president can maintain some leverage in the economic sphere, even without a clear policy or legislative basis. In almost all cases, participation in policy-making does not extend to representatives of more broadly based citizens' groups.

A continuing problem is the inefficacy of policy implementation. Under Communist rule, the party's control over political appointments enforced at least some degree of conformity to central mandates. Under Yeltsin, fragmented and decentralized political power gave the executive branch few resources to ensure compliance. Pervasive corruption, including bribery and selective enforcement, hindered enforcement of policy decisions. Although Putin stated his commitment to restrict these types of irregularities, they no doubt continue. However, his commitment to reestablishing order and a rule of law has been an important foundation of his public support and his justification for the centralization of power we have discussed in this chapter.

Summary

When the Russian Federation was formed in 1991, new political structures needed to be constructed. A constitution was adopted in 1993, which involved a directly elected president who had strong political powers. In addition, a federal system was established with the result that the central government had difficulty controlling actions of regional governments in the 1990s. Since 1999, the political system saw increased centralization under Vladimir Putin's leadership, including a harmonization of central and regional laws, quasi-appointment of regional governors, and a more unified executive structure in the country. Under Putin the role of the security forces increased; the military lost its previous stature; and the judiciary took on increased, although not complete, independence. Policy-making is largely under the guidance of the executive organs of the state with little real input or influence from society or political parties. Whereas in the 1990s the relationship between the executive and legislative branches (Federal Assembly) was characterized by conflict that often produced political deadlock, under Putin's leadership the legislative branch was relatively compliant, reinforcing the president's dominant role.

SECTION 4 Representation and Participation

Gorbachev's policies in the 1980s brought a dramatic change in the relationship between state and society, as *glasnost* sparked new public and private initiatives. Most restrictions on the formation of social organizations were lifted, and a large number of independent groups appeared. Hopes rose that these trends might

civil society refers to the space occupied by voluntary associations outside the state, for example, professional associations, trade unions, and student groups.

indicate the emergence of **civil society**, an autonomous sphere of social life that could act on the state without being dependent on it. However, just a few years later, only a small stratum of Russian society was actively engaged; the demands of everyday life as well as cynicism about politics has led many people to withdraw into private life. With minor fluctuations, Putin's approval rating stabilized at 65 to 70 percent after his election in 2000, while trust in public institutions remained low and the public's ability to affect policy seemed questionable.

The Legislature

FOCUS QUESTIONS
What are the functions of the chambers in the Russian legislature? Can the Russian legislature act as an effective check on the executive branch or in representing the population?

The Russian legislature, the Federal Assembly, came into being after the parliamentary elections of December 12, 1993, when the referendum ratifying the new Russian constitution was also approved. The upper house, the Federation Council, represents Russia's constituent federal units. The lower house, the *Duma*, has 450 members and involves direct popular election of candidates and parties. The first Federal Assembly served only a two-year term. Subsequent elections to the *Duma* have occurred every four years, in 1995, 1999, 2003, and 2007.

Within the *Duma*, factions unite deputies from the same or allied parties. The *Duma* also has a number of standing committees; in 2005 all twenty-nine heads came from the dominant United Russia faction, with just six committees having first deputy chairs from other party factions.[23] The *Duma* elects its own speaker (or chair); since July 2003 this has been Boris Gryzlov, head of the United Russia Party, who, in Putin's circles, enjoys the highest level of support next to the president.[24] After the 1995 and 1999 elections, the speaker of the *Duma* came from the Communist Party, which had the highest electoral showing in those votes.

Compared to the Communist period, deputies reflect less fully the demographic characteristics of the population at large. For example, in 1984, 33 percent of the members of the Supreme Soviet were women;[25] in 2005 they constituted less than 10 percent. In 2000, manual workers made up less than 1 percent of *Duma* deputies, in contrast to 35 percent in the 1985 Supreme Soviet.[26]

The upper house of the Federal Assembly, the Federation Council, has two members from each of Russia's federal regions and republics, but the method of selection has varied over time. A new procedure, phased in between 2000 and 2002, involves appointment of one representative by the regional executive and the other by the regional legislature, whereas from 1995 until that time, the elected governor/president of each region and the regional legislative head were themselves members. Many prominent businessmen are among the appointees, and in some cases the posts may be granted in exchange for political loyalty, raising doubts about the likelihood that the body adequately represents interests of the regions.

The constitution grants parliament powers in the legislative and budgetary areas, but if there is conflict with the president or government, these powers can be exercised effectively only if parliament operates with a high degree of unity. In practice, the president can often override the parliament through mechanisms such as the veto of legislation. Each house of parliament has the authority to confirm certain presidential appointees, in addition to the prime minister. The Federation Council must also approve presidential decrees relating to martial law and state emergency, as well as deploying troops abroad.[27]

Following electoral rebuffs in the 1993 and 1995 parliamentary elections, Yeltsin confronted a parliament that obstructed many of his proposed policies, but the parliament did not have the power or unity to offer a constructive alternative. Since the 2003 election, however, the *Duma* has cooperated with the president; in 2006 over two-thirds of the deputies were tied to the dominant United Russia faction, closest to the president, even though this party won only 49 percent of the seats in 2003 Duma election (2003).[28]

Society's ability to affect particular policy decisions through the legislative process is minimal. Parties in the parliament are isolated from the public at large, suffer low levels of popular respect, and the internal decision-making structures of parties are generally elite-dominated. Interest associations to lobby the parliament are weak, and public hearings on controversial issues are rare.

Political Parties and the Party System

FOCUS QUESTIONS

What are the bases of support of the most important Russian political parties?

How has the United Russia Party been able to gain a dominant position in such a short period of time?

One of the most important political changes following the collapse of communism was the shift from a single-party to a multiparty system. In the USSR, the CPSU not only dominated state organs but also oversaw all social institutions, such as the mass media, trade unions, youth groups, educational institutions, and professional associations. It defined the official ideology for the country, set the parameters for state censorship, and ensured that loyal supporters occupied all important offices. Approximately 10 percent of adults in the Soviet Union were party members, but there were no effective mechanisms to ensure accountability of the party leadership to its members.

National competitive elections were held for the first time in the USSR in 1989, but new political parties were not formal participants in Russia until 1993. Since then, a confusing array of political organizations has run candidates in elections (see Table 5.3). Until 2003, these included not only political parties but also political and socioeconomic movements. A new law on political parties went into effect in July 2001; the law tightened the conditions for party formation and registration, which were further strengthened in 2006. Although critics have portrayed these changes as artificially reducing voter choice, defenders argue that they will help to bring order to a chaotic and fragmented party system.

In the 1990s, many parties formed around prominent individuals, making politics very personalistic. Most Russian parties do not have a firm social base or stable constituency. Furthermore, other than the Communist Party, Russian parties are young, so deeply rooted political identifications have not had time to develop. Finally, many citizens do not have a clear conception of their own interests or of how parties might represent them. In this context, image making is as important as programmatic positions, so parties appeal to transient voter sentiments.

TABLE 5.3

Top Parties in the State Duma Elections[a]

Party or Bloc[b]	Percent of 1995 Party List Vote[c]	Percent of 1999 Party List Vote[c]	Percent of 2003 Party List Vote[c]	Percent of Duma Seats 2003[d]	Percent of 2007 Party List Vote[e]	Percent of Duma Seats Based on 2007 Vote	Comments	Party Leader
Centrist/Establishment								
United Russia	—	(23.3)	37.6	49.3	64.1	70.0	Formed as Unity Party in 1999, then merged with Fatherland, All-Russia to form United Russia	Boris Gryzlov, party chair, but Vladimir Putin to head the party list on the ballot (2007)
A Just Russia	—	—	—	—	7.8	8.4	Formed in 2006 from three political parties: Life, Rodina, and the Russian Party of Pensioners	Sergey Mironov
Fatherland, All-Russia	—	13.3	—	—	—	—	Merged into United Russia in 2001	Yuri Lyzhkov, Evgenii Primakov (1999)
Our Home Is Russia	10.1	1.2	—	—	—	—	Chernomyrdin was prime minister, 1992–1998	Viktor Chernomyrdin (1995, 1999)
Liberal/Reform								
Union of Rightist Forces	(3.9)	8.5	4.0	0.7	—	—	Russia's Choice (1993), Russia's Democratic Choice/ United Russia (1995)	Nikita Belykh
Yabloko	6.9	5.9	4.3	0.9	—	—	Opposition liberal/reform party	Grigoriy Yavlinsky

Communist/Socialist

Communist Party of the Russian Federation	22.3	24.3	12.6	11.6	11.6	12.7	Gennady Zyuganov

Nationalist/Patriotic

Liberal Democratic Party of Russia	11.2	6.0	11.5	8.0	8.2	8.9	In 1999 participated in elections as Bloc Zhirinovsky	Vladimir Zhirinovsky
Rodina (Motherland Bloc)	—	—	9.0	8.2	—	—	Left/center nationalist party; merged into A Just Russia	Dmitry Rogozin, Sergey Glaziev (2003)

[a] As of 2008, blocs of parties were not permitted to stand in elections.

[b] Figures may not add to 100 percent or to the total number of deputies in the State Duma because smaller parties and independents are excluded. Table includes only parties winning at least 4.0 percent of the national party list vote in one of the three elections (but not all such parties).

[c] Percentage of the total popular vote the party or bloc received on the proportional representation portion of the ballot in the year indicated. A dash indicates that the party or bloc was not included on that ballot or did not win a significant portion of the vote. Numbers in parentheses are votes for predecessor parties, similar to the one running in 2003.

[d] The sum of seats won in the proportional representation (party list) vote and the single-member district vote. Number of deputies in the faction changed over time following the elections.

[e] In 2007 all of the seats were allocated according to the party list (proportional representation) ballot for parties receiving at least 7% of that vote; the single-member district vote was discontinued. The final distribution of seats in the Duma is an estimate at the time of printing, based on results reported by the Russian Electoral Commission, December 3, 2007.

Source:

Revised from DeBardeleben, Joan, "Russia" in *Introduction to Comparative Politics*. Copyright 2004 by Houghton Mifflin Company. Reprinted with permission; and for the 2003 figures, *The Economist, Country Briefings: Russia*. http://www.economist.com, April 25, 2005.

Since 2003, one political party, United Russia, has taken on political dominance at both the national and regional levels. Although Putin is neither a leader nor member of this party, United Russia serves as a major source of political support for the system of power that has been erected under his leadership.

While individual leaders play an important role in political life in Russia, some key issues have divided opinions in the post-1991 period. One such issue is economic policy. Nearly all political parties have mouthed support for creation of a market economy to replace the centralized Soviet economy. However communist/socialist groupings have been more muted in their support and have argued for a continued state role in providing social protection and benefits for vulnerable parts of the population. The liberal/reform groupings, on the other hand, have advocated more rapid market reform, including privatization, free prices, and limited government spending. The now dominant United Russia party charts a middle ground, appealing to voters from a wide ideological spectrum.

Another dividing line relates to national identity. The nationalist/patriotic parties emphasize the defense of Russian interests over Westernization. They strongly criticize the westward expansion of NATO into regions neighboring Russia; they favor a strong military establishment, protection from foreign economic influence, and reconstitution of some former Soviet republics into a larger federation. Liberal/reform parties, on the other hand, advocate integration of Russia into the global market and the adoption of Western economic and political principles. Again, the United Russia party has articulated an intriguing combination of these viewpoints, identifying Europe as the primary identity point for Russia, but at the same time insisting on Russia's role as a regional power, pursuing its own unique path of political and economic development.

Ethnic and regional parties have not had a significant impact on the national scene. Amendments to the party law make it even more difficult than previously for regional parties to form. Similarly, religion, although an important source of personal meaning, has not emerged as a significant source of political identity for ethnic Russians, who are primarily Russian Orthodox Christians. Nonetheless, in recent years, rising expressions of Russian nationalism and ethnic intolerance, have erupted, particularly in relation to the primarily Muslim Chechens.

Russian political parties do not fit neatly on a left-right spectrum. Nationalist sentiments crosscut economic ideologies, producing the following party tendencies:

- The traditional left, critical of market reform and often mildly nationalistic

- Liberal/reform forces, supporting assertive Western-type market reform and political norms

- Centrist "parties of power," representing the political elite

- Nationalist/patriotic forces, primarily concerned with identity issues and national self-assertion

The most important parties in all four groupings have not challenged the structure of the political system but have chosen to work within it.

The Dominant Centrist Party: United Russia

United Russia's predecessor, the Unity Party, rose to prominence together with Vladimir Putin in the elections of 1999 and 2000. Although Putin is neither head nor member of the party, United Russia is clearly a vehicle for cementing his political power. Following its formation in the late 1990s, the party made a meteoric rise, finishing a close second runner to the CPRF in the 1999 *Duma* elections and winning nearly 50 percent of seats in the *Duma* in 2003. By 2005, through party mergers and individual shifts, 67 percent of *Duma* deputies joined the United Russia faction. In the 2007 Duma elections the party won 64 percent of the vote.

What explains United Russia's success? An important factor is the association with Putin, but the party has also built an effective political machine that could generate persuasive incentives for regional elites. A bandwagon effect and desire to be on the winning side have bolstered the party's fortunes. The party has a rather poorly defined program, which emphasizes the uniqueness of the Russian approach (as distinct from Western models), an appeal to values of order and law, and a continued commitment to moderate reform. The party is truly a party of power, focused on winning to its side prominent and powerful people, who will then use their influence to further bolster the party's support. By 2005, United Russia had, through a combination of carrots and sticks, brought sixty-four regional executives into the fold, along with increased influence in regional legislatures.[29] Combined with increasingly centralized control within the party, the result is a powerful political machine reinforced by the president's power over gubernatorial appointments. At the same time, United Russia's voters represent a broad spectrum of the population and the party has drawn support from every other part of the political spectrum, making the party a catchall electoral organization. A major question in the run-up to the 2007–2008 election cycle in Russia was whether an opposition party would be able pose a real and viable challenge to United Russia's dominance. Some observers speculated that the formation of a second centrist party, A Just Russia, had the blessing of the Kremlin in order to impart the impression that real competition existed in a situation where various informal mechanisms of power were increasingly marginalizing opposition political parties, though, for example, selective enforcement of complex electoral and party legislation. In the 2007 Duma elections the party A Just Russia won just under 8 percent of the vote, reducing its credibility as a viable competitor to United Russia.

The Russian Left: The Communist Party of the Russian Federation

The CPRF was by far the strongest parliamentary party after the 1995 elections, winning over one-third of the seats in the *Duma*. Since then its strength has steadily declined. In May 2005, only 10.4 percent of deputies were in the CPRF faction.[30] The CPRF, the clearest successor of the old CPSU, appears to be a party in decline. With the second strongest showing after United Russia in the 2007 Duma elections, the party nonetheless got only 11.7 percent of the vote.

In addition to its socialist economic approach, the CPRF espouses its own brand of Russian patriotism. The party defines its goals as being democracy, justice, equality, patriotism and internationalism, a combination of civic rights and duties, and socialist renewal. Primary among the party's concerns are the social costs of the reform process. Thus, it has supported state subsidies for industry to ensure timely payment of wages and to prevent enterprise bankruptcies. Support for the party is especially strong among older Russians, the economically disadvantaged, and rural residents. It appears to represent those who have adapted less successfully to the radical and uncertain changes of recent years, as well as some individuals who remain committed to socialist ideals. Its principal failures have been an inability to adapt its public position to attract significant numbers of new adherents, particularly among the young, as well as the absence of a charismatic and attractive political leader. Although one might expect Russia to offer fertile ground for social democratic sentiments like those that have been successful in the Scandinavian countries of Western Europe, the CPRF has not capitalized on these sentiments, nor has it made room for a new social democratic party that could be more successful.

Liberal/Reform Parties

The liberal/reform parties have found it hard to build a stable and unified electoral base. Many Russians held aspects of the liberal program, such as privatization and shock therapy, responsible for Russia's economic decline. Since the first competitive elections in 1993, various liberal/reform parties have split the vote among themselves. On November 21, 1998, the brutal murder by contract killers of the liberal/reform politician and *Duma* member Galina Starovoitova (one of Russia's most prominent female politicians) resulted in renewed efforts to form a united political bloc in the form of the Union of Rightist Forces (URF).[31] In 1999, the URF received only 8.5 percent of the party-list vote, while another liberal reform party, Yabloko, with its more critical stance toward the government, ran separately, polling just 5.9 percent. In 2003, for the first time, neither Yabloko nor the URF reached the 5 percent cutoff; thus, this tendency is currently not represented in the *Duma* at all, following further electoral declines in 2007.

These groups espouse a commitment to traditional liberal values, such as a limited economic role for the state, support for free-market principles, and the protection of individual rights and liberties. The unpopularity of Yeltsin's reform approach undermined their support. Although liberal/reform figures are often referred to as the "democrats" many Russians associate them with Russia's economic and national decline, thus giving the word *democrat* a negative connotation in some circles. Support for liberal/reform parties generally is stronger among the young, the more highly educated, urban dwellers, and the well-off.

Nationalist/Patriotic Parties

The Liberal Democratic Party of Russia (LDPR), headed by Vladimir Zhirinovsky, got the strongest support on the party ballot in 1993, winning almost 23 percent of the vote; this declined to 11 percent in 1995 and 6 percent in 1999, but rebounded to 11.5 percent in 2003, and 8.2 percent in 2007, placing a close third behind the Communist Party. Neither liberal nor particularly democratic in its platform, the party might more properly be characterized as nationalist and populist. Zhirinovsky openly appeals to the anti-Western sentiments that grew in the wake of Russia's decline from superpower status and the government's perceived groveling for Western economic aid. Concern with the breakdown of law and order seems to rank high among its priorities. Zhirinovsky's support has been especially strong among working-class men and military personnel. Continuing support for the LDPR and the increasingly nationalist tone in the programs of other parties suggest that nationalist sentiment in Russia is increasing, not declining.

Elections

FOCUS QUESTIONS

In what ways have Russian elections come to resemble elections in the United States or Western Europe? In what ways are they different?

The initial euphoria with the competitive electoral structure has been replaced by voter fatigue, although turnout in federal elections remains respectable, generally between 60 and 70 percent, but somewhat lower (56 percent) in the 2003 *Duma* election. In 2006 national legislation removed the requirement of a minimum 50 percent turnout to make an election valid. National elections receive extensive media coverage, and campaign activities begin as long as a year in advance. Elections are now big business, involving extensive use of polling firms and public relations experts. Up until 2003, national elections were generally considered to be reasonably fair and free, but international observers expressed serious concerns about the conduct of the 2003 and 2007 votes and the campaigns that preceded them.[32]

Up through 2003, the electoral system for selecting the *Duma* resembled the German system, combining **proportional representation** with winner-take-all districts. Half of the 450 deputies were selected on the basis of nationwide party lists, with any party gaining 5 percent of the national vote entitled to a proportional share of these 225 seats. The remaining 225 deputies were elected in **single-member plurality districts**; these races usually involved local notables. The final balance of forces in the parliament was determined by the combined result of the party-list vote and the single-member district votes. Some independent candidates joined party factions once they are in the *Duma*. Until 1999, despite the electoral rebuffs in 1993 and 1995, Yeltsin did not install a prime minister reflecting party strength in the *Duma*. In 1999 and 2003, parliamentary elections offered qualified support for the government.

In 2005, changes to the electoral law were approved, to take effect with the 2007 *Duma* elections. These involved abolition of the single-member districts, subsuming selection of all 450 deputies on the party-list ballot into one national proportional representation district, with a minimum threshold for representation raised to 7 percent. Parties are required to include regional representatives on their lists from across the country. Although this aspect of the legislation appears to prevent dominance by Moscow-based or other regional cliques, it is not clear whether this will be the actual effect, given strong central control within some

proportional representation (PR) a system of political representation in which seats are allocated to parties within multi-member constituencies, roughly in proportion to the votes each party receives.

single-member plurality district an electoral system in which candidates run for a single seat from a specific geographic district.

party structures. In addition, the overall reform has a strongly centralizing character. Over time, the number of successful parties is likely to decline, and these parties will probably be more dependent on national party machines. Higher hurdles for competing parties to gain representation may mean reduced opportunities for public input. These changes, plus allegations of interference with nomination and party registration processes, may reduce the effectiveness of elections as vehicles of popular control.

Since 1999, opposition parties have experienced a sharp decline in electoral success, with the rapid ascent of the United Russia party. One reason is genuine popular support for Putin, as well as the failure of the opposition parties to develop appealing programs or field attractive candidates. Media coverage has also favored the "party of power" and the president. Administrative control measures and selective enforcement have delimited the scope of acceptable political opposition, particularly when this has involved potential elite support for challengers. In addition, the carrot-and-stick method has wooed regional elites, producing a bandwagon effect, reinforced by the abolition of gubernatorial elections. Dependent on the president's nomination for reappointment, regional leaders have a further incentive to support the president's political position. Finally, potential opposition forces have been co-opted through party mergers and through formation of fellow-traveler parties (such as the Rodina Party before the 2003 election and A Just Russia before the 2007 election).

Results of presidential elections have not mirrored parliamentary election outcomes, and Russia has yet to experience a real transfer of power from one political grouping to another, which some scholars consider a first step in consolidating democratic governance. Under the Russian constitution, presidential elections are held every four years. If no candidate receives a majority of the votes in the first round, a runoff election is held between the two top contenders. In the 2000 and 2004 elections, runoff election was not required because Putin gained over 50 percent of the popular vote in the first round of voting.

Political Culture, Citizenship, and Identity

FOCUS QUESTIONS

How has Russian political culture evolved since the Soviet era?
Has Russian political culture become closer to Western patterns, or is it evolving in unique directions?

Political culture can be a source of great continuity in the face of radical upheavals in the social and political spheres. Attitudes toward government that prevailed in the tsarist period seem to have endured with remarkable tenacity. These include a tradition of personalistic authority, highly centralized leadership, and a desire for an authoritative source of truth. The Soviet regime embodied these and other traditional Russian values, such as egalitarianism and collectivism. At the same time, the Soviet development model glorified science, technology, industrialization, and urbanization—values superimposed on the traditional way of life of the largely rural population. When communism collapsed, Soviet ideology was discredited, and the government embraced Western political and economic values. Many citizens and intellectuals are skeptical of this "imported" culture, partly because it conflicts with other traditional civic values such as egalitarianism, collectivism, and a broad scope for state activity.

Public opinion surveys suggest considerable support for liberal democratic values such as an independent judiciary, a free press, basic civil liberties, and competitive elections. Colton and McFaul conclude from survey results that "a significant portion of the Russian population acquiesces in the abstract idea of democracy without necessarily looking to the West for guidance."[33] The authors find that Russians are divided on the proper balance between defense of individual rights and the maintenance of order. Other experts conclude that Russians' desire for a strong state and strong leaders does not imply support for authoritarian government.[34] On the other hand, democratic values may not be deeply enough entrenched to provide a safeguard against authoritarian rule.

In the USSR, just over 50 percent of the population was ethnically Russian. Since most of the major ethnic minorities now reside in other Soviet successor states, Russians now make up just under 80 percent of the population. The largest minority group is the Tatars, a traditionally Muslim group residing primarily in Tatarstan, a republic of Russia. Other significant minorities are the neighboring Bashkirs, various indigenous peoples of the Russian north, the many Muslim groups in the northern Caucasus region, and ethnic groups (such as Ukrainians and Armenians) of other former Soviet republics. Some 25 million ethnic Russians reside outside the Russian Federation in other former Soviet republics.

The Russian language itself has two distinct words for *Russian: russkii*, which refers to an ethnicity, and *Rossiiskii*, a broader concept referring to people of various ethnic backgrounds included in Russia as a political entity. Although the civic definition forms the basis of citizenship, both anti-Semitic and anti-Muslim sentiments surface in everyday life. Muslim groups from Russia's southern regions have been the target of ethnic stereotyping. In addition, refugee flows from some of the war-torn regions of the Tran-Caucasus (Georgia, Azerbaijan, and neighboring regions of southern Russia such as Chechnya and Ingushetia) have heightened national tensions.

Today, the Russian Orthodox Church appeals to many citizens who are looking for a replacement for the discredited values of the Communist system. A controversial law, directed primarily at Western proselytizers, passed in 1997, made it harder for new religious groups to organize. Human rights advocates and foreign observers protested strongly, again raising questions about the depth of Russia's commitment to liberal democratic values.

In the Soviet period, the mass media, the educational system, and a variety of other social institutions played a key role in propagating the party's political values. Now, students are presented with a wider range of views, and the print media represent a broad spectrum of political opinion. But the electronic media increasingly reflects the government position. The electronic media are particularly susceptible to political pressure, given the costs and limited availability of the technology needed to run television stations. Unequal media access, in favor of the pro-presidential forces, was criticized by international observers in relation to recent elections. Financial interests and mafia attacks on investigative journalists have inhibited press freedom, and journalists have been frequent targets of political killings.

Interests, Social Movements, and Protest

FOCUS QUESTIONS
What kinds of social movements have become prominent since the fall of the Soviet Union? Do these movements reflect longstanding Russian values, or are they reactions to changing social conditions?

Since the collapse of the USSR, numerous political and social organizations have sprung up in every region of Russia, representing the interests of groups such as children, veterans, women, environmental advocates, pensioners, and the disabled. Many observers saw such blossoming activism as the foundation for a fledgling civil society that would nurture the new democratic institutions established since 1991. Despite limited resources and small staffs, these nongovernment organizations (NGOs) provided a potential source of independent political activity. However, there have been many obstacles to realizing this potential. In the past, many groups relied on Western aid to support their activities, potentially diverting them from concerns of their constituents to priorities of their foreign sponsors. Others depend on support from local governments or commercial activities.

In January 2006 Putin signed legislation amending laws on public associations and noncommercial organizations. These controversial changes, protested widely by Western governments, placed new grounds for denying registration to such organizations, established new reporting requirements (particularly for organizations receiving funds from foreign sources), and increased government supervisory functions. Particular requirements are placed on foreign noncommercial nongovernmental organizations operating in Russia; accordingly, several foreign organizations, such as Amnesty International and Human Rights Watch, were forced to temporarily suspend activities while seeking to comply with the new requirements. The new measures were justified as necessary to respond to external terrorist threats, but many commentators saw them as an effort to reduce the likelihood that civil society activists with external contacts might foment a colored revolution in Russian similar to what happened in Ukraine in 2004 or in Georgia in 2005.

The government has also attempted to channel public activism through official forums, such as the Civic Forum, an unprecedented all-Russian congress of nongovernmental organization activists held in November 2001 in Moscow. A new initiative is the Public Chamber, created in 2005 by legislation proposed by the president. Based on voluntary participation by presidential appointees and representatives recommended by national and regional societal organizations, the organization is presented as a mechanism for public consultation and input, as well as a vehicle for creating public support for government policy. It appears to reflect a corporatist approach that might serve to co-opt public activists from more disruptive forms of self-expression. Putin supporters have encouraged the formation of public associations, such as the youth group Nashi ('Our') that support the president's approach.

The year 2005 commenced with an outburst of public protests, mainly associated with cutbacks in social benefits, as noted in Section 2. Despite such sporadic outbursts, at present, one cannot say that civil society has really formed in Russia. Social forces still do not easily find avenues to exert constructive and organized influence on state activity. Russian citizens seem to sway between

The U.S. Connection

Journalism and Freedom of the Press in the United States and Russia

Freedom of the press is considered a fundamental safeguard of democracy in the United States, protected by the constitution itself. The Russian constitution also states that "freedom of the mass media shall be guaranteed. Censorship shall be prohibited." This is an important statement, since censorship was a key element of the system of political control in the Soviet Union.

In the United States, the media not only provide up-to-date information about current issues, but journalists often perform an important watchdog function, helping to keep public figures accountable to the public. Investigative journalists can have a big impact; investigative work on the Watergate break-in, carried out by *Washington Post* reporters Carl Bernstein and Bob Woodward, laid the groundwork for the eventual resignation of Richard M. Nixon.

Most Americans wouldn't consider journalism a particularly dangerous profession unless posted abroad to a war zone. However in Russia journalists investigating sensitive topics are often at risk. A high profile victim, Anna Politkovskaia, was shot on October 7, 2006, at her apartment building in Moscow. Politkovskaia, a reporter for the independent newspaper *Novaia gazeta*, was an outspoken critic of the government, focusing on violations of human rights in Chechnya. Another prominent victim, Dmitriy Kholodov (1994), died when a bomb exploded in the editorial office of the popular Russian newspaper *Moskovskii Komsomolets*. Khodolov had highlighted corruption in the Russian army.

According to the Committee to Protect Journalists, an international NGO devoted to protecting press freedom, these cases are among forty-three journalists murdered in Russia since 1993, making Russia one of the most dangerous countries for journalists in the world.* Although many of the deaths are related to reporting in war-torn Chechnya, others could be classified as contract murders or assassinations. Why are journalists at risk in Russia? A fundamental cause is the incapacity of the state to protect the security of its citizens. Businessmen, politicians, and even scholars have also been targets of contract murders.

Freedom of the press faces other threats in Russia too. Although Russians have access to a wide range of independent newspapers, readership has declined radically since the Soviet period, and news coverage in particular outlets is often openly biased. The lack of a vibrant civil society may also partly explain the inadequate public base to generate newspapers in Russia with high professional standards comparable to the *New York Times* or the *Washington Post*.

An independent international organization, Reporters Without Borders, placed Russia 147th out of 168 countries surveyed, based on a press freedom index. The organization cited increasing control of major media outlets by industrial groups close to Putin. While powerful economics interests own major media outlets in the United States as well, their direct impact on media operations is limited by public expectations about journalistic standards and media objectivity.

Although ranking substantially better than Russia, the United States placed fifty-third on the index, along with Botswana, Tonga, and Croatia. In commenting on this evaluation, the organization's website notes the failure of federal courts to protect journalists' right not to reveal sources, as well as President Bush's suspicion of journalists questioning the war on terrorism. ❖

---

*Committee to Protect Journalists, "Journalists Killed: Statistics and Background," http://www.cpj.org/killed/killed_archives/stats.html (accessed Dec. 31, 2006).

activism and apathy, and the political system wavers along a path between fledgling democratic innovations and renewed authoritarianism.

Summary

The bicameral legislature of the Russian parliament has played a relatively ineffective role in policy-making throughout the postcommunist period, despite its legal power to approve legislation. In the 1990s the legislature lacked the necessary unity to act decisively. Despite the introduction of competitive elections, political parties have had a hard time establishing themselves as credible vehicles of popular influence; most political parties have weak linkages to society, are strongly marked by the image of their leaders, and have not played a significant role in forming the government. High levels of political party fragmentation characterized Russian politics until 2003, when United Russia, a party of the political establishment, established itself as the dominant political force in the country, enjoying a rapid rise in electoral success and popular support. This was in part due to its close association with Vladimir Putin and partly due to a "bandwagon" effect in which regional politicians and other important political figures have rushed to join the "party of power." While elections in the 1990s were considered by most international observers to be relatively fair, observers now have greater doubts about whether there is a level playing field, as opposition forces have been subject to various types of political controls that limit their ability to gain support or even compete in elections.

SECTION 5: Russian Politics in Transition

In April 2005, Putin made a dramatic admission: "Above all, we should acknowledge that the collapse of the Soviet Union was a major geopolitical disaster of the century. As for the Russian nation, it became a genuine drama."[35] About the same time, in several cities throughout Russia, local officials decided to erect new monuments to Joseph Stalin to commemorate the sixtieth anniversary of the end of World War II, a move Putin neither approved nor obstructed. President George Bush, in visiting Latvia before arrival in Moscow to celebrate the events, also evoked images of the past, referring to the Soviet Union's unlawful annexation and occupation of the Baltic states.[36] A Kremlin spokesperson vehemently denied this depiction of the postwar events. The verbal sparring was followed by two apparently congenial leaders in Moscow, honoring the veterans who brought the defeat of Germany. These events show how the Soviet past continues to haunt and obscure not only Russia's path forward, but also relations with neighbors and potential allies.

Political Challenges and Changing Agendas

FOCUS QUESTION
Describe three of the most important political challenges now facing the Russian state. For each one, outline how you think Russia will meet these challenges.

When the first edition of this book was published in 1996, five possible scenarios for Russia's future were presented:

- A stable progression toward marketization and democratization
- The gradual introduction of "soft authoritarianism"
- A return to a more extreme authoritarianism of a quasi-fascist or communist variety
- The disintegration of Russia into regional fiefdoms or de facto individual states
- Economic decline, civil war, and military expansionism[37]

Just before Putin's appearance as a major political figure, it appeared that the more pessimistic scenarios were the more likely. Under Putin, optimism grew that a strong leader might move Russia toward its own self-defined version of democracy. At the time of this writing, the "soft authoritarian" scenario seems to the most likely.

Russia in the World of States

In the international sphere, Russia's flirtation with Westernization in the early 1990s produced ambiguous results, including severe recession, social dislocation, and dependence on the West for economic aid. Russia's protests against international developments such as NATO expansion, the Desert Fox operation against Iraq in December 1998, and NATO's bombing of Yugoslavia in 1999 revealed Moscow's underlying resentment against Western dominance, as well as the country's relative powerlessness in affecting global developments. Russia could do little more than issue verbal protests. The West's recognition that Russia's involvement was crucial to finding a diplomatic solution to the Kosovo crisis in 1999 marked a turning point, heralding a new period of increased cooperation between Russia and the Western world. The events of September 11 reinforced these cooperative ventures. Evidence of warmer relations included the formation of a NATO-Russia Council in May 2002, marking an era of closer cooperation in areas such as control of international terrorism, arms control, nonproliferation, and crisis management.[38]

New tensions have emerged, however, in the face of American withdrawal from the Anti-Ballistic Missile Treaty, Russian objections to the American incursion into Iraq, and the American proposal to place a missile defense system in Central Europe. Russian leaders have expressed particular irritation at the possibility of NATO membership for former Soviet republics on the border of Russia, particularly Georgia and Ukraine. At the same time, Russian actions toward Ukraine and Belarus have added to the tension. For example when Russian increased prices for energy exports to these countries, conflicts ensued that temporarily jeopardized the flow of energy resources to Western Europe.

Although criticism of Russia's Chechnya policies by Western governments was tempered after the events of September 11, organizations such as Human Rights Watch have continued to charge Russia with acts of violence against the Chechen civilian population, as well as instances of arbitrary arrests and sexual attacks on women in Chechnya.[39] Since 2004 American officials have more generally criticized Putin's centralizing moves as antidemocratic. Figures in American business circles viewed attacks on prominent Russian businessmen as interference in business operations, producing inhibitions to investments in the crucial energy sector.

A critical element of Russia's relations with both the United States and its West European neighbors rests with Russia's rich endowment of oil and natural gas. It is the source of about 10 percent of the world's oil production and the country most richly endowed with natural gas (about a third of the world's total reserves). (See Figure 5.7) The United States began an "energy dialogue" with Russia in 2002, hoping to increase energy imports from Russia to diversify its international energy dependence. An energy dialogue had been initiated between the EU and Russia even earlier, in 2000, with a goal of increased integration of EU-Russian energy markets and assurances of energy security for the EU.[40] Russian imports support almost 20 percent of EU gas consumption and 16 percent of oil consumption. In 2004, the EU agreed to support Russia's bid to join the WTO in an implicit quid pro quo involving Russian ratification of the Kyoto climate change protocol, but also Russian agreement to bring a gradual adjustment of its domestic gas prices to bring them closer to world market levels. Will Russia be able to leverage energy and other resources to reestablish itself as a regional and potentially a global power? This may depend on whether the leadership can build a stable economic and political structure within the country.

Governing the Economy

The upturn in the Russian economy that began in 1999 may have been a watershed in the struggle to overcome the transitional recession that plagued Russia from the late 1980s onward. Nevertheless, severe disparities in income and wealth remain. A restoration of economic growth has raised consumption levels and disposable income for large parts of the population, but vulnerable population groups still fall below the poverty line. Questions also remain about whether income from oil and gas exports will feed the investment needs of other sectors of the economy, or whether they will be appropriated by a privileged elite. Making the economy attractive to foreign investors will require a continued development of the banking sector, legal institutions to ensure enforcement of contracts, and controls on crime and corruption. Although the 1998 devaluation of the ruble brought decreased reliance on Western

FIGURE 5.7

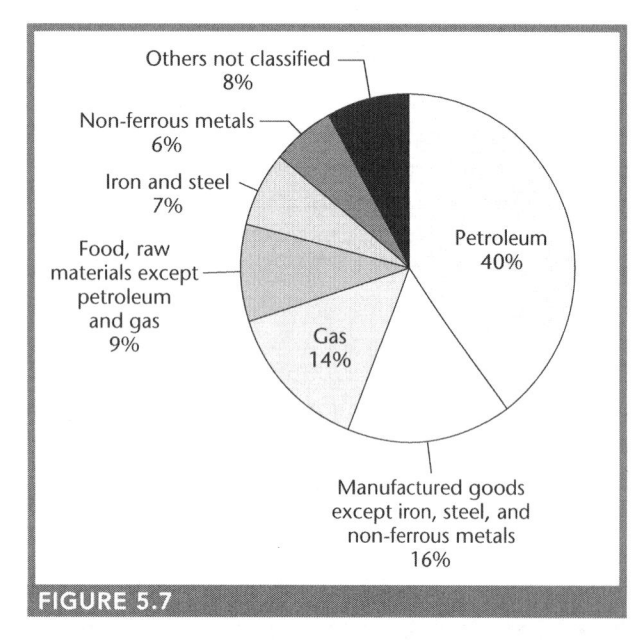

Exports from Russia, 2003

- Petroleum 40%
- Manufactured goods except iron, steel, and non-ferrous metals 16%
- Gas 14%
- Food, raw materials except petroleum and gas 9%
- Others not classified 8%
- Iron and steel 7%
- Non-ferrous metals 6%

Source: OECD Economic Survey of the Russian Federation 2004: The Sources of Economic Growth, p. 15, 2004.

imports (as they become too expensive), the so-called Dutch disease, in which heavy reliance on export income pushes the value of the currency up, now threatens again to undermine prospects for domestic producers. Reverberations in international markets and foreign economies can now have a direct impact on the Russian economy as well. Perhaps the greatest economic challenge facing the Putin administration is to establish policies to ensure a greater diversity of Russia's economic base.

The Democratic Idea

Russia's attempted democratization has been formally successful, but it is marred by corruption, the power of big money, and the limited accountability of its leaders. The political structures put in place by the 1993 constitution have not produced the strong and effective government most Russians desire. The continuing disjuncture between high personal support for Vladimir Putin and a continuing lack of confidence in the ability of political central institutions to address the country's problems suggests that the legitimacy of the system is still on thin ice. The more positive working relationship between the executive and legislative branches that emerged under Putin's leadership, as well as efforts to regularize relations between the center and regions, provides prospects for improved institutional performance. But the reduction of vehicles for popular input already shows signs of producing poor policy choices.

Although it is difficult to conceive that the freedoms that have been exercised since 1986 could be easily withdrawn, a reversion to a more centralized and predictable set of political practices may, on a conscious or unconscious level, seem familiar and therefore comfortable for many Russians. If the security and stability can be combined with rising prosperity, then many Russians may be willing to sacrifice democratic rights in exchange for economic improvement and political stability.

The Politics of Collective Identities

The formation of new political identities remains unfinished business. Most people are preoccupied by the struggle to make ends meet or to increase personal welfare. They have little time or energy to forge new forms of collective action to address underlying problems. Under such circumstances, the appeal to nationalism and other basic sentiments can be powerful. Indications of this are already evident in the fact that political parties with nationalist messages seem to be doing better than liberal forces. The weakness of Russian intermediary organizations (interest groups, political parties, or associations) means that politicians can more easily appeal directly to emotions because people are not members of groups that help them evaluate the politicians' claims. These conditions are fertile ground for authoritarian outcomes, which the government itself might use to keep the public compliant. Still, the high level of education and increasing exposure to international media may work in the opposite direction. Also, many Russians identify their country as part of Europe and its culture, an attitude echoed by the government. (See Table 5.4.) Exposure to alternative political systems and cultures may make people more critical of their own political system and seek opportunities to change it.

TABLE 5.4

Attitudes toward Foreign Countries

In general, what is your attitude toward the following foreign countries?

	USA	The European Union	Ukraine
Very positive	6%	6%	7%
Basically positive	57	67	60
Basically negative	22	12	19
Very negative	7	3	4
Hard to say	8	12	10

Note:
Based on a survey carried out April 15–18, 2005, among 1,600 residents of Russia (128 sampling points in 46 regions).

Source:
Levada Center, http://www.levada.ru/press/2005050401.html.

Russia remains in what seems to be an extended period of transition. In the early 1990s, Russians frequently hoped for "normal conditions," that is, an escape from the shortages, insecurity, and political controls of the past. As the new situation becomes familiar, *normality* has been redefined in less glowing terms than those conceived in the late 1980s.

Russian Politics in Comparative Perspective

FOCUS QUESTIONS

In what ways is Russia's transition to a market economy similar to or different from such transitions in other countries? How has Russia's previous industrialization complicated this transition?

The ways in which politics, economics, and ideology were intertwined in the Soviet period has profoundly affected the nature of political change in all of the former Soviet republics and generally made the democratization process more difficult. Unlike developing countries currently experiencing democratization and economic transformation, Russia is a highly industrialized country with a skilled and educated work force. Although this offers advantages, the high level of development is associated with a host of problems: a heavily damaged natural environment, obsolescent industries, entrenched bureaucratic structures, a nuclear arsenal that must be monitored and controlled, and a public that expects the state to provide a stable system of social welfare. These problems make it more difficult for the state to manage the domestic and international challenges it confronts.

How is Russia faring compared to some of the other postcommunist systems that faced many of these same challenges? The nations of Eastern Europe and the former Soviet Union were all subjected to a similar system of economic, political, and ideological power during the period of communist rule. Some were under communist rule for a shorter period of time, but most parts of the Soviet Union shared with Russia more than seven decades of the communist party state. Despite the efforts of the Soviet leadership to establish conformity throughout the region, national differences did emerge. The countries of Eastern Europe had a history of closer ties and greater cultural exposure to Western Europe; ideas of liberalism,

Joining the West or Aid Recipient?

The Russian Federation is now open to global influences, in contrast to the isolation imposed by the Soviet government. The Russian government has sought equal membership in some international organizations from which it was previously excluded, and it has forged partnerships with others. In the 1990s, Western governments and international agencies were welcomed by Russian authorities as they provided aid to Russia's developing market economy and fledgling democratic political structures, but now Russia's leaders are more resistant to Western influence with Russia.

An important aspect of these processes in the 1990s was the notion of **conditionality**, namely, the requirement that Russia meet certain conditions to be eligible to receive international assistance or to join certain international clubs. Conditionality is a controversial foreign policy tool because it grants foreign governments and agencies a certain leverage in domestic political and economic policy of recipient countries. It has been a particularly powerful tool used by the European Union in relation to candidate countries since strict conditions are set for membership. These requirements speeded transition processes in Central Europe (Czech Republic, Slovakia, Poland, Hungary, Slovenia) and the Baltic States before they were admitted as members in May 2004. Russia, viewing itself as a regional power that should have an equal partnership role, has been resistant to conditionality. This may be one reason that Russia has not adopted the goal of EU accession.

Following are some of the most important international agencies that Russia has become involved with in one way or another over the past fifteen years.

The International Monetary Fund (IMF). The IMF was founded in 1944, and during most of the 1990s it was the most influential international agency in Russia. Its general mandate is to oversee the international monetary system and help maintain stability in exchanges between its 184 member countries, which can draw on the fund's resources. The Soviet Union applied for membership in 1991 but was dissolved before acceptance. Russia was admitted to the IMF in 1992, and funds were issued to Russia as short- and medium-term credits to help stabilize the ruble and Russia's internal and external monetary balance. The disbursement of these funds was made contingent on the fulfillment of certain conditions by the Russian government, particularly the maintenance of noninflationary fiscal and monetary policies. These policies, in turn, necessitated cutbacks in social services and subsidies to troubled economic sectors. In 1999, a final loan was granted, and since then Russia has forgone further credits, choosing to manage its own macroeconomic fiscal policy. By 2004, Russia had paid off its IMF debt (www.imf.org).

The World Bank. Also founded in 1944, the World Bank has as its purpose to promote and finance economic development in the world's poorer countries. After World War II, this involved assistance in financing reconstruction in war-torn Europe. The agency is an investment bank with 184 member countries. As with the IMF, the Russian Federation was admitted in 1992. Through its International Bank for Reconstruction and Development (IBRD), the World Bank has provided loans to support development programs in Russia in sectors such as agriculture, the environment, energy, and social welfare. From 1991 to 2002, Russia borrowed US$12.5 billion from the IBRD, and in January 2005 its outstanding debt stood at $5.7 billion* (www.worldbank.org).

---

conditionality the requirement that certain commitments be made by receiving governments in exchange for credits or other types of assistance provided by international or foreign agencies, to ensure that the goals of the donor agency are respected.

*Central Bank of the Russian Federation website, at http://www.cbr.ru/statistics/credit_statistics/print.asp?file=debt.htm (accessed May 10, 2005).

continued

continued

The European Bank for Reconstruction and Development (EBRD). EBRD, formed in 1991, promotes the development of market economies in postcommunist countries. Specific current priorities include measures to "advance technological modernization and efficiency improvements in key sectors of the economy"[†] and helping economic diversification as well as supporting small business development. The EBRD provides loans and guarantees, and supports equity investments (www.ebrd.com).

The European Union (EU). The EU initiated the Tacis program in 1991 as a vehicle for providing grants to finance the transfer of knowledge to Russia and other countries in the former Soviet Union. Now the largest source of aid to Russia, annual contributions ran at about 90 million euros in 2002 and 2003. In addition to such assistance efforts, the EU's Partnership and Cooperation Agreement with Russia sets out a strategy for development of four "Common Spaces": Common Economic Space (to create an integrated market), Common Space for Freedom, Security, and Justice (relating to media, travel, human contact); Common Space for External Security (multilateralism, crisis management, antiterrorism); and Common Space for Research, Education, and Culture (http://europa.eu.int/comm/external_relations/russia/summit_05_05/index.htm).

North Atlantic Treaty Organization (NATO). NATO was formed in 1949 by ten European countries, the United States, and Canada to safeguard the security of its members in response to the perceived Soviet threat. Following the collapse of the communist system in Eastern Europe, NATO has had to rethink its mandate and the nature of potential threats. Among its duties are crisis management, peacekeeping, opposing international terrorism, and prevention of nuclear proliferation. In 2004, Bulgaria, Estonia, Latvia, Lithuania, Romania, Slovakia, and Slovenia became NATO members, following Hungary, the Czech Republic, and Poland in 1999. Albania, Croatia, and Macedonia (FYROM) are preparing for possible future membership. While raising strong objections to NATO expansion into its former sphere of influence, Russia has, over time, also developed a stronger working relationship with the organization. The Partnership for Peace program was the first important step in the process in 1994, and in 1997, the NATO-Russia Founding Act on Mutual Relations, Cooperation and Security was concluded. A further step was taken in 2002 with the establishment of the NATO-Russia Council, in which Russia holds an equal seat with the twenty-six NATO member states. Working groups deal with issues such as peacekeeping actions, international terrorism, and nuclear proliferation (http://www.nato.int/issues/nrc/index.html).

The G-8 and Russia. In 1998, Russia was accepted as a full member into the G-8 (Group of Eight), an expanded G-7. The G-8 is an informal international body consisting of the leading industrial nations; G-8 countries hold regular summits dealing with such issues as the international economy, trade relations, and foreign exchange markets. Although Russia is still too weak to exert much influence on G-8 issues, its membership in the organization is valuable, allowing Russia to maintain a presence on the world stage. In July 2006, Russia hosted the G-8 for the 2006 summit.

The World Trade Organization (WTO). The WTO is a powerful international organization, responsible for regulating international trade, settling trade disputes, and designing trade policy through meetings of its 148 member countries. Because of the increasingly global nature of trade, membership in the WTO is an essential prerequisite for increasing economic prosperity and for avoiding international economic isolation. Russia's membership is supported by powerful actors such as the European Union, but Russia still must conclude bilateral agreements with some member countries before accession can proceed. An agreement with the United States was reached in November 2006. The World Bank estimates that membership will bring Russian annual benefits of $19 billion through increased exports, opening the country to multilateral services and increased foreign direct investment[††] (www.wto.org). ❖

[†]European Bank for Reconstruction and Development website, at http://www.ebrd.com/about/strategy/country/russia/main.htm (accessed May 10, 2005).

[††]"Russian Economic Report #10: April 2005," *The World Bank Group*, http://194.84.38.65/mdb/upload/RER10_eng.pdf (accessed May 10, 2005).

private property, and individualism were less foreign to citizens in countries such as Czechoslovakia, East Germany, and Hungary than in regions farther east, including Russia. Within the Soviet Union, too, there was also considerable variation among the union republics. The Baltic republics of Latvia, Lithuania, and Estonia took a more experimental approach in many spheres of activity and had a more Western European atmosphere. At the other extreme, the Central Asian republics retained aspects of traditional Muslim culture, preserved the extended family structure, and maintained within the structure of the communist party a greater prominence for links rooted in the clan system indigenous to the region.

All fifteen countries that gained independence after the collapse of the Soviet Union, as well as several countries of Central and Eastern Europe, have experienced the collapse of the communist system of power since 1989. Given the diversity characterizing these countries, it is not surprising that their postcommunist experiences also varied. A rule of thumb, simple as it seems, is that the further east one goes in the postcommunist world, the more difficult and prolonged the transition period has been. This is partly because the more westerly countries of Central Europe that were outside the USSR (Poland, Hungary, Czech Republic, Slovakia), as well as the Baltic states, faced the realistic prospect of joining the EU and thus had a strong motivation to embark on fundamental reform to meet the EU's conditions. Also, these countries were under communist rule for a shorter period of time. Although political and economic liberalization generally follows this West-East axis, an exception is Belarus, which has liberalized less than Russia.

In terms of economic performance, postcommunist countries that liberalized the least, such as Uzbekistan and Belarus, suffered lesser recessions in the 1990s because state institutions remained more fully intact. However, these less-reformed economies may face painful adjustments in the future. Russia has had the advantage of possessing rich deposits of natural resources (including energy resources), giving it better possibilities than most other postcommunist states for coping with the ruptured economic ties resulting from the collapse of the Soviet. Ukraine and particularly Belarus are still suffering from the severe economic and health effects of the accident at the 1986 Chernobyl nuclear power plant. The Central Asian states confront the disastrous effects of Soviet-imposed emphasis on cotton production and associated environmental degradation (the Aral Sea crisis). On the other hand, Russia (along with Ukraine) has been the focal point of international economic assistance because of its large nuclear arsenal, its size, and its geopolitical importance (see "Joining the West or Aid Recipient?").

Progression along the various dimensions of the postcommunist transition are uneven across postcommunist countries, and Russia seems now to be progressing economically, while regressing politically, with nationalism on the rise and aspirations to status of a regional superpower resurfacing. In the political sphere, virtually all of the postcommunist states claim to be pursuing some form of democratization, but in some cases, this is more in name than in practice, particularly in Central Asia. Belarus has a distinctively authoritarian government. In all of the postcommunist states, the attempt to construct democratic political institutions has been characterized by repeated political crises, weak representation of popular interests, executive-legislative conflict, faltering efforts at constitutional revision, and corruption. In Russia, there is considerable skepticism about adopting the Western model of political development. Although the concept of democracy has a distinct appeal in the region, to much of the population it means, above all, personal freedom rather than support for notions of political accountability, rule of law, or the civic role of the citizen.

Although Russian politics has been highly contentious and the government has operated at very low levels of efficacy and legitimacy for most of the past decade, with the exception of the Chechnya conflict, Russia has escaped major domestic violence and civil war, unlike Yugoslavia, Armenia, Azerbaijan, Georgia, Moldova, and the Central Asian state of Tajikistan. For all their problems, Russian politicians have conducted themselves in a relatively civil manner. Citizenship rights for all ethnic groups have been maintained. State-sponsored racism is largely absent. The Russian government can be credited with avoiding marginalization of major social groups.

Russia will undoubtedly continue to be a key regional force in Europe and Asia. Its vast geographic expanse, rich resource base, large and highly skilled population, and the legacy of Soviet rule will ensure this. Yet its former allies in Central Europe, as well as the Baltic states, are gradually drifting into the orbit of Western Europe economically and politically. Following the 2004 EU enlargement, Russia's most important Western neighbor, Ukraine, aspires to EU membership, a goal the Russian leadership has not articulated. Although Ukraine is divided internally over its future course, the European dream is an increasingly important reference point. Russian leaders seem to appreciate the isolation this could imply, but seem unwilling to adopt certain crucial aspects of Western political practice. Thus, over the past few years, while Russia has resisted a monopolar world order dominated by the United States and its leaders have shown a desire and willingness to identify as a European country, Russia has an ambivalent relationship to accepting crucial norms that would underlie an effective and enduring partnership with the EU.

Will Russia be able to find a place for itself in the world of states that meets the expectations of its educated and sophisticated population? If Russia's experiment produces a stable outcome that benefits the majority of the population, then it may offer a path of quasi-democratic development that could serve as a model for countries further east. If instability and popular discontent rise, then incipient democracies elsewhere in the region may also take a further backward step.

Summary

Russia's political course since 1991 has been profoundly influenced by the fact that the country underwent simultaneous and radical transformations in three spheres: politics, economics, and ideology. Managing so much change in a short time has been difficult and has produced mixed results. Efforts to democratize the political system have been only partially successful, and experts disagree about whether Putin's efforts to strengthen the central state have contributed to rising authoritarian tendencies or whether they are needed to provide the stability that is necessary for democratic development. In the economic sphere, after recovering from a period of deep economic decline, Russia's renewed growth depends largely on exports of energy and natural resources. The country faces the challenge of effectively using its natural resource wealth to rebuild other sectors of the economy. In terms of ideology, nationalism threatens to reinforce intolerance and undermine social unity. Continuing high levels of corruption also undermine popular confidence in state institutions. Whereas those postcommunist countries that have joined the European Union seem, for the most part, to have successfully established viable democratic systems with functioning market economies, other post-Soviet states in Eastern Europe and Central Asia face similar challenges to Russia's in consolidating democracy and market reform. With its increased economic power, Russia has sought to reassert its role as a regional and global force, but increasing tensions have come to characterize Russia's relationship with the West as Russia sees its influence under challenge in neighboring countries.

Key Terms

patrimonial state
democratic centralism
vanguard party
collectivization
perestroika
glasnost
demokratizatsiia
market reform
shock therapy
joint-stock companies
insider privatization
privatization voucher
oligarchs
mafia
pyramid debt
nomenklatura
autonomous republics
krai
oblast
okrug
siloviki
power vertical
civil society
proportional representation
single-member plurality district
conditionality

Suggested Readings

Aslund, Anders. *Building Capitalism: The Transformation of the Former Soviet Bloc.* Cambridge, UK, and New York: Cambridge University Press, 2002.

Black, J. L. *Vladimir Putin and the New World Order: Looking East, Looking West?* Lanham, Md.: Rowman and Littlefield, 2004.

Blasi, R. Joseph, Maya Kroumova, and Douglas Kruse. *Kremlin Capitalism: The Privatization of the Russian Economy.* Ithaca, N.Y.: Cornell University Press, 1997.

Colton, Timothy J. *Transitional Citizens: Voters and What Influences Them in the New Russia.* Cambridge: Harvard University Press, 2000.

DeBardeleben, Joan, ed. *Soft or Hard Borders: Managing the Divide in an Enlarged Europe.* Aldershot, UK: Ashgate, 2005.

Eckstein, Harry, Frederic J. Fleron, Jr., Erik P. Hoffman, and William M. Reisinger. *Can Democracy Take Root in Russia? Explorations in State-Society Relations.* Lanham, Md.: Rowman & Littlefield, 1998.

Fish, M. Steven. *Democracy Derailed in Russia: The Failure of Open Politics.* Cambridge University Press, 2005.

Freeland, Chrystia. *Sale of the Century: Russia's Wild Ride from Communism to Capitalism.* New York: Doubleday, 2000.

Getty, J. Arch. *Origins of the Great Purges: The Soviet Communist Party Reconsidered.* Cambridge: Cambridge University Press, 1985.

Hoffman, David E. *The Oligarchs: Wealth and Power in the New Russia.* New York: Public Affairs Press, 2002.

Hough, Jerry, and Merle Fainsod. *How the Soviet Union Is Governed.* Cambridge: Harvard University Press, 1979.

Humphrey, Caroline. *The Unmaking of Soviet Life: Everyday Economies after Socialism.* Ithaca, N.Y.; London: Cornell University Press, 2002.

Karlkins, Rasma. *The System Made Me Do It: Corruption in Postcommunist Societies.* M.E. Sharpe, 2005.

Ledeneva, Alena V., *How Russia Really Works.* Cornell University Press, 2006.

Lewin, Moshe. *The Gorbachev Phenomenon: A Historical Interpretation.* Berkeley: University of California Press, 1991.

Motyl, Alexander J., Blair A. Ruble, and Lilia Shevtsova, eds. *Russia's Engagement with the West: Transformation and Integration in the Twenty-First Century.* Armonk, New York: M. E. Sharpe, 2005.

Pål, Kolsto, and Helge Blakkisrud, eds. *Nation-Building and Common Values in Russia.* Lanham, Md.: Rowman and Littlefield Publishers, 2004.

Pipes, Richard. *Russia Under the Old Regime.* New York: Scribner, 1974.

Reddaway, Robert, and Robert Orttung, eds. *The Dynamics of Russian Politics: Putin's Reform of Federal-Regional Relations.* 2 vols. Rowman & Littlefield, 2004 (volume 1); 2005 (volume 2).

Remington, Thomas F. *Politics in Russia.* 3rd ed. Boston: Pearson Education, 2004.

Sakwa, Richard. *Putin: Russia's Choice.* London and New York: Routledge, 2004.

Shevstsova, Lilia, *Putin's Russia.* rev. ed. Moscow: Carnegie Institute, 2004.

Solomon, Peter H., Jr., and Todd S. Fogelson. *Courts and Transition in Russia: The Challenge of Judicial Reform.* Boulder, Colo.: Westview Press, 2000.

Tolz, Vera. *Russia.* London: Arnold; New York: Oxford University Press, 2001.

Wilson, Andrew. *Virtual Politics: Faking Democracy in the Post-Soviet World.* Yale University Press, 2005.

Notes

[1] Richard Pipes, *Russia Under the Old Regime* (London: Widenfeld & Nicolson, 1974, pp. 22–24.

[2] Mikhail Gorbachev, *Perestroika: New Thinking for Our Country and the World* (New York: Harper, 1987).

[3] Sergei Peregudov, "The Oligarchic Model of Russian Corporatism," in Archie Brown (ed.), *Contemporary Russian Politics: A Reader* (New York: Oxford University Press, 2001), p. 259.

[4] Jacques Sapir, "Russia's Economic Rebound: Lessons and Future Directions," *Post-Soviet Affairs* 18, no. 1 (January–March 2002): 6.

[5] Economist Intelligence Unit (EIU), *Country Report: Russia* (London: EIU, March 8, 2005).

[6] Central Intelligence Agency, CIA Factbook, 2004, Russia https://www.cia.gov/cia/publications/factbook/geos/rs.html.

[7] EIU, Country Report: Russia (March 2005).

[8] EIU, *Country Report: Russia* (March 2002), 13; *Rossiiskii statisticheskii ezhegodnik* (Russian Statistical Yearbook), Moscow: Goskomstat, 2004.

[9] Levada Centre, *Vestnik obshchestvennogo mnenia* (November–December 2004), p. 104; and Levada Center data, http://www.levada.ru/economic.htmlonlinel (January 2, 2007).

[10] Sarah Ashwin and Elaine Bowers, "Do Russian Women Want to Work?" in Mary Buckley (ed.), *Post-Soviet Women: From the Baltics to Central Asia* (Cambridge: Cambridge University Press, 1997), p. 23. Also *Rossiiskii statisticheskii ezhegodnik* (2004).

[11] Goskomstat (Russian Statistical Agency), http://www.gks.ru/bgd/free/b05_00/IswPrx.dll/Stg/d010/i010180r.htm (accessed January 2, 2007).

[12] *Rossiiskii statisticheskii ezhegodnik* (Russia Statistics Annual). Moscow: Federal Service of State Statistics, 2004.

[13] Victor Zaslavsky, "From Redistribution to Marketization: Social and Attitudinal Change in Post-Soviet Russia," in Gail W. Lapidus (ed.), *The New Russia: Troubled Transformation* (Boulder, Colo.: Westview Press, 1994), 125.

[14] "*Putin Urges Early Repayment of Russia's Whole External Debt*," Moscow News Online, Feb. 11, 2005, http://www.mosnews.com/money/2005/02/11/putindebt.shtml (accessed April 14, 2005).

[15] Economist Intelligence Unit, Russia: Country Profile 2004, pp. 53, 63.

[16] Vladimir Putin, Address to the Federal Assembly, April 25, 2005, http://www.kremlin.ru/eng/speeches/2005/04/25/2031_type70029type82912_87086.shtml (accessed January 2, 2007).

[17] Thomas Remington, *Politics in Russia*, 2nd ed. (New York: Longman, 2001), 53–54.

[18] Ibid.

[19] Fred Weir, "Putin's Endgame for Chechen Bear Trap," *Christian Science Monitor*, January 25, 2001.

[20] "Society Is Afraid of Our Army," interview with Defense Minister Sergei Ivanov, April 13, 2005, http://mosnews.com/interview/2005/04/13/ivanov.shtml (accessed April 20, 2005). Interview conducted by Natalia Kalashnikova.

[21] Svetlana Mikhailova, "Constitutional Court Confirms Federal Authorities' Ability to Fire Governors, Disband Legislatures," *Russian Regional Report*, April 10, 2002, http://se2.isn.ch/serviceengine/FileContent?serviceID=RESSpecNet&fileid=219CFDBC-C014-1DC1-C198-FFF9F76C3522&lng=en (accessed January 2, 2007).

[22] On corporatism, see Philippe C. Schmitter and Gerhard Lehmbruch, *Trends Towards Corporatist Intermediation* (Thousand Oaks, Calif.: Sage, 1979).

[23] Compiled by the author from the website of the State Duma, http://www.duma.gov.ru/ (accessed December 12, 2006).

[24] Levada Center, public opinion poll, March 18, 2005, http://www.levada.ru/press/2005041801.html (accessed May 2, 2005).

[25] David Lane, *State and Politics in the USSR* (Oxford: Blackwell, 1985), 184–185.

[26] Thomas Remington, *Politics in Russia* (New York: Longman, 2001), 102.

[27] See the Constitution of the Russian Federation, Article 102.

[28] http://www.duma.gov.ru (May 2, 2005).

[29] Darrell Slider, "'United Russia' and Russia's Governors: The Path to a One-Party System," paper presented the American Assocation for the Advancement of Slavic Studies National Convention, Washington, D.C., November 17, 2006.

[30] These numbers also include seats won in single-member districts, as discussed below.

[31] See the official website at http://www.sps.ru/ (accessed January 2, 2007).

[32] Office for Democratic Institutions and Human Rights, "Russian Federation: Election to the State Duma 7 December 2003, OSCE/ODHIR Election Observation Mission Report" (Warsaw, January 27, 2004), http://unpan1.un.org/intradoc/groups/public/documents/UNTC/UNPAN016105.pdf (accessed January 2, 2007).

[33] Timothy J. Colton and Michael McFaul, "Are Russians Undemocratic," *Post-Soviet Affairs* 18 (April–June 2002): 102.

[34] William M. Reisinger, Arthur H. Miller, Vicki L. Hesli, and Kristen Hill Maher, "Political Values in Russia, Ukraine, and Lithuania: Sources and Implications," *British Journal of Political Science* 24 (1994): 183–223.

[35] http://www.kremlin.ru/eng/speeches/2005/04/25/2031_type70029type82912_87086.shtml (accessed January 2, 2007).

[36] Elisabeth Bumille, "Bush, Arriving in Baltics, Steps Into Argument With Russia," *New York Times*, May 7, 2005.

[37] Joan DeBardeleben, "Russia," in Mark Kesselman, Joel Kreiger, and William A. Joseph (eds.), *Comparative Politics at the Crossroads* (Lexington, Mass.: Heath, 1996): 355–357.

[38] For the official statement, see the NATO website, "NATO-Russia Relations: A New Quality," Declaration by Heads of State and Government of NATO Member States and the Russian Federation, http://www.nato.int/docu/basictxt/b020528e.htm (accessed January 2, 2007).

[39] Human Rights Watch webpage, http://hrw.org/english/docs/2005/05/07/russia10586.htm (accessed January 2, 2007).

[40] EU-Russia Energy Dialogue, Fifth Progress Report, November 2004, Moscow-Brussels http://europa.eu.int/comm/energy/russia/joint_progress/doc/progress5_en.pdf (accessed January 2, 2007).

Official Name:	People's Republic of China (*Zhonghua Remin Gongheguo*)
Location:	East Asia
Capital City:	Beijing
Population (2007):	1.3 billion
Size:	9,596,960 sq. km.; slightly smaller than the United States

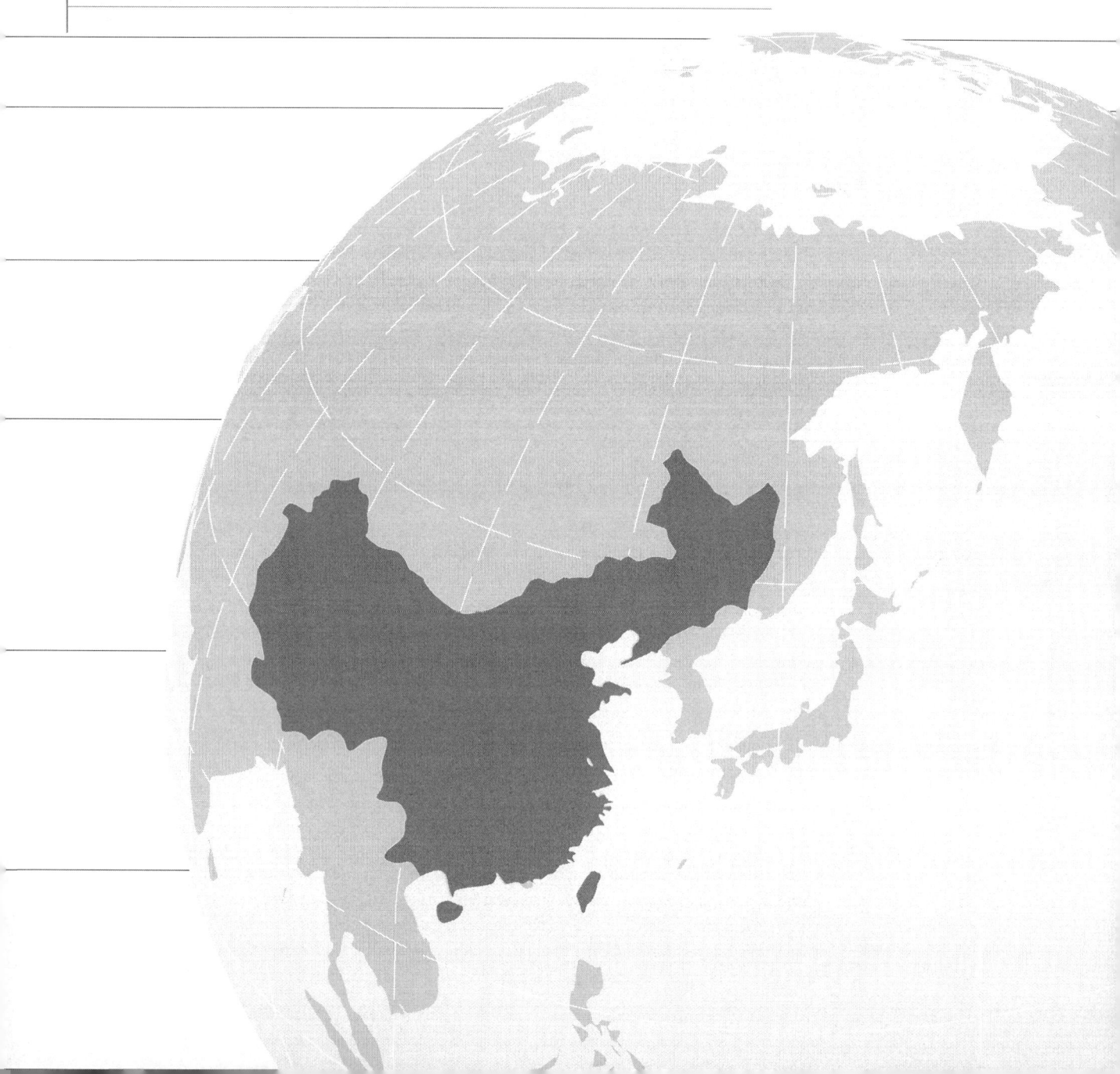

CHAPTER 4 China

■ William A. Joseph

SECTION 1	The Making of the Modern Chinese State
SECTION 2	Political Economy and Development
SECTION 3	Governance and Policy-Making
SECTION 4	Representation and Participation
SECTION 5	Chinese Politics in Transition

Chronology of Modern China's Political Development

1911 Revolution led by Sun Yat-sen overthrows 2,000-year-old imperial system and establishes the Republic of China.

1912 Sun Yat-sen founds the Nationalist Party (*Guomindang/Kuomintang*) to oppose warlords who have seized power in the new republic.

1921 Chinese Communist Party (CCP) is founded.

1927 Civil war between Nationalists (now led by Chiang Kai-shek) and Communists begins.

1934 Mao Zedong becomes leader of the CCP.

1937 Japan invades China, marking the start of World War II in Asia.

1949 Chinese Communists win the civil war and establish the People's Republic of China.

SECTION 1: The Making of the Modern Chinese State

FOCUS QUESTION
What is the major contradiction, or tension, in contemporary Chinese politics?

Politics in Action

In the center of Beijing, China's capital, is one of the world's largest and most magnificent public spaces, Tiananmen ("Gate of Heavenly Peace") Square. It is about a square mile in size—vast enough to hold ninety football fields. It is named after the entrance to a palace ten times bigger than the square, the Forbidden City, which housed China's emperors for nearly 500 years, that frames its northern border.

Over the last century Tiananmen has been the site of some of the most momentous events in Chinese history.[1] In 1919, large protests by intellectuals and students against the country's weak government set in motion the revolutionary process that led to the founding of the Chinese Communist Party (CCP). In 1949, the leader of the communist party, Chairman Mao Zedong, stood atop Tiananmen gate to proclaim the establishment of the People's Republic of China (PRC) after his forces had triumphed in the Chinese civil war. In 1966, Chairman Mao stood on the same spot, this time to greet and give his political blessing to more than a million Red Guards, high school and college students—the shock troops in his bloody crusade to rid China of those he believed were betraying his vision of Chinese communism. In 1989, more than ten years after Mao's death, Tiananmen again witnessed huge student protests, this time calling for greater democracy, that were brutally crushed when China's communist leaders sent in the army to clear the square.

More recently, in July 2001, over 200,000 Chinese citizens joyfully poured into Tiananmen Square to celebrate the announcement of the International Olympic Committee (IOC) that Beijing would be the site of 2008 summer games. They saw the awarding of the Olympics as long overdue recognition of the remarkable modernization of the Chinese economy, the stunning successes of Chinese athletes in international sports competitions, and the emergence of the PRC as a major global power.

1958–1960	1966–1976	1976	1978	1989	1997	2002–2003
Great Leap Forward.	Great Proletarian Cultural Revolution.	Mao Zedong dies.	Deng Xiaoping becomes China's most powerful leader.	Tiananmen massacre.	Deng Xiaoping dies; Jiang Zemin becomes China's top leader.	Hu Jintao succeeds Jiang as head of the CCP and president of the People's Republic of China.

But many voices around the world were extremely critical of the IOC's decision to give the games to Beijing. Human rights organizations such as Amnesty International argued that the decision rewarded one of the world's most oppressive governments. Some compared the Beijing Games to the ones in Berlin, in 1936, shortly after Hitler had come to power—games that the Nazis used to gain international legitimacy. Others argued that China has become much more open economically and that further involvement with the international community, including hosting the 2008 Olympics, could be a force for positive political change. They cite as a parallel, not the 1936 Berlin games, but the 1988 Olympics in Seoul, which helped bring about South Korea's transition from military dictatorship to democracy.

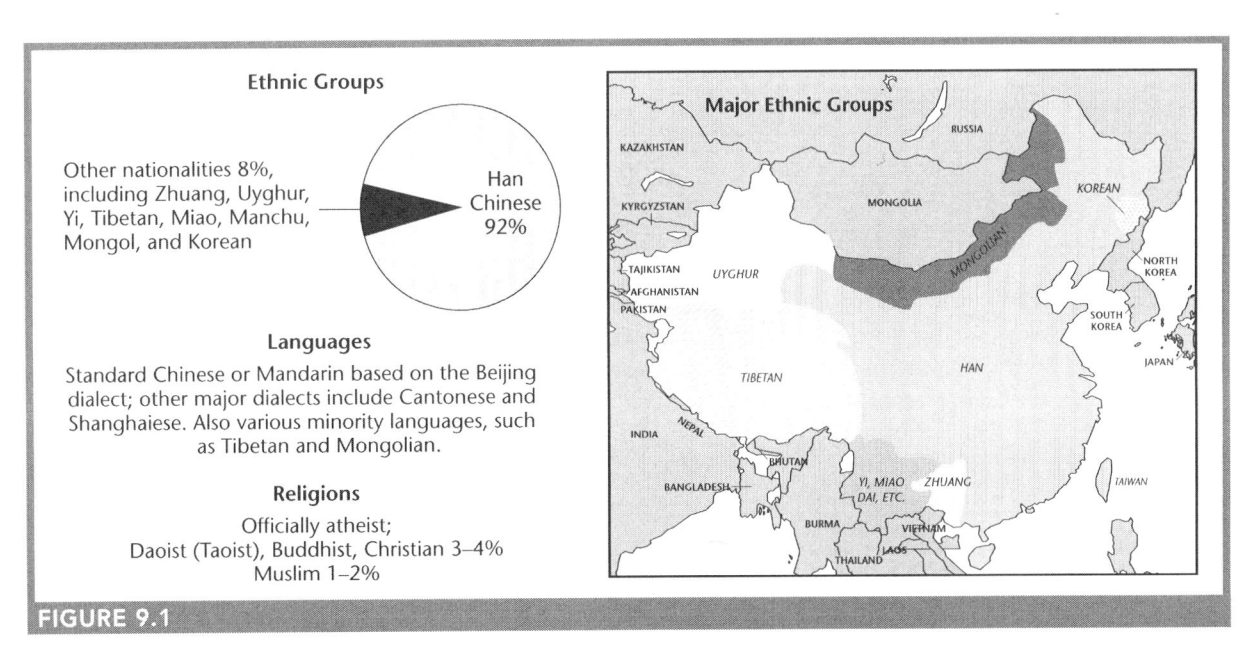

Ethnic Groups

Han Chinese 92%

Other nationalities 8%, including Zhuang, Uyghur, Yi, Tibetan, Miao, Manchu, Mongol, and Korean

Languages

Standard Chinese or Mandarin based on the Beijing dialect; other major dialects include Cantonese and Shanghaiese. Also various minority languages, such as Tibetan and Mongolian.

Religions

Officially atheist; Daoist (Taoist), Buddhist, Christian 3–4% Muslim 1–2%

FIGURE 9.1

The Chinese Nation at a Glance

communist party-state a type of nation-state in which the Communist Party attempts to exercise a complete monopoly on political power and controls all important state institutions.

Marxism-Leninism the theoretical foundation of communism based on the ideas of the German philosopher, Karl Marx (1818–1883), and the leader of the Russian Revolution, V. I. Lenin (1870–1924).

FOCUS QUESTION

How does China compare with the United States in terms of area and population?

autonomous region in the People's Republic of China, a territorial unit equivalent to a province that contains a large concentration of ethnic minorities.

The controversy over the Beijing Olympics reflects the fundamental contradiction of Chinese politics today. The People's Republic of China is one of only a few countries in the world that is still a **communist party-state** where the ruling party claims an exclusive monopoly on political power and proclaims allegiance (at least officially) to the ideology of **Marxism-Leninism**. But the country has experienced dramatic economic and social reform—and even considerable political relaxation since the Tiananmen bloodshed in 1989. It is more fully integrated into the world than at any other time in its history. But the Chinese Communist Party rejects any meaningful movement toward democracy. The rift between China's dictatorial political system and its increasingly open economy and globalized society remains deep and ominous.

Geographic Setting

China is located in the eastern part of mainland Asia. It is at the heart of one of the world's most strategically important regions. It is slightly smaller than the United States in land area, and is the fourth-largest country in the world, after Russia, Canada, and the United States.

The PRC is made up of twenty-two provinces, five **autonomous regions**, four centrally administered cities (including the capital, Beijing), and two Special Administrative Regions (Hong Kong and Macau), former European colonies that are only indirectly ruled by China. The vast, sparsely populated western part of the country is mostly mountains, deserts, and high plateaus. The northeast is much like the U.S. plains states in terms of weather and topography. This wheat-growing area is also China's industrial heartland. Southern China has a much warmer climate. In places it is even semitropical, which allows year-round agriculture and intensive rice cultivation. The country is very rich in natural resources, particularly coal and petroleum (including significant, but untapped onshore and offshore reserves). It has the world's greatest potential for hydroelectric power. Still, China's astounding economic growth in recent decades has created an almost insatiable demand for energy resources. This, in turn, has led the PRC to look abroad for critical raw materials.

Although China and the United States are roughly equal in geographic size, China's population (1.3 billion, the world's largest) is more than four times greater. Less than 15 percent of its land, however, is usable for agriculture. The precarious balance between people and the land needed to feed them has been a dilemma for China for centuries. It remains one of the government's major concerns.

China has nearly 150 cities with a population of a million or more. The three largest cities are Shanghai (17.8 million), Beijing (15.4 million), and Tianjin (10.4 million). In 1997, the former British colony of Hong Kong became part of the PRC. It is one of the world's great commercial centers (population 6.9 million). Nevertheless, about 60 percent of China's people still live in rural areas. The countryside has played—and continues to play—a very important role in China's political development.

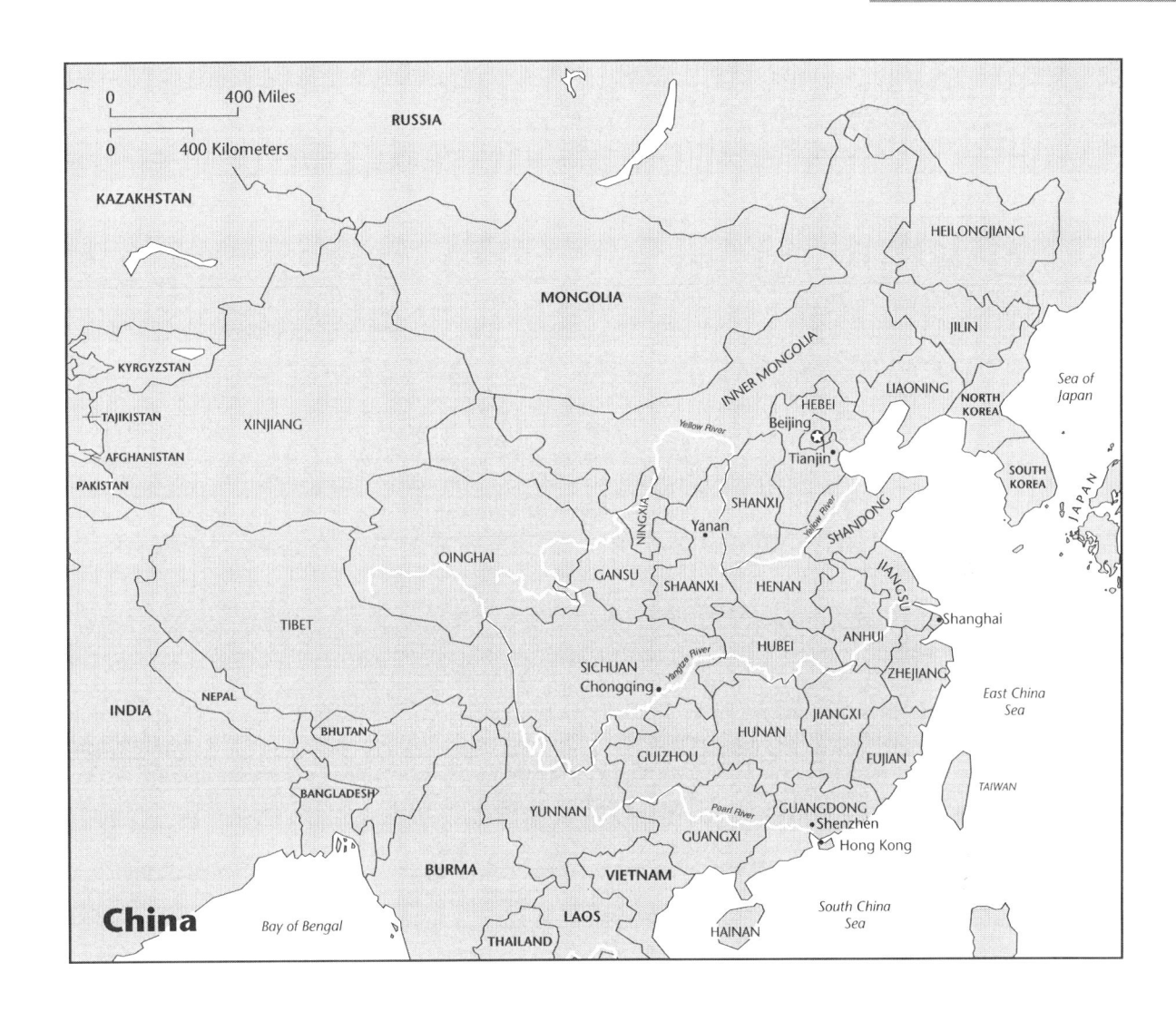

Critical Junctures

Chinese history falls into three broad periods. In the imperial period (221 BCE–1911 CE), a series of dynasties and emperors ruled China. During the relatively brief republican period (1912–1949), civil war and foreign invasion plagued the country. The communist period began in 1949.

From Empire to Republic (221 BCE–1911 CE)

Traditional Chinese culture was based on the teachings of the ancient philosopher, Confucius (551–479 BCE). Confucianism emphasizes obedience to authority, respect for your superiors and elders, as well as the responsibility of rulers to govern benevolently, and the importance of education. The Chinese empire took political shape in 221 BCE, when China's first emperor unified a

---

FOCUS QUESTIONS

How and why did the Chinese Communist Party come to power in China?

What impact did Mao Zedong and Deng Xiaoping have on China's political and economic development?

TABLE 9.1

Political Organization

Political System	Communist party-state; officially, a socialist state under the people's democratic dictatorship.
Regime History	Established in 1949 after the victory of the Chinese Communist Party (CCP) in the Chinese civil war.
Administrative Structure	Unitary system with twenty-two provinces, five autonomous regions, four centrally administered municipalities, and two Special Administrative Regions (Hong Kong and Macau).
Executive	Premier (head of government) and president (head of state) formally elected by legislature, but only with approval of CCP leadership; the head of the CCP, the general secretary, is in effect the country's chief executive, and usually serves concurrently as president of the PRC.
Legislature	Unicameral National People's Congress; about 3000 delegates elected indirectly from lower-level people's Congresses for five-year terms. Largely a rubber-stamp body for Communist Party policies, although in recent years it has become somewhat more assertive.
Judiciary	A nationwide system of people's courts, which is constitutionally independent but, in fact, largely under the control of the CCP; a Supreme People's Court supervises the country's judicial system and is formally responsible to the National People's Congress, which also elects the court's president.
Party System	A one-party system, although in addition to the ruling Chinese Communist Party, there are eight politically insignificant "democratic" parties.

number of small kingdoms. He laid the foundation of an imperial system that lasted for more than twenty centuries until it was overthrown by a revolution in 1911. During those many centuries, about a dozen different family-based dynasties ruled China. The country went through extensive geographic expansion and far-reaching changes. But the basic political and social institutions remained remarkably consistent. One of the most distinctive aspects of imperial China was its national bureaucracy, which developed much earlier than similar government institutions in Europe. Imperial bureaucrats were appointed by the emperor only after they had passed a series of very difficult examinations that tested their mastery of the classic books of Confucianism.

Imperial China experienced many internal rebellions, often quite large in scale. Some led to the downfall of the ruling dynasty. But new dynasties always kept the Confucian-based imperial political system. However, in the late eighteenth and nineteenth centuries, the Chinese empire faced an unprecedented combination of internal crises and external challenges. A population explosion (resulting from a long spell of peace and prosperity) led to economic stagnation and growing poverty. Official corruption in the bureaucracy and exploitation of the peasants by both landlords and the government increased. This caused widespread social unrest. One massive revolt, the Taiping Rebellion (1850–1864), took 20 million lives and nearly overthrew the imperial government.

By the early nineteenth century, the European powers had surged far ahead of China in industrial and military development and were pressing the country to open its markets to foreign trade. China tried to limit the activities of Westerners. But Europe, most notably Britain, was in the midst of its era of great commercial and colonial expansion. Britain was importing huge amounts of tea from China, and in order to balance the trade, used its superior military power to compel China to buy opium from the British colony of India. After a humiliating defeat by the British in the so-called Opium War (1839–1842), China was forced to sign a series of unequal treaties. These opened its borders to foreign merchants, missionaries, and diplomats on terms dictated by Britain and other Western powers. China also lost significant pieces of its territory to foreigners (including Hong Kong, which remained a British colony until 1997). Important sectors of the Chinese economy fell under foreign control.

There were many efforts to revive or reform the imperial government in the late nineteenth and early twentieth centuries. But political power in China remained in the hands of staunch conservatives who resisted change. When change came in 1911, it was a revolution that toppled the ruling dynasty and ended the 2,000-year-old empire.

Warlords, Nationalists, and Communists (1912–1949)

The Republic of China was established in 1912. Dr. Sun Yat-sen,* then China's best-known revolutionary, became president. However, the American-educated Sun could not hold on to power. China soon fell into a lengthy period of conflict and disintegration. Rival military leaders known as warlords ruled large parts of the country. Sun organized another revolution to try to reunify the country under his Nationalist Party (the *Guomindang* or *Kuomintang*).

In 1921, a few intellectuals, inspired by the Russian revolution in 1917 founded the Chinese Communist Party. They were looking for more radical solutions to China's problems than that offered by Sun Yat-sen and his Nationalist Party. But, encouraged by the Soviet Union, the small Chinese Communist Party joined with the Nationalists to fight the warlords. After initial successes, this alliance came to a tragic end in 1927. Chiang Kai-shek, a military leader who had become the head of the Nationalist Party after Sun's death in 1925, turned against his communist partners. He ordered a bloody suppression that nearly wiped out the CCP. Chiang proceeded to unify the Republic of China under his personal rule. He did this largely by striking deals with some of the country's most powerful remaining warlords who supported him in suppressing the communists.

---

*In China, family names come first. For example, Sun Yat-sen's family name was "Sun," and his given name was Yat-sen, and he is referred to as Dr. Sun.

The Republic of China on Taiwan

Despite being defeated by Mao Zedong and the communists on the mainland in October 1949, Chiang Kai-shek's Nationalist Party and the Republic of China (ROC) continued to function on the island of Taiwan, just 90 miles off the coast. The Chinese communists would probably have taken over Taiwan if the United States had not intervened to prevent an invasion. Taiwan remains politically separate from the People's Republic of China and still formally calls itself the Republic of China.

The Nationalist Party imposed a harsh dictatorship on Taiwan after its forced exile from the mainland in 1949. This deepened the sharp divide between the mainlanders who had arrived in large numbers with Chiang in 1949 and the native Taiwanese majority, whose ancestors had settled there centuries before and who spoke a distinctive Chinese dialect.

But with large amounts of U.S. aid and advice, the Nationalist government under Chiang Kai-shek sponsored a successful, peaceful program of land reform and rural development. It attracted extensive foreign investment and promoted economic growth by producing very competitive exports. This made Taiwan a model **newly industrializing country (NIC)**. The government also modernized Taiwan's roads and ports. It implemented policies that have given the island health and education levels that are among the best in the world. Its standard of living is one of the highest in Asia.

After Chiang Kai-shek died in 1975, his son, Chiang Ching-kuo, became president of the Republic of China and head of the Nationalist Party. Most people expected him to continue **authoritarian** rule. Instead, he permitted some opposition and dissent. He gave important government and party positions, previously dominated by mainlanders, to Taiwanese. When he died in 1988, the Taiwanese vice president, Lee Teng-hui, became president and party leader.

Under President Lee, Taiwan made great strides toward democratization. Laws used to imprison dissidents were revoked, the media were freed of all censorship, and open multiparty elections were held for all local and island-wide positions. In the 1996 presidential elections, Lee won 54 percent of the vote in a hotly contested four-way race. Lee's relatively small margin of victory reflected the new openness of the political system, but his victory reflected the credit that voters gave the Nationalist Party for the island's progress.

In 2000, an opposition party candidate, Chen Shui-bian of the Democratic Progressive Party (DPP), won the presidency. Chen's victory was partly due to a combination of the desire for change, especially in light of a serious downturn in the island's economic growth and a split within the Nationalist Party. It was also evidence of the further maturing of Taiwan's democracy.

The most contentious political issue in Taiwan is whether the island should continue to work, however slowly, toward reunification with the mainland. This was the Nationalists' policy under Lee Teng-hui. Or should it declare formal independence from China? A big factor in Chen's election in 2000 was the growing popularity of the DPP's position that Taiwan should seriously consider independence. Public opinion is sharply divided on this issue. But most people seem to prefer the status quo in which Taiwan is, for all intents and purposes (including its own strong military), a separate political entity from China, but not an internationally recognized independent country.

Chen was re-elected in 2004 in a close and contentious election. He and the DPP have toned down their independence rhetoric. The United States is committed to a "peaceful solution" of the Taiwan issue. It continues to sell military technology to Taiwan so it can defend itself. China regards Taiwan as a part of China, and Beijing has refused to renounce the use of force if the island moves toward formal separation. The PRC government often criticizes American policy toward Taiwan as interference in China's internal affairs, even though

---

newly industrializing countries (NICs) a group of countries that achieved rapid economic development beginning in the 1960s, stimulated by robust international trade and guided by government policies.

authoritarianism a system of rule in which power depends not on popular legitimacy but on the coercive force of the political authorities.

the United States only has informal diplomatic relations with Taiwan. Taiwan actually has formal diplomatic relations with very few other countries because doing so would anger the PRC.

Taiwan and China have developed extensive economic relations. Millions of people from Taiwan go to the mainland to do business, visit relatives, or just sightsee. The PRC and ROC have engaged in negotiations about further reconciliation and possible reunification. In 2005 the current head of the Nationalist Party went to the mainland and held talks with CCP leader (and PRC president) Hu Jintao. This was the first direct contact between the two political parties since the end of the civil war. In 2008, the Nationalists were returned to power and promised to seek closer ties with the PRC. ❖

Taiwan

Land area	13,895 sq mi/35,980 sq km (slightly smaller than Maryland and Delaware combined)
Population	23 million
Ethnic composition	Taiwanese 84%, mainland Chinese 14%, aborigine 2%
GDP at purchasing power parity (US$)	$690 billion, which ranks it 18th in the world behind Australia and ahead of Turkey
GDP per capita at purchasing power parity (US$)	$29,800, about the same as Greece or New Zealand

To survive, the Communist Party relocated its headquarters deep into the Chinese countryside. Ironically, this retreat created the conditions for the eventual rise to power of the man who would lead the CCP to nationwide victory, Mao Zedong. Mao had been one of the junior founders of the Communist Party. He had strongly advocated paying more attention to China's suffering peasants as a potential source of support. "In a very short time," he wrote in 1927, "several hundred million peasants will rise like a mighty storm, like a hurricane, a force so swift and violent that no power, however great, will be able to hold it back."[2] While the CCP was based in the rural areas Mao began his climb to the top of the party leadership.

In late 1934, the CCP was surrounded by Chiang Kai-shek's army and forced to begin a year-long, 6000-mile journey called the Long March, which took them across some of the most remote parts of China. In October 1935, the communists established a base in an impoverished area of northwestern China. It was there that Mao consolidated his political and ideological control of the CCP, sometimes through ruthless means. He was elected party chairman in 1943. He held this position until his death in 1976.

In 1937 Japan invaded China, which started World War II in Asia. The Japanese army pushed Chiang Kai-shek's Nationalist government to the far southwestern part of the country. This effectively eliminated the Nationalists as an active combatant against Japanese aggression. In contrast, the CCP base in the northwest was on the front line against Japan's troops. Mao and the Communists successfully mobilized the peasants to use **guerrilla warfare** to fight the invaders. This gained them a lot of support among the Chinese people.

By the end of World War II in 1945, the CCP had vastly expanded its membership. It controlled much of the countryside in north China. The Nationalists

guerrilla warfare a military strategy based on small bands of soldiers (guerrillas) who use hit-and-run tactics to attack a numerically superior and better-armed enemy.

were isolated and unpopular with many Chinese because of corruption, political repression, and economic mismanagement.

After the Japanese surrender, the Chinese civil war quickly resumed. The communists won a decisive victory over the U.S.-backed Nationalists. Chiang Kai-shek and his supporters had to retreat to the island of Taiwan, 90 miles off the Chinese coast. On October 1, 1949, Mao Zedong declared the founding of the People's Republic of China.

Mao in Power (1949–1976)

The CCP came to power on a wave of popular support because of its reputation as a party of social reformers and patriotic fighters. Chairman Mao and the CCP quickly turned their attention to some of the country's most glaring problems. A nationwide land reform campaign redistributed property from the rich to the poor and increased agricultural production in the countryside. Highly successful drives eliminated opium addiction and prostitution from the cities. A national law greatly improved the legal status of women in the family. It allowed many women to free themselves from unhappy arranged marriages. The CCP did not hesitate to use violence to achieve its objectives and silence opponents. Nevertheless the party gained considerable legitimacy among many parts of the population because of its successful policies during the first period of its rule.

Between 1953 and 1957, the PRC implemented a Soviet-style five-year economic plan. The complete takeover of industry by the government and the **collectivization** of agriculture in these years were decisive steps toward **socialism**. The plan achieved good economic results for the country. But Mao disliked the growth of the government bureaucracy and the persistence of inequalities, especially those caused by the emphasis on industrial and urban development and the relative neglect of the countryside.

This discontent led Mao to launch the **Great Leap Forward** (1958–1960). The Leap was a utopian effort to speed up the country's development so rapidly that China would catch up economically with Britain and the United States in just a few years. It relied on the labor power and revolutionary enthusiasm of the masses while at the same time aiming to propel China into an era of true **communism** in which there would be almost complete economic and social equality.

The Great Leap Forward turned into "one of the most extreme, bizarre, and eventually catastrophic episodes in twentieth-century political history."[3] In the rural areas, bad weather, irrational policies, wasted resources, poor management, and Mao's willful refusal to slow down the Great Leap combined to produce a famine. Between 20 and 30 million people died. An industrial depression soon followed the collapse of agriculture. China suffered a terrible setback in economic development.

In the early 1960s, Mao took a less active role in day-to-day decision making. Two of China's other top leaders at the time, Liu Shaoqi and Deng Xiaoping, were put in charge of reviving the economy. They used a combination of careful government planning and market-oriented policies to stimulate production, particularly in agriculture.

---

collectivization a process undertaken in the Soviet Union under Stalin in the late 1920s and early 1930s and in China under Mao in the 1950s, by which agricultural land was removed from private ownership and organized into large state and collective farms.

socialism an economic system in which the state plays a leading role in organizing the economy, and most business firms are publicly owned.

Great Leap Forward a movement launched by Mao Zedong in 1958 to industrialize China very rapidly and propel it toward communism.

communism a system of social organization based on the common ownership and coordination of production.

This strategy did help the Chinese economy. Once again, however, Mao became profoundly unhappy with the consequences of China's development. By the mid-1960s, the chairman had concluded that the policies of Liu and Deng had led to a resurgence of elitism and inequality. He thought they were threatening his revolutionary goals by setting the country on the road to capitalism. China also broke relations with the Soviet Union, which Mao had concluded was no longer a revolutionary country. The two communist countries nearly went to war in the late 1960s.

The **Great Proletarian Cultural Revolution** (1966–1976) was an ideological crusade designed to jolt China back toward Mao's radical vision of communism. Like the Great Leap Forward, the Cultural Revolution was a campaign of mass mobilization and utopian idealism. Its methods, however, were much more violent. Its main objective was not accelerated economic development, but the political purification of the party and the nation through struggle against so-called class enemies. Using his unmatched political clout and charisma, Mao put together a potent coalition of radical party leaders, loyal military officers, and student rebels (called Red Guards) to support him and attack anyone thought to be guilty of betraying his version of communist ideology known as Mao Zedong Thought.

In the Cultural Revolution's first phase (1966–1969), 20 million or so Red Guards rampaged across the country. They harassed, tortured, and killed people accused of being class enemies, particularly intellectuals and discredited party officials. During the next phase (1969–1971), Mao used the People's Liberation Army (PLA) to restore political order. Many Red Guards were sent to live and work in the countryside. The final phase of the Cultural Revolution (1972–1976) involved intense power struggle over who would succeed the old and frail Mao as the leader of the Chinese Communist Party.

Mao died in September 1976 at age eighty-two. A month later, a group of relatively moderate leaders settled the power struggle. They arrested their radical rivals, the so-called Gang of Four, led by Mao's wife, Jiang Qing. This marked the end of the Cultural Revolution. It had claimed at least a million lives and brought the nation close to civil war.

Great Proletarian Cultural Revolution the political campaign launched in 1966 by Chairman Mao Zedong to stop what he saw as China's drift away from socialism and toward capitalism.

Deng Xiaoping and the Transformation of Chinese Communism (1977–1997)

To repair the damage caused by the Cultural Revolution, China's new leaders restored to power many veteran officials who had been purged by Mao and the radicals. These included Deng Xiaoping. By 1978, Deng had clearly become the country's most powerful leader, although he never took for himself the formal positions of head of either the Communist Party or the Chinese government. Instead he appointed younger, loyal men to those positions.

Deng's policies were a profound break with the Maoist past. He had long believed that Mao put too much emphasis on politics and not enough on the economy. That was why he had been purged by Mao during the Cultural Revolution. Under Deng, state control of the economy was significantly reduced.

Market forces were allowed to play an increasingly important role. Private enterprise was encouraged. The government allowed unprecedented levels of foreign investment. Chinese artists and writers saw the shackles of party control that had bound them for decades greatly loosened. Deng took major steps to revitalize China's government by bringing in younger, better-educated officials. After decades of stagnation, the Chinese economy experienced spectacular growth throughout the 1980s. (See Section 2.)

Then came June 1989 and the Tiananmen Square massacre. For more than a year, discontent had been growing over inflation and official corruption. Many people, especially students and intellectuals, desired more political freedom. Large-scale demonstrations began in Beijing and several other Chinese cities that spring. At one point more than a million people from all walks of life gathered in and around Tiananmen. For several months, CCP leaders disagreed about how to handle the protests. They did little other than engage in threatening rhetoric in the hope that the demonstrators would leave. But they stayed, and China's leaders ran out of patience. The army received orders to clear the Square during the very early morning hours of June 4. By the time dawn broke in Beijing, the army had indeed cleared Tiananmen Square. The Chinese government has never revealed the exact death toll which very likely numbered in the hundreds. Indeed, the government still insists that it did the right thing in the interests of national stability.

Following the Tiananmen crisis, China went through a few years of intense political repression and a slowdown in the pace of economic change. Then in early 1992, Deng Xiaoping took some bold steps to accelerate reform of the economy. He hoped reform would help the PRC avoid a collapse of China's communist system such as had happened in the Soviet Union in 1991.

This cartoon captures the contradiction between economic reform and political repression that characterized China under the leadership of Deng Xiaoping. (© *Tribune Media Services, Inc. All Rights Reserved. Reprinted with permission.*)

From Revolutionaries to Technocrats (1997 to the Present)

In mid-1989, Deng Xiaoping had promoted the former mayor and communist party leader of Shanghai, Jiang Zemin, to become the head of the CCP. Although Deng remained the power behind the throne, he gradually turned over greater authority to Jiang, who, in addition to his positions as head (general secretary) of the CCP and chair of the powerful Central Military Commission, became president of the PRC in 1993. When Deng Xiaoping died in February 1997, Jiang was secure in his position as China's top leader.

Under Jiang's leadership, China continued its economic reforms and remarkable economic growth. The PRC became an even more integral part of the global economy. It enhanced its regional and international stature. But the country also faced serious problems, including mounting unemployment, pervasive corruption, and widening gaps between the rich and the poor. Overall, China was politically stable during the Jiang era. But the CCP still repressed any individual or group it perceived as challenging its authority.

Upon Jiang's retirement, Hu Jintao, China's vice president, became CCP general secretary in November 2002 and PRC president in March 2003. Hu was sixty years old when he took over the highest party and government offices, which was considerably younger than most of China's recent leaders. But both Jiang and Hu represented a new kind of leader for the PRC. Mao Zedong and Deng Xiaoping were career revolutionaries. They had participated in the CCP's long struggle for power dating back to the 1920s. They were among the founders of the Communist regime in 1949. In contrast, Jiang and Hu were **technocrats**. They were officials with academic training (in their cases, as engineers) who had worked their way up the party ladder by professional competence and political loyalty.

The transfer of power from Jiang to Hu was remarkably predictable and orderly. Some observed that it was the first relatively tranquil top-level political succession in China in more than 200 years. Jiang had retired after two terms in office, as required by both party rules and the state constitution, and Hu had, for several years, been expected to succeed Jiang.

Hu Jintao has tried to project himself as a leader who not only wants to promote economic growth, but who is also more concerned than his predecessor about some of the country's serious problems, such as the enormous inequalities between regions, rural poverty, and the environment. But Hu has also taken a hard line on political dissent. There is little reason to expect he will deviate significantly from the combination of economic reform and political repression that has been the CCP's formula for retaining power since the days of Deng Xiaoping.

> **technocrats** career-minded bureaucrats who administer public policy according to a technical rather than a political rationale.

Themes and Implications

Historical Junctures and Political Themes

The World of States. At the time the People's Republic was established in 1949, China occupied a weak position in the international system. For more than a century, its destiny had been shaped by incursions and influences from abroad that it could do little to control. Mao made many tragic and terrible blunders. But one of his great achievements was to build a strong state able to affirm and defend its sovereignty. China's international stature has increased as its economic and military strength have grown. Although still a relatively poor country by many per capita measures, the sheer size of its economy makes the PRC an economic powerhouse. Its import and export policies have an important impact on many other countries. China is a nuclear power with the world's largest conventional military force. It is an active and influential member of nearly all international organizations, including the United Nations, where it sits as one of the five permanent members of the Security Council. China has become a major player in the world of states.

> **FOCUS QUESTIONS**
> In what ways might China be compared to other countries? In what ways is it unique?

Governing the Economy. Since coming to power in 1949, the Chinese Communist Party has experimented with a series of very different economic systems for China: a Soviet-style bureaucratic planning system in the early 1950s, the radical egalitarianism and mass mobilization of the Maoist model, and market-oriented policies implemented by Deng Xiaoping and his successors. Ideological disputes over these development strategies were the main cause of ferocious political struggles within the CCP. Deng began his bold reforms in the hope that improved living standards would restore the legitimacy of the CCP, which had been badly tarnished by the economic failings and political chaos of the Maoist era. The remarkable successes of those reforms have sustained the CCP at a time when most of the world's other Communist regimes have disappeared.

The Democratic Idea. Any hope that democracy might take root in the early years of Communist rule in China quickly vanished by the mid-1950s with the building of a one-party Communist state and Mao's unrelenting campaigns against alleged enemies of his revolution. The Deng Xiaoping era brought much greater economic, social, and cultural freedom. But time and again the CCP strangled the stirrings of the democratic idea, most brutally in Tiananmen Square in 1989. Jiang Zemin and Hu Jintao have been faithful disciples of Deng. They have vigorously championed economic reform in China. They have also made sure that the CCP retains its firm grip on power.

The Politics of Collective Identity. Because of its long history and ancient culture, China has a very strong sense of national identity. China's cultural and ethnic homogeneity has also spared it the kind of widespread communal

In an act of outrage and protest, an unarmed civilian stood in front of a column of tanks leaving Tiananmen Square the day after the Chinese army had crushed the pro-democracy demonstration in June 1989. This "unknown hero" disappeared into the watching crowd. Neither his identity nor his fate are known. *(Source: Jeff Widener/AP Images)*

violence that has plagued so many other countries in the modern world. The exception has been in the border regions of the country where there is a large concentration of minority peoples, including Tibet and the Muslim areas of China's northwest (see Section 4).

Implications for Comparative Politics

The PRC can be compared with other countries that have been or are ruled by a communist party. From this perspective, China raises intriguing questions: Why has China's communist party–state so far proved more durable than that of the Soviet Union and nearly all other such regimes? By what combination of reform and repression has the CCP held onto power? What signs are there that it is likely to continue to be able to do so for the foreseeable future? What signs suggest that Communist rule in China may be weakening?

China can also be compared with other developing nations that face similar economic and political challenges. Although the PRC is part of the Third World as measured by the average standard of living of its population, its record of growth in the past several decades has far exceeded almost all other developing countries. Furthermore, the educational and health levels of the Chinese people are quite good when compared with many other countries at a similar or somewhat higher level of development, for example, India and Mexico. How has China achieved such relative success in its quest for economic and social development? By contrast, much of the Third World has become democratic in recent decades. How and why has China resisted this wave of democracy? What does the experience of other developing countries say about how economic modernization might influence the prospects for democracy in China?

Napoleon Bonaparte, emperor of France in the early nineteenth century, is said to have remarked, "Let China sleep. For when China wakes, it will shake the world."[4] It has taken awhile, but China certainly has awakened. Will it shake the world?

Summary

China has experienced more dramatic changes over the last century than almost any other country. Until 1912, it was an imperial system headed by an emperor. From then until 1949 it was known as the Republic of China, but the government was never in full control. Warlords ruled various parts of the country. China suffered terribly from a brutal invasion by Japan during World War II. In 1949, a civil war that had been waged for two decades ended when the Chinese Communist Party under Chairman Mao Zedong came to power and established the People's Republic of China. From then until his death in 1976, Mao imposed a kind of radical communism on China. This had a mostly disastrous political and economic impact. Deng Xiaoping became China's most powerful leader in 1978. He implemented major reforms that helped make China the fastest growing economy in the world. But he and his successors have suppressed all challenges to the authority of the Communist Party.

SECTION 2

Political Economy and Development

State and Economy

FOCUS QUESTION

What are the major differences between Mao Zedong's approach to governing the economy and Deng Xiaoping's?

The Maoist Economy

When the Chinese Communist Party came to power in 1949, China's economy was suffering from more than a hundred years of rebellion, invasion, civil war, and bad government. The country's new communist rulers seized much property from wealthy landowners, rich industrialists, and foreign companies. Nevertheless, it allowed some private ownership and many aspects of capitalism to continue in order to gain support for the government and revive the economy.

In early 1950s, the CCP followed the socialist model of a **command economy** as practiced in the Soviet Union. The state owned or controlled most economic resources. Government planning and commands, not market forces, drove economic activity.

At first, China's command economy yielded impressive results. But it also created huge bureaucracies and new inequalities, especially between the heavily favored industrial cities and the investment-starved rural areas. Both the Great Leap Forward (1958–1961) and the Cultural Revolution (1966–1976) embodied the unique and radical Maoist approach to economic development. This was intended to be less bureaucratic and more egalitarian than the Soviet model.

Under Mao, the PRC built a strong industrial base. The people of China became much healthier and better educated. But the Maoist economy was plagued by political interference, poor management, and ill-conceived projects. This led to wasted resources of truly staggering proportions. Overall, China's economic growth rates, especially in agriculture, barely kept pace with population increases. The average standard of living changed little between the 1950s and Mao's death in 1976.

command economy a form of socialist economy in which government decisions ("commands") rather than market mechanisms (such as supply and demand) are the major influences in determining the nation's economic direction.

China Goes to Market

After Deng Xiaoping consolidated power in 1978, he took China in an economic direction far different from Mao's or that of any other communist party-state. In 1962 Deng had remarked in a speech, "It doesn't matter whether a cat is white or black, as long as it catches mice."[5] He meant that the CCP should not be overly concerned about whether a particular policy was socialist or capitalist if it helped the economy. Such sentiments got Deng in trouble with Mao. They made Deng one of the principal victims of the Cultural Revolution.

Once in charge, Deng spearheaded sweeping reforms that transformed the Chinese economy. They also touched nearly every aspect of life in the PRC. They redefined the role of the communist party and the meaning of socialism in China. These reforms greatly reduced the role of government control and increased that of the market economy. Authority for making economic decisions passed from government bureaucrats to families, factory managers, and even the owners of private businesses. Individuals were encouraged to work harder and more efficiently to make money rather than to "serve the people" as had been the slogan during the Maoist era.

In most sectors of the economy the state no longer dictates what to produce and how to produce it. Almost all prices are now set according to supply and demand, as in a capitalist economy, rather than by administrative decree. Many government monopolies have given way to fierce competition between state-owned and non–state-owned firms. A decade ago there were over 100,000 state-owned enterprises (SOEs) in China; now there are about a quarter of that number. In 1978, SOEs generated about 80 percent of China's gross domestic product; by 2004 that number had dropped to about 25 percent. But state-owned enterprises still employ nearly 70 millions workers. They also dominate critical parts of the economy such as steel and petroleum.

But even SOEs must now respond to market forces. If they cannot turn a profit, they have to restructure or even go into bankruptcy. Some have been semiprivatized. But many are vastly overstaffed. Many are economic dinosaurs with outdated facilities and machinery that make them unattractive to potential foreign or domestic investors. The state-owned sector remains a huge drain on the country's banks (mostly government-controlled), which are still required to bail out many failing SOEs. These large loans are rarely, if ever, paid back. Many economists think that even more drastic SOE reform is needed. The country's leaders understandably fear the political and social consequences that would result from a massive layoff of industrial workers.

Although it is somewhat ironic, the Chinese Communist Party now strongly encourages and supports private businesses. The private sector is the fastest growing part of China's economy. It now accounts for more than two-thirds of the PRC's industrial output and employs nearly 200 million workers.

The results of China's move from a command toward a market economy have been phenomenal (see Figure 9.2). The PRC has been the fastest-growing major economy in the world for more than two decades. China's GDP per capita (that is, the total output of the economy divided by the total population) grew at an average rate of nearly 9 percent per year from 1990 to 2006. During the same period, the per capita GDP of the United States grew at a little under 2 percent per year during the same period, Japan's at about 1 percent, and India's at around 4 percent.

There has also been a consumer revolution in China. In the late 1970s, people in the cities could only shop for most consumer goods at state-run stores. These carried a very limited range of products, many of which were of shoddy quality. Today most of China's urban areas are becoming shopping paradises. They have domestic and foreign stores of every kind, huge malls, fast-food outlets, and a great variety of entertainment options. A few decades ago, hardly anyone owned a television. Now nearly every urban household and 75 percent of rural households have a color TV. Cell phones are everywhere. In the cities, the new middle class is starting to buy houses, condominiums, and cars.

FIGURE 9.2

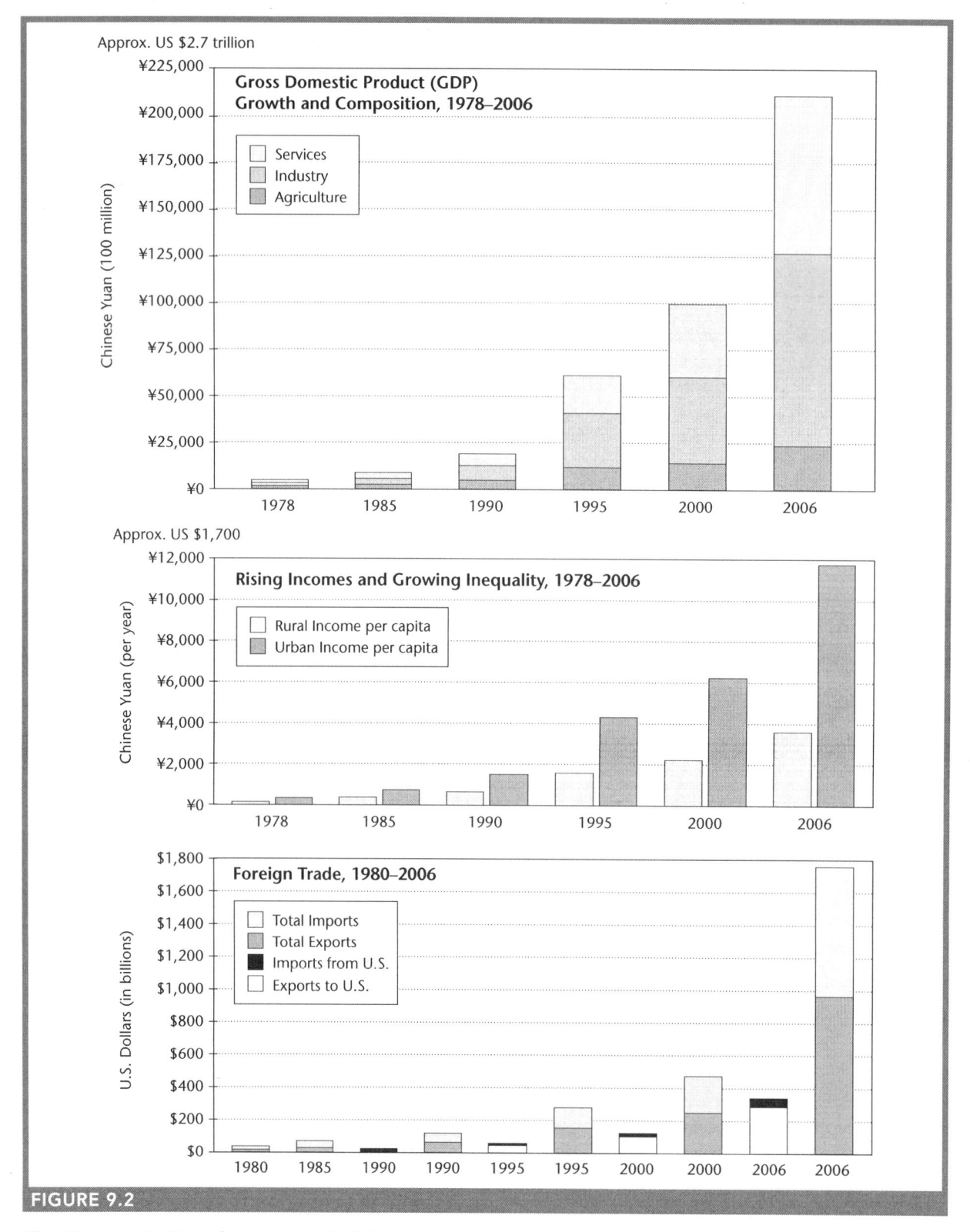

The Economic Transformation of China

These charts show how dramatically the Chinese economy has been transformed since the market reforms were introduced by Deng Xiaoping in 1978.

Source: *China Statistical Yearbooks*, United States-China Business Council.

Despite these changes, government commands and central planning, although greatly refined and reduced, have not disappeared altogether. China is still not fully a free market economy. National and local bureaucrats continue to exercise a great deal of control over the production and distribution of goods, resources, and services. The extent of private property is still restricted. Market reforms have gained substantial momentum that would be nearly impossible to reverse. But the CCP still wields the power to decide the direction of China's economy.

Remaking the Chinese Countryside

One of the first revolutionary programs launched by the Chinese Communist Party when it came to power in 1949 was land reform that confiscated the property of landlords and redistributed it as private holdings to the poorer peasants. But in the mid- to late 1950s peasants were reorganized by the state into collective farms and communes in which the village, not individuals, owned the land and government officials directed all production and labor. Individuals were paid according to how much they worked on the collective land. Most crops and other farm products had to be sold to the state at low fixed prices. The system of collectivized agriculture was one of the weakest links in China's command economy because it was very inefficient and people had little incentive to work hard. Per capita agricultural production and rural living standards were stagnant from 1957 to 1977.

Deng Xiaoping made the revival of the rural economy one of his top priorities when he became China's most powerful leader in the late 1970s. He abolished collective farming and established a **household responsibility system**, which remains in effect today. Farmland is now contracted out by the villages (which still technically own the land) to individual families, who take full charge of the production and marketing of crops. Agricultural productivity and income have sharply increased for most farm families. It is estimated that more than 200 million rural residents have been lifted out of extreme poverty in the last two decades.

Economic life in the Chinese countryside has also been transformed by the remarkable growth of rural industry and commerce. Rural factories and businesses range in size from a handful of employees to thousands; some are privately owned, but many are run by local governments. They even attract considerable foreign investment.

Certainly life is much better for the vast majority of the more than 600 million people who still live in China's rural areas. But there are also serious problems in the countryside. Health care, education, disability pay, and retirement funds for people in the countryside receive little government support. They now depend almost entirely on the relative wealth of families and villages. Rural protests, sometimes violent, have increased significantly in recent years. The protests have been about high taxes, corrupt local officials, pollution, illegal land seizures by developers, and delays in payments for agricultural products purchased by the government.

---

household responsibility system the system put into practice in China beginning in the early 1980s in which the major decisions about agricultural production are made by individual farm families based on the profit motive rather than by a people's commune or the government.

A view of Shanghai's ultramodern skyline. The city is China's financial and commercial center and one of the world's busiest ports. *(Source: © Xiaoyang Liu/Corbis)*

FOCUS QUESTION

What have been some of the major downsides to China's spectacular economic growth over the last two or three decades?

Society and Economy

Market reform and globalization have made Chinese society much more diverse and open. People are vastly freer to choose jobs, travel about the country and internationally, practice their religious beliefs, buy private homes, join nonpolitical associations, and engage in a wide range of other activities that were prohibited or severely restricted during the Maoist era. But economic change has also caused serious social problems. Crime, prostitution, and drug use have sharply increased. Although such problems are still far less prevalent in China than in many other countries, they are severe enough to worry national and local authorities.

Economic reform has also brought significant changes in China's basic system of social welfare. The Maoist economy was characterized by what was called the **iron rice bowl**. As in other communist party-state economies such as the Soviet Union, the government guaranteed employment, a certain standard of living (although, a low one), and basic cradle-to-grave benefits to most of the urban and rural labor force. In the cities, the workplace was more than just a place to work and earn a salary. It also provided housing, health care, day care, and other services.

China's economic reformers believed that such guarantees led to poor work motivation and excessive costs for the government and businesses. They implemented policies designed to break the iron rice bowl. Income and employment are no longer guaranteed. They are now directly tied to individual effort. An estimated 45 to 60 million workers have been laid off from state-owned

iron rice bowl a feature of China's socialist economy during the Maoist era (1949–76) that provided guarantees of lifetime employment, income, and basic cradle-to-grave benefits to most urban and rural workers.

Despite China's spectacular economic progress in recent decades, tens of millions of people still live in dire poverty in rural areas such as that shown in this photograph. Inequality between city and countryside is one of the biggest challenges facing China's government. *(Source: © Keren Su/Corbis)*

enterprises in recent years. Many are too old or too unskilled to find good jobs. The official unemployment rate is about 4 percent of the urban labor force. But it is generally believed to be at least twice that and to be as high as 40 percent in some parts of the country. China has very little in the way of unemployment insurance or social security for its displaced workers. Work slowdowns, strikes, and large-scale demonstrations are becoming more frequent, particularly in China's northeastern rust belt, where state-owned industries have been particularly hard hit. If unemployment continues to surge, labor unrest could be a political time bomb for China's communist party-state.

Welfare subsidies have been greatly reduced or eliminated entirely. China's health care system is in shambles. Less than a quarter of the urban population, and only 10 percent of those who live in the rural areas, have health insurance.

Market reforms have also opened China's cities to a flood of rural migrants. After the agricultural communes broke up in the early 1980s, many peasants headed to the urban areas to look for jobs. The more than 150 million people in this so-called floating population reflect the biggest population movement in human history. They are mostly employed in low-paying jobs, but fill an important niche in China's changing labor market, particularly in boom areas like construction. But they also put increased pressure on urban housing and social services. Their presence in Chinese cities could become politically destabilizing if they find their economic aspirations thwarted by a stalled economy or if they are treated too roughly or unfairly by local governments, which often see them as intruders.

China's economic boom has also created enormous opportunities for corruption. Officials still control numerous resources and retain power over many economic transactions from which large personal profits can be made. The government recognizes the threat corruption poses to its legitimacy. It has repeatedly launched well-publicized campaigns against official graft, with severe punishment, including execution, for some serious offenders. In the fall of 2006, even the head of the communist party in Shanghai was kicked out of office and charged with misuse of nearly $400 million in pension funds.

The benefits of economic growth have reached most of China. But the market reforms and economic boom have created sharp class differences, and inequalities between people and parts of the country have risen significantly.

A huge gap separates the average incomes of urban residents and those in the countryside (see Fig. 2.1). Farmers in China's poorer areas have faced years of stagnating or even declining incomes. The gap is also widening between the prosperous coastal regions and the inland areas of the country.

Such inequalities are an embarrassing contradiction for a party that still claims to believe in communist ideals. The current administration of Hu Jintao has begun to promote the development of what it calls a "harmonious society." This emphasizes not only achieving a higher average standard of living, but a more equitable distribution of income and basic social welfare, including health and education. There is more attention being paid to the rural economy, and new poverty alleviation programs and increased investment have brought some progress to the less developed western regions. In early 2006, the government announced that it was abolishing all taxes on agriculture.

Gender inequalities also appear to have grown in some ways since the introduction of the economic reforms. There is no doubt that the social status, legal rights, employment opportunities, and education of women in China have improved enormously since 1949. Women have also benefited from rising living standards and economic modernization of recent decades. But the trend toward a market economy has not benefited men and women equally. In the countryside, it is almost always the case that only male heads of households sign contracts for land and other production resources. And so men dominate rural economic life. This is true even though farm labor has become increasingly feminized as many men move to jobs in rural industry or migrate to the cities.

Economic and cultural pressures have also led to an alarming suicide rate (the world's highest) among rural women. Over 70 percent (about 120 million) of illiterate adults in China are female. Although China has one of the world's highest rates of female urban labor participation, the market reforms have "strengthened and in some cases reconstructed the sexual division of labor, keeping urban women in a transient, lower-paid, and subordinate position in the workforce."[6] Women workers are the first to be laid off or are forced to retire early when a collective or state-owned enterprise downsizes.

Finally, the momentous economic changes have had serious environmental consequences. Industrial expansion has been fueled primarily by highly polluting coal. The air in China's cities and even many rural areas is among the dirtiest in the world. Soil erosion, the loss of arable land, and deforestation are serious. The dumping of garbage and toxic wastes goes virtually unregulated. It is estimated that 80 percent of China's rivers are badly polluted. One of the most serious problems is a critical water shortage in north China due to urbanization and industrialization. Private automobile use is just starting to take off. This will greatly add to the country's pollution concerns (and demand for more oil) in the very near future. **Sustainable development**, which balances economic growth and environmental concerns, is a key part of the party-state's current emphasis on building a "harmonious society."

Dealing with some of the negative consequences of fast growth and market reforms is one of the main challenges facing China's government. The ability of citizen associations—including labor, women's, and environmental organizations—to place their concerns about these problems on the nation's political agenda remains limited by the party's tight control of political life and by restrictions on the formation of autonomous interest groups (see Section 4).

sustainable development an approach to promoting economic growth that seeks to minimize environmental degradation and depletion of natural resources.

China in the Global Economy

FOCUS QUESTION

In what ways has China's economy become globalized?

China was not a major trading nation when Deng Xiaoping took power in 1978. Total foreign trade was around $20 billion (approximately 10 percent of GDP). Foreign investment in China was minuscule. The stagnant economy, political instability, and heavy-handed bureaucracy did not attract potential investors from abroad.

In the early 1980s, China embarked on a strategy of using trade as a central component of its drive for economic development. In some ways it followed the model of export-led growth pioneered by Japan and newly industrializing countries (NICs) such as the Republic of Korea (South Korea). This model takes advantage of low-wage domestic labor to produce goods that are in demand internationally. It then uses the earnings from those goods to modernize the economy.

In terms of goods and services, China is now the world's second-largest trading nation behind the United States. China's main exports are office machines, data-processing and telecommunications equipment, clothing and footwear, toys, and sporting goods. It mostly imports industrial machinery, technology and scientific equipment, iron and steel, and raw materials (including oil) needed to support economic development. In 2007, a large number of Chinese goods, including pet food, seafood, toys, and tires were recalled from the American market because of health and safety concerns. This reflected both the enormous growth of China as a key part of the global factory of the twenty-first century and the lack of effective regulation in many sectors of China part-command, part-market economy.

The U.S. Connection
Sino*–American Relations

China and the United States were allies during World War II. At that time, the Chinese government was controlled by the pro-American Nationalist Party of Chiang Kai-shek. The United States supported Chiang and the Nationalists in the civil war against the Chinese Communist Party. When the CCP took power and established the People's Republic of China in 1949, Sino-American relations plunged into a period of Cold War hostility that lasted for more than two decades.

The United States continued to support Chiang and the Nationalists after they fled to Taiwan and protected Taiwan from an attack by the PRC. China and the United States also fought against each other in the Korean War (1950–1953). That war ended in a stalemate. That is why the Korean peninsula is still divided between a communist North Korea and a democratic, capitalist South Korea.

Furthermore, the PRC was closely allied with its communist big brother, the Soviet Union, America's archenemy, for much of the 1950s. Relations between Moscow and Beijing soured in the early 1960s, and the two communist powers became ideological rivals. But China and the United States still saw each other as enemies, and, for example, backed different sides in the Vietnam War.

In the early 1970s, Sino-American relations began to warm up. Each country saw the Soviets as its main enemy and decided to cooperate with each other in order to weaken their common foe. In 1972, Richard Nixon became the first U.S. president to visit the People's Republic (in fact, he was the first U.S. president ever to visit China). Formal diplomatic relations between Washington and Beijing were established in 1978. Since then, economic, cultural, and even military ties have deepened, despite some disruptions, such as following the Tiananmen massacre in 1989, and recurring tensions over Taiwan, Tibet, trade, human rights, and other issues. Many scholars and diplomats believe that U.S.-China relations are the most important bilateral relationship in the post–Cold War world.

Economic relations between China and the United States are particularly important and complex. China now trades with the United States more than it does with any other country, while China is America's third-largest trading partner (after Canada and Mexico). The United States imports far more from China than it exports (over $200 billion dollars more). Wal-Mart alone buys about $20 billion of goods from China. Wal-Mart also runs over sixty stores in China and recently bought a chain that will add another hundred.

There are many people in the United States who think that importing such a huge quantity of "cheap" products from China means lost jobs and lower wages for Americans. They argue that American firms can't compete with Chinese companies because labor costs in China are so much lower. They also say that China engages in unfair trade practices, exploits sweat-shop labor, and suppresses independent union activity. Since exports are so vital to the PRC's economic growth, they conclude that America's huge trade deficit with China indirectly helps keep the Chinese Communist Party in power. They want the United States government to put more restrictions on trade with China, particularly on imports.

On the other side, there are those who say that the benefits of U.S. trade with China far outweigh the negative impacts. First of all, consumers benefit greatly by the availability of a large variety of less-expensive products. Furthermore, in their view, the United States should focus on developing more high-tech businesses to create jobs rather than trying to compete with China and other countries in "old-fashioned" labor-intensive industries. They point out that many American firms have huge investments in China, which will grow—as will demand for American products—as that country becomes more modern and prosperous. Chinese investments in the United States and the PRC's purchase of several hundred billion dollars worth of U.S. government bonds has helped keep inflation low and the economy growing in the United States. Finally, the pro-China trade side argues that Sino-American economic engagement is one important way to promote not only the free market in China but also a more open society and democracy. ❖

Sino is a term derived from Latin that is often used to refer to China. For example, scholars who specialize in the study of China are "sinologists." Sino-American relations is another way of saying United States–China relations.

Foreign investment in the PRC has also skyrocketed. China is now one of the world's largest targets of foreign direct investment. Each year tens of billions of dollars are invested in tens of thousands of businesses and projects. More than 400 of the world's 500 top corporations have operations in the PRC. Foreign firms operating in China generally pay their workers considerably more than the average wage of about 60 cents per hour in Chinese-owned factories. But the low cost of labor in China is still a major attraction to investors from abroad.

Another lure to foreign investment is the huge Chinese domestic market. As incomes rise, corporations like Coca-Cola, General Motors, Starbucks, and Wal-Mart have poured vast amounts of money into China. American tobacco companies are hoping that China's 350 million smokers can make up for sharply declining cigarette sales in the United States. In 2005, Philip Morris signed an agreement with a Chinese company to jointly produce Marlboros (2 billion in the first year!) to be sold in China.

China is itself becoming a major investor in other countries. In a sign of how far the PRC has come as a world economic power, the Chinese company, the Lenovo Group, bought IBM's personal computer business in late 2004 and is now actively marketing its machines in the United States and elsewhere.

China occupies an important, but somewhat contradictory, position in the global economy. On the one hand, the PRC's relatively low level of economic and technological development makes it very much a part of the Third World. On the other hand, the total output and rapid growth of its economy, expanding trade, and vast resource base (including its population) make it a rising economic superpower among nations.

Summary

During the Maoist era (1949–1976), the communist party-state thoroughly dominated the economy. It did this both through a system of central planning in which government bureaucrats determined economic policies and by radical politics that suppressed any kind of private economic activity as counterrevolutionary. This approach achieved some success in promoting industrialization and raising the educational and health standards of the Chinese people. But, overall, it left China as a very poor country with little involvement in the global economy. Under Deng Xiaoping and his successors, the party-state has given up much of its control of the economy and encouraged free market forces, private ownership, international trade, and foreign investment. Living standards, modernization, and globalization have all increased dramatically. But serious problems challenge China's current leaders. For example, there is enormous inequality between city and countryside. More than 150 million people have moved from the rural to urban areas. Health care and other social services have collapsed in many parts of the country. The environment has been badly damaged. The government is now showing concern about these downsides to China's economic miracle. It remains to be seen how this concern will be translated into action.

SECTION 3

Governance and Policy-Making

FOCUS QUESTIONS

What are the most important features of a communist party-state as a type of political system? What is the relationship between the government of the People's Republic of China and the CCP? How does the CCP justify its continuing rule?

Organization of the State

The People's Republic of China, Cuba, Vietnam, North Korea, and Laos are the only remaining communist party-states in the world. Like the Soviet Union before its collapse in 1991, the political systems of these countries are characterized by Communist Party domination of all state (or government) institutions; that is why they are called "party-states"). Such political systems also have an official state ideology based on Marxism-Leninism, and, to varying and changing degrees, government control of key aspects of the economy. Ruling communist parties assert that only they can govern in the best interests of the entire nation. Therefore they claim the right to exercise what is called the "leading role" throughout society. Political opposition is not permitted in communist party-states.

The government of communist party-states like China is organizationally and functionally distinct from the Communist Party. But the government essentially acts as the administrative agency for carrying out and enforcing policies made by the party. The Communist Party exercises direct or indirect control over all government organizations and personnel. High-ranking government officials with any substantive authority are also members of the Communist Party.

Ideology is an important feature of a communist party-state. Despite China's sharp move toward a market economy, the CCP still asserts that it is building socialism in China with the ultimate objective of creating an egalitarian and classless communist society. It claims to be guided by the fundamental principles of Marxism-Leninism. Marxism refers to the part of communist ideology based on the writing of Karl Marx (1818–1883) that is centrally concerned with economic exploitation of the poor working classes (the "proletariat") by the rich property owners (the "capitalists"). Leninism refers to the theories developed by the Russian revolutionary, Vladimir Lenin (1870–1924) who founded the Soviet Union. It emphasizes how the proletariat should be organized and led by a communist party to seize political power from the capitalists.

The CCP says that Mao Zedong made a highly original and significant contribution to communist ideology. He adapted Marxism-Leninism, which had evolved in Europe and Russia, to China's special circumstances. In particular he emphasized the peasant-based revolution that brought the communist party to power in China. The party continues to praise Mao and what they call "Mao Zedong Thought." But they acknowledge that Mao made serious mistakes, such as in his views about class struggle that led to the Cultural Revolution.

Chinese communist ideology has continued to develop in ways that reflect the priorities of the leadership. In 1997, the CCP added "Deng Xiaoping Theory" to its official ideology. This reflected Deng's use of market forces to promote the economy in a socialist country led by a communist party. In 2002, when Jiang Zemin retired as general secretary, his ideas (called the "Three Represents") about expanding the CCP to incorporate all sectors of Chinese society, including owners of private businesses, became part of the party's core ideology. And, in 2007, party leader Hu Jintao's goals for creating a "harmonious society" were added to the CCP constitution and referred to as "the Scientific Outlook on Development."

The focus of Chinese communism, in both theory and practice, has shifted from revolutionary change to economic development. But most people in China have lost faith in communist ideology because of the CCP's erratic and repressive leadership. Or else they simply consider it largely irrelevant to their daily lives. Many of those who join the party now do so mainly for career advancement. But the latest Chinese communist variant of Marxism-Leninism still provides the framework for governance and policy-making. And it sets the boundaries for what is permissible in politics.

The underlying organizing principles of China's party-state appear in the constitution of the People's Republic (which is a separate document from the party constitution). The preamble of the PRC constitution repeatedly declares that the country is under "the leadership of the Communist Party of China." Article 1 defines the PRC as "a socialist state under the people's democratic dictatorship." It declares that "disruption of the socialist system by any organization or individual is prohibited." Such provisions imply that the Chinese "people" (implicitly, supporters of socialism and the leadership of the party) enjoy democratic rights and privileges. But the constitution also gives the CCP authority to exercise dictatorship over any person or organization that, it believes, opposes socialism and the party.

China's constitution is less a governing document of enduring principles than a political statement. Constitutional change (from minor amendments to total replacement) during the last fifty years has reflected the shifting political winds in China. The character and content of the state constitution in force at any given time bear the ideological stamp of the prevailing party leadership. The constitution of the Mao era stressed the importance of continuing the revolution and class struggle while the current one emphasizes national unity in the pursuit of economic development and modernization.

The Executive

FOCUS QUESTIONS

What are the most powerful executive positions and organizations in the PRC and the CCP? What is the relationship between government and party executives?

The government of the People's Republic of China and the Chinese Communist Party have separate, but connected executive offices and organizations. The party executive is clearly the more powerful.

The Party Executive

According to the constitution of the Chinese Communist Party, the "highest leading bodies" of the party are the National Party Congress and the Central Committee (see Figure 9.3). But the National Party Congress meets for only one week every five years, and it has more than 2,200 delegates. This means that the role of the Congress is more symbolic than substantive. The essential function of the National Party Congress is to approve decisions already made by the top leaders and to provide a showcase for the party's current policies. There is little debate about policy and no contested voting of any consequence. The party congress

182   Chapter 4: China

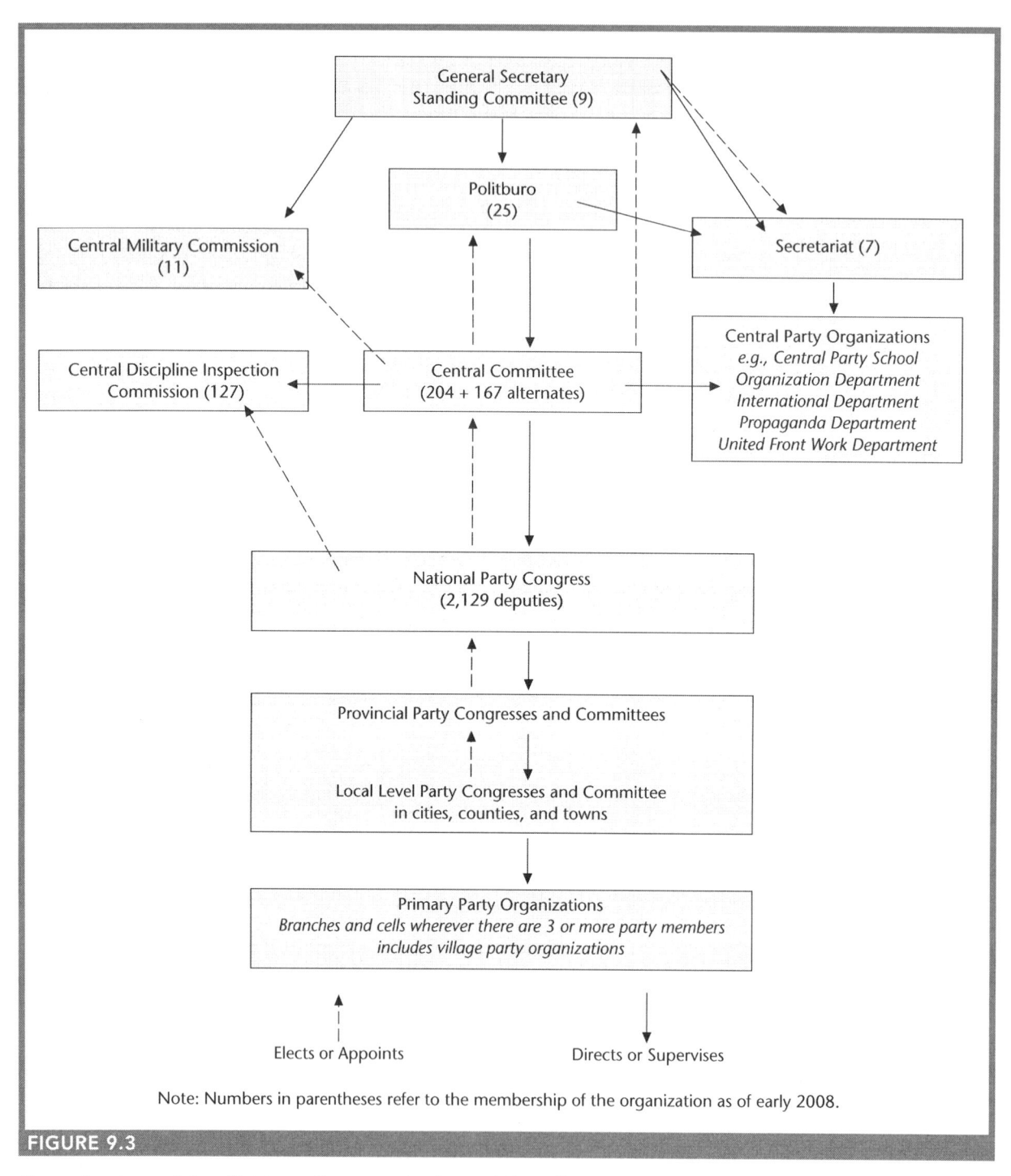

FIGURE 9.3

Organization of the Chinese Communist Party (73 million)

does not function as a legislative check or balance of the power of the party's executive leadership.

The Central Committee (currently 204 full members and 167 alternates) is the next level up in the pyramid of party power. It consists of CCP leaders from around the country who meet annually for about a week. Members are elected for a five-year term by the National Party Congress by secret ballot, with a limited choice of candidates. Contending party factions may jockey to win seats, but the overall composition of the Central Committee is closely controlled by the top leaders to ensure compliance with their policies.

In theory, the Central Committee directs party affairs when the National Party Congress is not in session. But its size and short, infrequent meetings (called plenums) also greatly limit its effectiveness. However, Central Committee plenums and occasional informal work conferences do represent significant gatherings of the party elite. They can be a very important arena of political maneuvering and decision making.

The most powerful political organizations in China's communist party-state are the two small executive bodies at the very top of the CCP's structure: the Politburo (or Political Bureau) and its even more exclusive Standing Committee. These bodies are elected by the Central Committee from among its own members under carefully controlled and secretive conditions. The current Politburo has twenty-five members. Nine of them also belong to the Standing Committee, the formal apex of power in the CCP.

People who study Chinese politics scrutinize the membership of the Politburo and Standing Committee for clues about leadership priorities, the balance of power among party factions, and the relative influence of different groups in policy-making. Seven of the nine members of the Standing Committee elected in 2007 and about half of the members of the Politburo were trained as engineers before beginning political careers. Almost all the other members of the top leadership have university degrees in business, law, the social sciences, or the humanities. This is dramatic evidence of the shift in China's ruling circles from the revolutionary leaders of Mao's and Deng's generations to college-educated technocrats who place the highest priority on science and technology as the keys to the country's development. No wonder China's government is sometimes called a "technocracy": Time.com once even referred to the rise to power of the engineers and other well-educated leaders in China as "The Revenge of the Nerds" since intellectuals and technical specialists were persecuted during the Maoist era.[7]

The Politburo and Standing Committee are not responsible to the Central Committee or any other institution in any meaningful sense. The operations of these organizations are generally shrouded in secrecy. Key leaders work and often live in a huge walled compound called Zhongnanhai ("Middle Southern Sea") on a lake in the center of Beijing quite near the Forbidden City that once housed China's emperors. Zhongnanhai is not only heavily guarded as any government executive headquarters would be, but it also has no identifying signs on its exterior, nor does it appear on any public maps.

Profile
Hu Jintao

China's current president and Communist Party leader, Hu Jintao, is, in many ways, typical of the kind of people who now lead the country. For a Chinese leader, he was relatively young (60) when he assumed power in 2002–2003. He is also well-educated and had a more-or-less smooth rise to the top up the party career ladder. He fits the definition of a "technocrat," a term often used to describe China's current generation of leaders who have backgrounds in technical fields and spent most of their working lives as bureaucrats within the Chinese Communist Party.

Hu was born into a family of tea merchants in 1942, and grew up in a small city in the central coastal province of Jiangsu, not far from Shanghai. He was just six years old when the Chinese Communist Party came to power. Hu did very well in school and attended Qinghua University, China's best school of science and technology, where he studied hydroelectric engineering. He joined the Communist Party while at Qinghua. He graduated in 1965. This was right before the start of Chairman Mao's Great Proletarian Cultural Revolution, a period of political and social chaos when China's universities were shut down as part of the campaign to destroy those who were seen as enemies of Chinese Communist Party.

Hu Jintao did not participate as a Red Guard in the Cultural Revolution. But he did witness a lot of violence, and his father was persecuted for being a "capitalist" and imprisoned. This experience is one influence that made Hu turn against the kind of radical communism preached by Chairman Mao.

In the late 1960s, Hu was among the millions of young people sent to the rural areas and the frontier as part of their revolutionary education. He spent about a decade living and working in the poor, remote desert province of Gansu in China's far west. At first he did manual labor in housing construction, but he was transferred to work in the provincial ministry of water resources and electric power because of his high level of specialized training. It was then that he also became actively involved in Communist Party politics.

In Gansu, Hu formed a close relationship with the top party official in the province—also a Qinghua University graduate—who became a member of the CCP's powerful Standing Committee after Deng Xiaoping had consolidated his power as China's dominant leader in the early 1980s. Hu's political career rose with that of his mentor—a good example of the importance of *guanxi* ("connections") in Chinese politics. He was given the critical opportunity to study at the Central Party School in Beijing, which is a training ground for the CCP's future elite. He became a specialist in youth affairs and rose to the position of head of the Communist Youth League.

Hu was then appointed to be Communist Party leader in Guizhou province and Tibet. These appointments gave him an unusual amount of experience in areas of the country inhabited by large numbers of China's minorities (see Section 4). When he was the party leader in Tibet, he imposed **martial law** to suppress demonstrations in favor of Tibetan independence. In 1992, he joined the CCP Secretariat, a key group that manages the party leadership's day-to-day work. In the late 1990s, he became a member of the powerful Standing Committee and China's vice-president. He also emerged as Deng Xiaoping's choice to succeed Jiang Zemin as head of the Communist Party and country. The fact that Deng could anoint not only his successor, but also his successor's successor reflected both the extent of Deng's personal power and the informal means by which such important decisions are made in China.

Hu Jintao became general secretary of the Chinese Communist Party in 2002 (re-elected in 2007) and president of the People's Republic of China in 2003 (re-elected in 2008). Like Deng and Jiang, he has been committed both to promoting rapid economic growth and free market reforms and to maintaining the rule of the Communist Party. He has also proclaimed that his goal for China is to create a "harmonious society" that pays more attention to problems like growing inequality, rural poverty, and pollution that have accompanied the PRC's rapid development. In late 2007, the meeting of the National Congress of the Chinese Communist Party (held every five years) was a showcase for Hu's power and policies, and his "Scientific Outlook on Development" was added to the party's constitution as the CCP's current guiding version of Marxism-Leninism. ❖

martial law a period of time during which the normal procedures of government are suspended and the executive branch enforces the law with military power.

The party's top leader is the general secretary, who presides over the Politburo and the Standing Committee. Jiang Zemin (1989–2002) and Hu Jintao (2002–present) have held this position most recently. Neither Jiang nor Hu have had the personal clout or charisma of either Deng or Mao. They have governed as part of a collective leadership that included their fellow members on the Standing Committee and Politburo. Nevertheless, both have tried to put their own stamp on the party's major policy direction.

Below the national level, the CCP has a hierarchy of local party organizations in provinces, cities, and counties, each headed by a party secretary and party committee. There are also more than 3.5 million primary party organizations, called branches. These are found throughout the country in workplaces, government offices, schools, urban neighborhoods, rural towns, villages, and army units where there are three or more party members. Local and primary organizations extend the CCP's reach throughout Chinese society. They are also designed to ensure coordination within the vast and complex party structure and subordination to the central party authorities in Beijing.

The Government Executive

Government authority in China is formally vested in a system of people's congresses that begins at the top with the National People's Congress (NPC), which is a completely different organization than the National *Party* Congress. The NPC is China's national legislature and is discussed in more detail in Section 4. There are also people's congresses at the subnational levels of government, including provincial people's congresses, city people's congresses, and rural township people's congresses (see Figure 9.4). In theory, these congresses (the legislative branch) are empowered to supervise the work of the "people's governments" (the executive branch) at the various levels of the system. But in reality, government executives (such as cabinet ministers, provincial governors, and mayors) are more accountable to party authority than to the people's congresses. For example, the city of Shanghai has both a mayor and a party secretary, each with distinct and important powers. But the party secretary's power is more consequential.

The National People's Congress formally elects the president and vice president of China. But there is only one candidate, chosen by the Communist Party, for each office. The president's term is concurrent with that of the congress (five years). There is a two-term limit. The position is largely ceremonial, although a senior Communist Party leader has always held it. As China's head of state, the president meets and negotiates with other world leaders. Both Jiang Zemin and Hu Jintao served concurrently as CCP general secretary and PRC president.

The premier (prime minister) has authority over the government bureaucracy and policy implementation. The premier is formally appointed by the president with the approval of the National People's Congress. But in reality,

Chapter 4: China

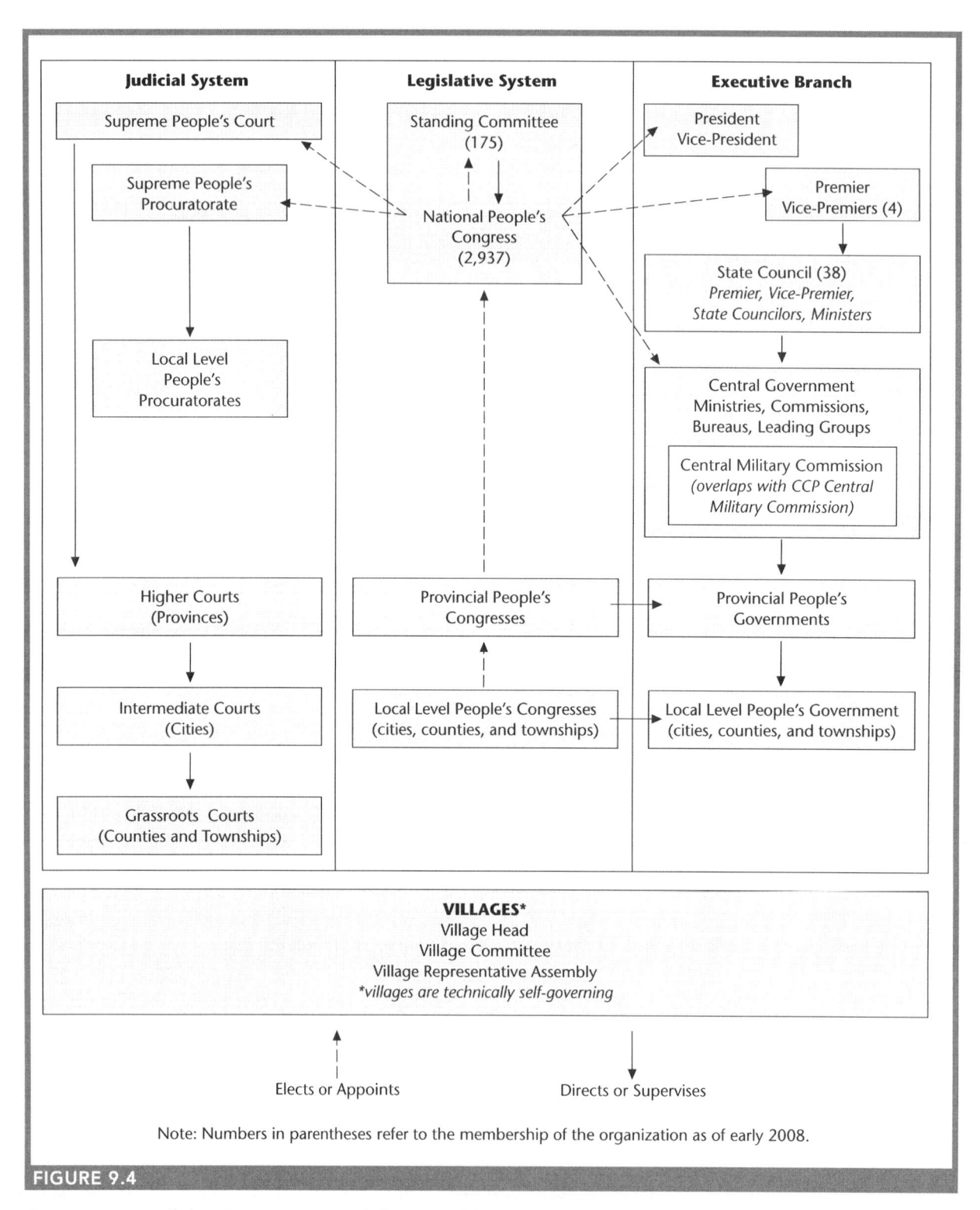

Judicial System

- Supreme People's Court
  - Supreme People's Procuratorate
    - Local Level People's Procuratorates
- Higher Courts (Provinces)
  - Intermediate Courts (Cities)
    - Grassroots Courts (Counties and Townships)

Legislative System

- Standing Committee (175)
- National People's Congress (2,937)
- Provincial People's Congresses
- Local Level People's Congresses (cities, counties, and townships)

Executive Branch

- President / Vice-President
- Premier / Vice-Premiers (4)
- State Council (38) — *Premier, Vice-Premier, State Councilors, Ministers*
- Central Government Ministries, Commissions, Bureaus, Leading Groups
  - Central Military Commission *(overlaps with CCP Central Military Commission)*
- Provincial People's Governments
- Local Level People's Government (cities, counties, and townships)

VILLAGES*
Village Head
Village Committee
Village Representative Assembly
*villages are technically self-governing

↑ Elects or Appoints   ↓ Directs or Supervises

Note: Numbers in parentheses refer to the membership of the organization as of early 2008.

FIGURE 9.4

Organization of the Government of the People's Republic of China (PRC)

The Chinese Communist Party Standing Committee. *(Source: Ng Han Guan/AP Images)*

the Communist Party decides who will serve as premier. A very high-ranking member of the CCP Standing Committee has always held that post. Like the president, the premier may serve only two five-year terms. The current premier, Wen Jiabao, was trained as a geological engineer and is another good example of the technocrats who now run China.

The premier directs the State Council, which is constitutionally "the highest organ of state administration" (Article 85) in the PRC. It functions much like the cabinet in a parliamentary system. It includes the premier, a few vice premiers, the heads of government ministries and commissions, and several other senior officials. The National People's Congress appoints the State Council, although its membership is determined by the party leadership.

State Council ministers run either functionally specific departments, such as the Ministry of Health, or organizations with more comprehensive responsibilities, such as the State Commission of Science, Technology and Industry for National Defense. Beneath the State Council is an array of support staffs, research offices, and bureaucratic agencies charged with policy implementation.

China's bureaucracy is immense in size and in the scope of its reach throughout the country. The total number of **cadres**—people in positions of authority paid by the government or party—in the PRC is around 40 million. A minority of these cadres work directly for the government or the CCP. The remainder occupy key posts in economic enterprises (such as factory directors); schools (such as principals); and scientific, cultural, and other state-run institutions. There have been important moves toward professionalizing the

cadre a person who occupies a position of authority in a communist party–state; cadres may or may not be Communist Party members.

bureaucracy, particularly at the city level of government. More official positions are now subject to competition through civil service exams rather than the still-prevalent method of appointment from above.

One of the most significant administrative reforms of the post-Mao era—quite unprecedented in a communist party-state—has been to take measures to limit how long officials can stay in their jobs. Depending on their position, both government and party cadres must now retire between the ages of sixty and seventy. A two-term limit has been set for all top cadres.

Other State Institutions

The Military, the Police, and the Judiciary

> **FOCUS QUESTIONS**
> What are the most important features of China's military, police, legal system, and local government? How and why does the CCP closely supervise these state institutions?

The China's People's Liberation Army (PLA) encompasses all the country's ground, air, and naval armed services. It is the world's largest military force, with about 2.3 million active personnel. The PLA also has a formal reserve of another 1 million or so and a backup people's militia of 12 to 15 million, which could be mobilized in the event of war. The level of training and weaponry available to the militia are generally minimal.

The PRC has increased military spending by double-digit percentages nearly every year for more than a decade (18 percent in 2007) in order to modernize its armed forces and raise the pay of military personnel. China said that it spent $45 billion on defense in 2007. Many analysts think that the PRC vastly understates its defense budget. They estimate that it is really closer to two or three times the official figures. Still, China spends much less in total and vastly less per capita on military expenditures than does the United States, which spent over $500 billion on defense in 2007.

The key organizations in charge of the Chinese armed forces are the Military Commissions (CMC) of the CCP and PRC. On paper, these are two distinct organizations. In fact, they overlap entirely in membership and function. The chair of the state Military Commission is "elected" by the National People's Congress, but is always the same person as the chair of the party CMC. The CMC chair is, in effect, the commander-in-chief of China's armed forces. This position has almost always been held by the most powerful party leader. Hu Jintao is the current chair of China's Central Military Commission.

China's internal security apparatus consists of several different organizations. The Ministry of State Security is responsible for combating espionage and gathering intelligence at home and abroad. A 1.5-million-strong People's Armed Police guards public officials and buildings and carries out some border patrol and protection. It also quells serious public disturbances, including worker or peasant unrest. The Ministry of Public Security is responsible for the maintenance of law and order, the investigation of crimes, and the surveillance of Chinese citizens and foreigners in China suspected of being a threat to the state. Local Public Security Bureaus are under the command of central ministry authorities in Beijing. In effect, China has a national police force stationed throughout the country. There are also local police forces, but they do little more than supervise traffic.

In addition to a regular prison system, the Ministry of Public Security maintains an extensive system of labor reform camps for people convicted of particularly serious crimes, including political ones. These camps, which are noted for their harsh conditions and remote locations, are estimated to have millions of prisoners. Public Security Bureaus have the authority to detain indefinitely people suspected of committing a crime without making a formal charge. They can also use administrative sanctions (penalties imposed outside the court system) to levy fines or sentence detainees for up to three years of "re-education through labor." A special system of more than 300 camps holds such detainees (estimated at 300,000). They include prostitutes, drug users, and petty criminals, as well as some who might be considered political prisoners.

China's criminal justice system works swiftly and harshly. Great faith is placed in the ability of an official investigation to find the facts of a case. The outcome of cases that actually do come to trial is pretty much predetermined. The conviction rate is 98–99 percent for all criminal cases. Prison terms are long and subject to only cursory appeal. A variety of offenses in addition to murder—including, in some cases, rape and especially major cases of embezzlement and other "economic crimes"—are subject to capital punishment. All death penalty sentences must be approved by the country's Supreme Court. But such appeals are handled very quickly. Capital punishment cases do not linger in the courts for years, or even months. Execution is usually by a single bullet in the back of the convicted person's head, although the country is moving toward lethal injection. Amnesty International said that China led the world in the application of the death penalty in 2006, with about 1100 executions that it could verify, followed by Iran (177), Pakistan (82), Iraq (65), Sudan (61), and the United States (53). However, death penalty statistics are officially a state secret in the PRC, and Amnesty estimates that the actual number of executions in China was in the 7000–8000 range.

China has a four-tiered "people's court" system. It reaches from a Supreme People's Court down through higher (provincial-level), intermediate (city-level), and grassroots (county- and township-level) people's courts. The Supreme People's Court supervises the lower courts and the application of the country's laws. It hears few cases and does not exercise judicial review over government policies.

There are now more than 100,000 lawyers in China (compared to about a million in the United States). Legal advisory offices throughout the country provide citizens and organizations with legal assistance. Many laws and regulations have been enacted, including new criminal and civil codes, to make the legal system much fairer than it was during the Maoist period.

Although the PRC constitution guarantees judicial independence, China's courts and other legal bodies remain under party control. The appointment of judicial personnel is subject to party approval. The CCP is still able to bend the law to serve its interests. Legal reform in China has been undertaken because China's leaders are well aware that economic development requires detailed laws, professional lawyers and judicial personnel, predictable legal processes, and binding documents such as contracts.

Subnational Government

China is not a federal system (like Brazil, Germany, India, Nigeria, and the United States) that gives subnational governments considerable policy-making autonomy. Provincial and local authorities in the PRC operate "under the unified leadership of the central authorities" (Article 3 of the state constitution). This makes China a unitary state like France and Japan. The national government in Beijing exercises a high degree of control over other levels of government.

There are four main layers of state structure beneath the central government in China: provinces, cities, counties, and rural towns. There are also four very large centrally administered cities (Beijing, Shanghai, Tianjin, and Chongqing) and five autonomous regions (areas of the country with large minority populations, such as Tibet and Mongolia). Each of these levels has a representative people's congress that meets infrequently, and plays a limited, but increasingly active, role in managing affairs in its area. Executive officials, such as governors and mayors, have much greater authority than they did in the recent past, but they, too, are always subject to supervision by the central government and the Communist Party organization at their level.

Beneath the formal layers of state administration are China's 700,000 or so rural villages. These are home to the majority of the country's population. These villages, with an average population of roughly 500–1,000 each, are technically self-governing and are not formally responsible to a higher level of state authority. In recent years, village leaders have been directly and competitively elected by local residents. Village representative assemblies have become more vocal. These trends have brought an important degree of grass-roots democracy to village government (see Section 4). However, the most powerful organization in the village is the Communist Party committee, and the single most powerful person is the local Communist Party leader (the party secretary).

The Policy-Making Process

FOCUS QUESTIONS
How does the CCP exercise control of the policy-making process?
What other factors influence the policy-making process in China?

Political power in China has become much more decentralized and institutionalized than during the Maoist era. Policies now evolve from a complex process of cooperation, conflict, and bargaining among actors and organizations at various levels of the system. Provincial and local governments have a lot more clout in the policy process. The national focus on economic development has also given growing influence to nonparty experts and organizations in the policy loop.

Nevertheless the Chinese Communist Party still ultimately controls policy-making in China. The top two dozen or so party leaders wield nearly unchecked power. The CCP uses a weblike system of organizational controls to make sure that the government bureaucracy complies with the party's will in policy implementation Almost all key government officials (such a mayors and provincial governors) are also party members. Various party organizations keep a careful eye on government agencies. The CCP exercises control over appointments to millions of positions in the government and elsewhere, including universities, banks, trade unions, and newspapers.

In recent years, "leading small groups" have become very important in policy-making at the national level. These groups are made up of leaders from different organizations who coordinate decision making on important issues that may cut across bureaucratic boundaries. Some are more-or-less permanent, such as the National Security Leading Small Group, while others are set up to deal with a short-term crisis, like a natural disaster or an epidemic. Since most of the members are high-ranking CCP officials, they are also meant to insure party supervision of policy in that particular area.

Any account of the policy process in China must also note the importance of **guanxi** ("connections"). These are personal relationships and mutual obligations based on family, friendship, school, military, professional, or other ties. The notion of *guanxi* has its roots in China's traditional Confucian culture. It has long been an important part of political, social, and economic life. In the bureaucracy, personal ties are often the key to getting things done. *Guanxi* can either cut red tape and increase efficiency or stiffen organizational rigidity and feed corruption.

The power of the Communist Party is the most basic fact of political life in the People's Republic of China. But the policy-making process still "wriggles with politics" of many kinds, both formal and informal.[8] It is important to look at how various influences, including policy disagreements, bureaucratic interests, *guanxi*, and even citizen input (discussed in the next section) shape the decisions ultimately made by Communist Party leaders and organizations.

guanxi a Chinese term that means "connections" or "relationships," and describes personal ties between individuals based on such things as common birthplace or mutual acquaintances.

Summary

China is a communist party-state. It is one of the few remaining countries in the world that is still ruled by a communist party. Even though the Chinese Communist Party (CCP) has moved China in the direction of a capitalist, free market economy, it proclaims that it is following communist ideology (Marxism-Leninism) and that its goal is to create a socialist China. The CCP insists that it is the only political party that can lead the country toward this goal, and it prohibits any serious challenge to its authority. Power in China is highly concentrated in the top two dozen or so leaders of the Communist Party, presided over by the general secretary of the CCP, who are chosen through secretive inner-party procedures. The government of the People's Republic of China (the "state") is technically separate from the CCP, and political reform in China has brought a degree of autonomy to government institutions, such as the national legislature and the judiciary. But, in fact, the state operates only under the close supervision of the Communist Party and almost all high-ranking government officials are also members of the Communist Party.

SECTION 4

Representation and Participation

socialist democracy the term used by the Chinese Communist Party to describe the political system of the People's Republic of China.

The People's Republic of China says that it is a **socialist democracy** under the leadership of the Chinese Communist Party, which is, in turn, said to represent the interests of the overwhelming majority of the people. Socialist democracy is claimed by the PRC to be different from democracy in capitalist countries like the United States where big business and the rich are able to influence politics in their favor to the disadvantage of working people.

Although power in China is highly concentrated in the hands of the top leaders of the Chinese Communist Party, representation and participation do play important, if limited, roles in the China's political system. Legislatures, elections, and organizations like labor unions provide citizens with ways of influencing public policy-making and the selection of some government leaders.

FOCUS QUESTIONS

What powers does the National People's Congress have? How does the CCP control the NPC? In what ways is it becoming more active and independent?

The Legislature

China's constitution grants the National People's Congress (NPC) the power to enact and amend the country's laws, approve and monitor the state budget, and declare and end war. The NPC is also empowered to elect (and recall) the president and vice president, the chair of the state Central Military Commission, the head of China's Supreme Court, and the procurator-general (something like the U.S. attorney general). The NPC has final approval over the selection of the premier and members of the State Council. On paper, China's legislature certainly looks to be the most powerful branch of government. In fact, these powers, which are not insignificant, are exercised only as allowed by the Communist Party.

The National People's Congress is elected for a five-year term and meets for only about two weeks every March. There are nearly 3,000 members (called "deputies") in the NPC. Deputies are not full-time legislators, but remain in their regular jobs and home areas except for the brief time when the congress is in session. All deputies, except those from the People's Liberation Army, are chosen on a geographic basis from China's provinces, autonomous regions, and major municipalities. There are representatives from China's two indirectly ruled Special Administrative Regions, the tiny former Portuguese colony and now gambling haven of Macau and the former British colony and now bustling commercial city of Hong Kong. To symbolize China's claim to Taiwan, deputies representing the island are chosen from among PRC residents with Taiwanese ancestry or other ties.

About 73 percent of the deputies elected in 2003 were members of the CCP. The others belonged to one of China's eight noncommunist (and powerless) political parties (see below) or had no party affiliation.

Workers and farmers made up about 18 percent of the deputies elected in 2003. Intellectuals and professionals made up another 21 percent. Government and party cadres accounted for a little under a third. Nine percent were from the

Hong Kong: From China to Britain—and Back Again

Hong Kong became a British colony in three stages during the nineteenth century as a result of what China calls the "unequal treaties" imposed under military and diplomatic pressure from the West following the Opium War. Two parts of Hong Kong were given *permanently* to Britain in 1842 and 1860. But the largest part of the small territory was given to Britain in 1898 with a ninety-nine-year lease. The anticipated expiration of that lease led to negotiations between London and Beijing in the 1980s. In December 1984, Britain agreed to return all of Hong Kong to Chinese sovereignty on July 1, 1997. On that date, Hong Kong became a Special Administrative Region (SAR) of the People's Republic of China.

Britain ruled Hong Kong for more than one hundred years in a traditional, if generally benevolent, colonial fashion. A governor from London presided over an administration in which British rather than local people exercised most of the power. There was a free press, a fair and effective legal system, and other important features of a democratic system. In the last years of their rule, the British appointed more Hong Kong Chinese to higher administrative positions. They also expanded the scope of elections for choosing some members of the colony's executive and representative bodies. The British, were criticized for taking steps toward democratization only on the eve of their departure from the colony. They allowed only a small number of Hong Kong residents to emigrate to the United Kingdom before the start of Chinese rule.

Hong Kong flourished economically under the free-market policies of the British. It became one of the world's great centers of international trade and finance. It now has the highest standard of living in Asia other than Singapore. Hong Kong is also characterized by extremes of wealth and poverty. When China took over Hong Kong in 1997, it pledged not to impose its political or economic system on the SAR for fifty years. The PRC has a strong motivation not to do anything that might destroy the area's economic dynamism.

Although the PRC took over full control of Hong Kong's foreign policy and has stationed troops of the People's Liberation Army in Hong Kong, Beijing has generally fulfilled its promise that the SAR will have a high degree of political as well as economic autonomy. Civil liberties, the independence of the judiciary, and freedom of the press have largely been maintained.

Nevertheless, China has made sure that it keeps a grip on power in Hong Kong. The SAR is headed by a chief executive, who along with other top civil servants must be approved by the PRC. Politicians favoring democracy in Hong Kong have a strong presence in the SAR's elected legislature, but the legislature itself is relatively powerless to make policy. In a telling example of the tug of war over the direction of Hong Kong's political future, the PRC's plan to implement a law prohibiting "any act of treason, secession, sedition, subversion against the Central People's Government [in Beijing], or theft of state secrets" was withdrawn in 2004 after large-scale protests by those who worry that British colonialism in Hong Kong might be replaced by Chinese authoritarianism. ❖

Hong Kong

Land area	401.5 sq mi/1,092 sq km (about six times the size of Washington, D.C.)
Population	7 million
Ethnic composition	Chinese, 95%; other, 5%
GDP at purchasing power parity (US$)	$293 billion, which ranks it 41st in the world and close to Austria and Norway
GDP per capita at purchasing power parity (US$)	$42,000, which ranks it above Switzerland and Canada

military. The remainder represented other occupational categories, such as business people. These numbers reflect the NPC's shift of emphasis from representing the working classes to taking economic development as its top priority. Women made up 20 percent of NPC deputies and ethnic minorities 14 percent.

Despite great fanfare in the press as examples of socialist democracy at work, legislation is passed and state leaders are elected in the National People's Congress by overwhelming majorities and little substantive debate. Nevertheless, some dissent does occur. In 1992, about a third of NPC deputies either voted against or abstained from voting on the hugely expensive ($70 billion) and ecologically controversial Three Gorges dam project now nearing completion on the Yangtze River. On very rare occasions, government legislative initiatives have even been defeated or tabled. But the NPC never takes up politically sensitive issues. The CCP also monitors the election process to make sure that no outright dissidents are elected as deputies.

Legislatures in communist party-states used to be called rubber stamps, meaning they automatically and without question approved party policies. But as economics has replaced ideology as the main motivation of China's leaders, the NPC has become a much more significant and lively part of the Chinese political system. Many NPC deputies are now chosen because of their ability to contribute to China's modernization rather than simply on the basis of political loyalty. Some have even become more assertive on issues like corruption and environmental problems. Debate and discussion can influence the final shape of legislation. The NPC is still not part of an independent branch of government in a system of checks and balances; but it also is no longer merely a rubber stamp of the Chinese Communist Party.

> **FOCUS QUESTIONS**
> How has the CCP changed over time? How has it adapted to China's emphasis on economic development and modernization? What role do China's noncommunist parties play?

Political Parties and the Party System

The Chinese Communist Party

With about 73 million members, the CCP is by far the largest political party in the world. But its membership makes up a very small minority of the population (about 8 percent of those over eighteen, the minimum age for joining the party). This is consistent with the party's view that it is a "vanguard" party that admits only those who are truly dedicated to the communist cause.

The social composition of the CCP's membership has changed considerably since the party came to power in 1949. In the mid-1950s, peasants made up nearly 70 percent. In 2007, "farmers, herdsmen, and fishermen" made up 31 percent of party members, while only 10.8 percent were industrial workers. The majority of CCP members are party-state officials, office workers, enterprise managers, military personnel, and professionals, including scientists, technical experts, and academics. The party now claims that rather than representing just workers and peasants, it represents the interests of the overwhelming majority of people in China and is open to all those who are committed to promoting national development and are willing to accept party leadership in achieving that goal.

The CCP has recently encouraged owners and employees of private businesses ("entrepreneurs") to join the party. It has also established party organizations in many private firms. This is quite a change from the Maoist era when any hint of capitalism was crushed. It is also recognition of the increasing importance of the private sector in China's economy. It is a strategy by which the party hopes to prolong its rule by adapting to a rapidly modernizing society.

Women make up only 20 percent of the CCP membership as a whole and just 6 percent of full members of the Central Committee (and 14 percent of alternates) elected in 2007. The Politburo has one female member, Liu Yandong, who has extensive experience working with youth and noncommunist organizations to help them articulate their interests and to make sure that they stay in line with party policies. No women serve on the party's most powerful organization, the Politburo Standing Committee.

Even though many Chinese believe that communist ideology is irrelevant to their lives and the nation's future, being a party member still provides unparalleled access to influence and resources. It remains a prerequisite for advancement in many careers, particularly in government. More than two million people join the CCP each year, most of them college graduates under the age of thirty-five.

China's Noncommunist "Democratic Parties"

China is usually called a one-party system because the country's politics are so thoroughly dominated by the Chinese Communist Party. In fact, China has eight political parties in addition to the CCP. These are officially referred to as China's "democratic parties," which is said to be another example of socialist democracy in the PRC. Each noncommunist party represents a particular group in Chinese society. For example, the Chinese Party for the Public Interest draws on overseas Chinese who have returned to live in China. But these parties, all of which were established before the founding of the PRC in 1949 and accept the "guidance" of the CCP, have a total membership of only a little over a half a million. They do not contest for power or challenge CCP policy. Their function is to provide advice to the CCP and generate support within their particular constituencies for CCP policies. Individual members of the parties may assume important government positions. But politically these parties are relatively insignificant. They certainly do not function as an opposition to the ruling communist party.

New political parties are not allowed to form. When a group of activists who had been part of the 1989 Tiananmen protests tried to establish a China Democracy Party in 1998 to promote multiparty politics, they were arrested or forced into exile abroad, and the party was banned.

> **FOCUS QUESTIONS**
>
> How are elections carried out in China? How have they become more democratic?

Elections

Elections in the PRC are basically mechanisms to give the communist party-state greater legitimacy by allowing large numbers of citizens to participate in the political process under very controlled circumstances. But elections are becoming a bit more democratic and more important in providing a way for citizens to express their views and hold some officials accountable.

Most elections in China are "indirect." In other words, it is the members of an already elected or established body that elect, mostly from among themselves, those who will serve at the next highest level in the power structure. For example, it is the deputies of a provincial people's congress, not all the eligible citizens of the province, who elect delegates to the National People's Congress.

Direct elections are elections in which all the voters in the relevant area get to cast a ballot for candidates for a particular position. Direct elections are most common in China at the village level, although there have been a few experiments with letting all voters choose officials and representatives at the next rung up the administrative ladder (the township). The authorities have been very cautious in expanding the scope of direct elections. The CCP wants to prevent them from becoming a forum for dissent or a vehicle to form an opposition party. The most powerful positions in the government, such a city mayors and provincial governors, are appointed, not elected.

Many direct and indirect elections now have multiple candidates, with the winner chosen by secret ballot. Any group of more than ten voters can nominate candidates for an election. A significant number of independently nominated candidates have defeated official nominees, although even independent candidates basically have to be approved by the CCP.

The most noteworthy progress toward real democratic representation and participation in China has occurred in the rural villages. Laws implemented since the late 1980s have provided for direct election of village leaders. These elections are generally multicandidate with a secret ballot. Villagers have used them to remove from office leaders they think are incompetent or corrupt.

The village CCP committee closely monitors such grass-roots elections. As noted in the previous section, the most powerful village leader is the head of the local Communist Party, and that is not an elected position. However, in many cases, the Communist Party leader has been chosen to serve simultaneously as the village head in a competitive election. This is often because the Communist Party leader is a well-respected person who has the confidence and support of the villagers. Only 1 percent of the leaders in China's 700,000 villages are women.

Village representative assemblies have members chosen from each household or group of households. The assemblies have taken a more active role in supervising the work of local officials and decision making in matters affecting community finances and welfare. Some outside observers believe such direct grass-roots elections and the representative assemblies are seeds of real democracy. Others believe they are merely a facade to appease international critics and give the rural population a way to express discontent with some officials without challenging the country's fundamental political organization.

Rural residents vote in a village election in China. In recent years, such grassroots democracy has become widespread in the countryside, although it is always closely monitored by the Chinese Communist Party. *(Getty Images)*

Recent electoral reform has certainly increased popular representation and participation in China's government. But elections in the PRC still do not give citizens a means by which they can exercise effective control over the party officials and organizations that have the real power in China's political system. Top Chinese communist leaders, from Mao to now, have repeatedly claimed that multiparty democracy is unsuited to China's traditions and conditions and would lead to chaos. In a major speech in June 2007, Chinese president and Communist Party leader, Hu Jintao, reaffirmed his support for the continuing development of socialist democracy in China, but he also noted "We must uphold the party's leadership" and that "unswervingly upholding the party's basic line is the most reliable safeguard ensuring that our cause is capable of standing the test and potential dangers and that we can smoothly arrive at our destination"[9]

Political Culture, Citizenship, and Identity

From Communism to Consumerism

Marxism-Leninism is still important in Chinese politics since the Communist Party proclaims that it is China's official ideology. Serious challenges to that ideology or the party are not permitted. The CCP also tries to keep communist ideology viable and visible by continued efforts to influence public opinion and values and limit opposition. For instance, the party ultimately controls the media, the arts, and education.

China's media are much livelier and more open than during the Maoist period when they were totally under CCP domination and did little other than convey party messages. However, freedom of the press is still quite limited.

FOCUS QUESTIONS

What is replacing communist ideology as a source of values, beliefs, and identity in China? How is the CCP responding to this change?

How large is China's ethnic minority population, and where do most of them live?

> What is their relationship to the Chinese communist party-state?

Reduced political control of the media has largely meant only the freedom to publish more entertainment news, human interest stories, local coverage, and some nonpolitical investigative journalism in areas that are consistent with party objectives. For example, in the summer of 2007, the news media helped expose the use of slave labor (including many children) in thousands of brick kilns and coal mines in two provinces in central China.

The arts are generally the area of life that has seen the greatest political change in China in recent years. There is much less direct (but not totally absent) censorship. The Chinese film industry has emerged as one of the best in the world.

Educational opportunities have expanded enormously in China since 1949. Primary school enrollment is close to 100 percent of the age-eligible population (ages six to eleven), but it drops to about 75 percent in middle and high school (ages eleven to eighteen) and 20 percent in college. Political study is still a required but now relatively minor part of the curriculum at all levels. Much greater attention goes to urging students to gain the skills and knowledge they need to further their own careers and help China modernize. More than 80 percent of China's students between the ages of seven and fourteen belong to the Young Pioneers, an organization designed to promote good social behavior, community service, patriotism, and loyalty to the party.

Internet access is exploding in China, with more than 200 million users by the end of 2007. Web connections are available even in some quite remote towns. The government worries about the influence of e-mail and electronic information it cannot control. It has blocked access to certain foreign websites and shut down unlicensed cyber cafés, which it likened to opium dens. It has arrested people it has accused of disseminating subversive material over the Internet.

Web access in China is tightly controlled by the licensing of just a few Internet Service Providers. They are responsible for who uses their systems and how. A special state organization, with an estimated 50,000 employees, polices the Internet. The government is investing huge sums to develop (with technical assistance from western companies) stronger firewalls and monitoring systems. Human rights organizations have criticized Microsoft, Yahoo, and Google for agreeing to political restrictions on websites, news sources, chat rooms, and blogs in exchange for the right to do business in China. The Chinese party-state knows that cutting-edge technology is critical to its modernization plans. Even the CCP has its own websites. The party wants citizens to become computer literate. As with so much else in China, however, the party-state wants to define the way and dictate the rules.

Alternative sources of socialization and belief are growing in importance in China. These do not often take expressly political forms, however, because of the threat of repression. In the countryside, peasants have replaced portraits of Mao and other Communist heroes with statues of folk gods and ancestor worship tablets. The influence of extended kinship groups such as clans often outweighs the formal authority of the party in the villages. In the cities, popular culture, including gigantic rock concerts, shapes youth attitudes much more profoundly than party propaganda. Consumerism ("buying things") is probably the most widely shared value in China today. Many observers have spoken of a moral vacuum in the country. This is not uncommon for societies undergoing such rapid, multifaceted change.

Organized religion, which was ferociously suppressed during the Mao era, is attracting an increasing number of adherents. Buddhist temples, Christian churches, and other places of worship operate more freely than they have in decades. However, despite the fact that freedom of religion is guaranteed by the PRC constitution (as is the freedom not to believe in any religion), religious life is strictly controlled and limited to officially approved organizations and venues. Clergy of any religion who defy the authority of the party-state are still imprisoned. Clandestine Christian communities, called house churches, have sprung up in many areas among people who reject the government's control of religious life and are unable to worship in public. Although local officials sometimes tolerate these churches, in numerous cases house church leaders and lay people have been arrested and the private homes where services are held have been bulldozed. The Chinese Catholic Church is prohibited from recognizing the authority of the pope, although there have been recent signs of a thaw between Beijing and the Vatican.

Citizenship and National Identity

The views of China's citizens about what ties them to the state—their sense of national identity—is going through a profound and uncertain transformation. Party leaders realize that most citizens are skeptical or dismissive of communist ideology and that appeals to socialist goals and revolutionary virtues no longer inspire loyalty. The CCP has turned increasingly to patriotic themes to rally the country behind its leadership. The official media put considerable emphasis on the greatness and antiquity of Chinese culture. They send the not-so-subtle message that it is time for China to reclaim its rightful place in the world order—and that only the CCP can lead the nation in achieving this goal.

In the view of some, such officially promoted nationalism could lead to a more aggressive foreign and military policy—especially with the country's growing need for energy resources—toward areas such as the potentially oil-rich South China Sea, where the PRC's historical territorial claims conflict with those of other countries including Vietnam and the Philippines.

It is, of course, the cultural tie of being "Chinese" that is the most powerful collective identity that connects people to the nation. The Chinese people are intensely proud of their ancient culture and long history. Their enthusiasm for hosting the 2008 Olympics in Beijing reflected this cultural pride. They can also be very sensitive about what they consider slights to their national dignity. Many Chinese feel that Japan has not done enough to acknowledge or apologize for the atrocities its army committed in China during World War II. This has been a strain in relations between the two countries and has sometimes led to spontaneous anti-Japanese demonstrations by Chinese students.

China's Non-Chinese Citizens

The PRC calls itself a multinational state with fifty-six officially recognized ethnic groups, one of which is the majority Han people (named after an early dynasty). The Han make up 91.5 percent of the total population. The defining elements of a minority group involves some combination of language, culture (including religion), and race that distinguish them from the Han. The fifty-five non-Han minorities number a little more than 100 million, or about 8.5 percent of the total population. These groups range in size from 16 million (the Zhuang of southwest China) to about 2,000 (the Lhoba in the far west). Most of these minorities have come under Chinese rule over many centuries through the expansion of the Chinese state rather than through migration into China.

China's minorities are highly concentrated in the five autonomous regions of Guangxi, Inner Mongolia, Ningxia, Tibet, and Xinjiang. Only in the last two, however, do minority people outnumber Han Chinese, who have been encouraged to migrate to these regions. The five autonomous regions are sparsely populated, yet they occupy about 60 percent of the total land area of the PRC. Some of these areas are resource rich. All are located on strategically important borders of the country, including those with Vietnam, India, and Russia.

The Chinese constitution grants these autonomous areas the right of self-government in certain matters, such as cultural affairs. But minority regions remain firmly under the control of the central authorities. Minority peoples enjoy some latitude to develop their local economies as they see fit. Religious freedom is generally respected, and the use of minority languages in the media and literature is encouraged, as is, to a certain extent, bilingual education. In order to keep the already small minority populations from dwindling further, China's stringent family planning policy is applied much more loosely among minorities, who are often allowed to have two or more children per couple rather than the one-child prescribed limit for most Chinese.

The most extensive ethnic conflict in China has occurred in Tibet. Tibet is located in the far west of China and has been under Chinese military occupation since the early 1950s. Tibetans practice a unique form of Buddhism and most are fiercely loyal to the Dalai Lama, a priest they believe is the incarnation of a divine being. China has claimed authority over Tibet since long before the Communist Party came to power. Tibetans have always disputed that claim and resisted Chinese rule, sometime violently, including in 1959, when the Dalai Lama fled to exile in India following the failure of a rebellion by his followers.

During the Maoist era, traditional Tibetan culture was suppressed by the Chinese authorities. Since the late 1970s, Buddhist temples and monasteries have been allowed to reopen, and Tibetans have gained a significant degree of cultural freedom; the Chinese government has also significantly increased investment in Tibet's economic development. However, China still considers talk of Tibetan political independence to be treason, and Chinese troops have crushed several anti-China demonstrations in Lhasa, the capital of Tibet.

There are more than 20 million Muslims in China. They live in many parts of the country and belong to several different ethnic minority groups. The highest concentration of Muslims is in the far west of China in the Ningxia Hui and Xinjiang Uyghur autonomous regions. The latter borders the Islamic nations of Afghanistan and Pakistan and the Central Asian states of the former Soviet Union.

The more secular Hui are well assimilated into Han Chinese society. But there is growing unrest among Uyghurs in Xinjiang. The Chinese government has clashed with Uyghur militants who want to create a separate Islamic state of "East Turkestan" and have sometimes used violence, including bombings and assassinations, to press their cause. The PRC became an eager ally of the United States in the post–9/11 war on terrorism in part because China could then justify its crackdown on the Xinjiang-based East Turkestan Islamic Movement (ETIM). Washington has included this group on its list of organizations connected to al Qaeda.

China's minority population is relatively small and geographically isolated. Ethnic unrest has been limited, sporadic, and easily quelled. Therefore, the PRC has not had the kind of intense identity-based conflict experienced by countries with more pervasive religious and ethnic cleavages, such as India and Nigeria. But it is possible that domestic and global forces will make ethnic identity a more visible and volatile issue in Chinese politics.

Interest Groups, Social Control, and Citizen Protest

FOCUS QUESTIONS
What is the difference between "mass organizations" and "nongovernmental organizations"? How does the CCP monitor and control the way in which citizens express their interests? What kinds of protests have been increasing in China?

Truly independent interest groups and social movements are not permitted to influence the political process in any significant way. The CCP supports official "mass organizations" as a means to provide a way for interest groups to express their views on policy matters—within strict limits.

Total membership of mass organizations in China reaches the hundreds of millions. Two of the most important are the All-China Women's Federation, the only national organization representing the interests of women in general, and the All-China Federation of Trade Unions (ACFTU), to which about 90 million Chinese workers belong. Neither constitutes an autonomous political voice for the groups they are supposed to represent. But they do sometimes act as an effective lobby in promoting the nonpolitical interests of their constituencies. For example, the Women's Federation has become a strong advocate for women on issues ranging from domestic violence to economic rights. The Trade Union Federation has pushed for legislation to reduce the standard workweek from six to five days. The ACFTU also represents individual workers with grievances against management, although its first loyalty is to the Chinese communist party-state.

Since the late 1990s, there has been a huge increase in the number of nongovernmental organizations (NGOs) less directly subordinate to the CCP than the official mass organizations. There is an enormous variety of national and local NGOs. These include ones that deal with the environment (such as the China Green Earth Volunteers), health (for instance, the China Foundation for the Prevention of STDs and AIDS), charitable work (such as the China Children and

Teenagers Fund), and legal issues (for instance, the Beijing Center for Women's Law Services). These NGOs, which must register with the government, have considerable latitude to operate within their functional areas without direct party interference *if* they steer clear of politics and do not challenge official policies.

Although China has certainly loosened up politically since the days of Mao Zedong, the party-state's control mechanisms still prevent the formation of movements that might defy the CCP's authority. In rural areas, the small-scale, closely knit nature of the village facilitates control by the local party and security organizations. Residents' committees are one of the major instruments of control in urban China. These neighborhood-based organizations, each of which covers 100 to 1,000 households depending on the size of the city, effectively extend the unofficial reach of the party-state down to the most basic level of urban society. They used to be staffed mostly by appointed retired persons (often elderly women). But now their functions are shifting from surveillance to service. Many are led by younger and better-educated residents. In some places neighbors elect committee members. The growth of private enterprise, increasing labor and residential mobility, and new forms of association (such as discos and coffeehouses) and communication (for example, cell phones, e-mail, fax machines) are just some of the factors that are making it much harder for the party-state to monitor citizens as closely as in the past.

Protest and the Party-State

The Tiananmen massacre of 1989 showed the limits of protest in China. The party leadership was particularly alarmed at signs that a number of independent student and worker grass-roots organizations were emerging from the demonstrations. The brutal suppression of the democracy movement was meant to send a clear signal that neither open political protest nor the formation of autonomous interest groups would be tolerated.

There have been few large-scale political demonstrations in China since 1989. Pro-democracy groups have been driven deep underground or abroad. Known dissidents are continuously watched, harassed, imprisoned, or expelled from the country, sometimes as a conciliatory diplomatic gesture.

Repression has not stopped all forms of citizen protest. The Falun Gong (literally, "Dharma Wheel Practice") has carried out the biggest and most continuous demonstrations against the party-state in recent years. The Falun Gong (FLG) is a spiritual movement with philosophical and religious elements drawn from Buddhism and Taoism along with traditional Chinese physical exercises (similar to *tai chi*) and meditation. It claims 70 million members in China and 30 million in more than seventy other countries. Its promise of inner tranquility and good health has proven very appealing to a wide cross-section of people in China as a reaction to some of the side effects of rapid modernization. The authorities began a crackdown in 1999, which intensified after approximately 10,000 Falun Gong followers staged a peaceful protest in front of CCP headquarters in the center of Beijing. The authorities have destroyed FLG books and tapes, jammed Web sites, and arrested thousands of practitioners. Despite a few small FLG demonstrations in recent years, the crackdown seems to have been successful.

Labor unrest is becoming more frequent, with reports of thousands of strikes and other actions in recent years. Workers have carried out big demonstrations at state-owned factories. They have protested the ending of the iron rice bowl system, layoffs, the nonpayment of pensions or severance packages, and the arrest of grass-roots labor leaders. Workers at some foreign-owned enterprises have gone on strike against unsafe working conditions or low wages. Most of these actions have remained limited in scope and duration, so the government has usually not cracked down on the protesters. On occasion, it has actually pressured employers to meet the workers' demands.

In mid-2007, the Chinese government implemented a new, rather sweeping labor law, which was largely designed to protect workers' rights. The law requires that employers, even foreign companies, give workers written contracts and regulates the use of temporary laborers. Workers cannot be fired without due process. Some observers see this as an effort to stem the tide of labor unrest. Others see it also as part of Hu Jintao's political platform to create a "harmonious society."

China's farmers have found ways to resist party-state policies that they believe hurt their interests. One such example is rural resistance to China's strict one-child population control policy.

The countryside has also seen a sharp increase of protest over other issues. In the poorer regions of the country, farmers have attacked local officials and rioted over corruption, exorbitant taxes and extralegal fees, and the government's failure to pay on time for agricultural products it has purchased. In areas benefiting from China's economic growth, people have protested environmental damage by factories whose owners care only for profit. Protests have also attacked illegal land seizures by greedy local officials working in cahoots with developers who want to build factories, expensive housing, or even golf courses.

These protests have not spread beyond the locales where they started. They have focused on the protestors' immediate material concerns, not on grand-scale issues like democracy. They have usually been contained by the authorities through a combination of coercion and concessions to some of the farmers' demands.

Grass-roots protests in both the countryside and cities most often target corrupt local officials or unresponsive employers, not the Communist Party. By responding positively to farmer and worker concerns, the party-state can win support and turn what could be regime-threatening activities into regime-sustaining ones.

The overall political situation in China remains rather contradictory. Although people are much freer than they have been in decades and most visitors find Chinese society quite open, repression can still be intense. Public political dissent is almost nonexistent. But there are many signs that the Chinese Communist Party is losing or giving up some of its ability to control the

China's One-Child Policy

As noted earlier, China and the United States are about the same size in terms of total area. But China has more than four times the population of the United States. This difference is reflected in the population density of each country: the United States has 31 people per square kilometer (80 per square mile); China has 137 per square kilometer (355 per square mile). The most heavily populated part of New York City (Manhattan) has 25,849 people per square kilometer (66,949 per square mile); in Shanghai, the Huangpu area has 126,500 per square kilometer (327,633 per square mile). Furthermore, the United States has more arable land (land that can be used to produce food) than does China. In the United States, much farmland goes unused (the government even pays some farmers *not* to grow crops); in China, literally every inch of land that can be used to produce food is under cultivation.

This should give you a sense of why China's government has long felt a need to control the growth of its population.

China experienced a huge surge in the size of its population beginning in the mid-eighteenth century. In fact, the economic pressures caused by this surge were one of the reasons for the collapse of China's imperial system and the revolution that brought the Communist Party to power in 1949. Mao Zedong did not promote population control because he believed that people were China's most precious resource and source of support for his radical policies.

By the 1970s, China's population exceeded 800 million. Greatly improved health conditions had allowed it to grow at about 2.8 percent per year, which is a very high rate of population increase. The Chinese population would double in just twenty-five years. Cutting the birthrate came to be seen by the country's post-Mao leaders as a major requirement to economic development. Since the 1980s, the Chinese government has enforced a strict population control policy that has, over time, used various means to encourage or even force couples to have only a single child. This is called the "One-Child Policy."

Intensive media campaigns laud the patriotic virtues and economic benefits of small families. Positive incentives such as more farmland or preferred housing have been offered to couples with only one child. Fines or demotions have punished violators. In some places, workplace medics or local doctors monitor contraceptive use and women's fertility cycles, and a couple must have official permission to have a child. Defiance has sometimes led to forced abortion or sterilization.

The combination of the one-child campaign, the modernizing economy, and a comparatively strong record in improving educational and employment opportunities for women have brought China's population growth rate to about 0.6 percent per year. This is even lower than the rate in the United States, which is 0.9 percent per year. China's rate of population increase is *very* low for a country at its level of economic development. India, for example, has also had some success in promoting family planning. But its annual population growth rate is 1.4 percent. Nigeria's is 2.4 percent. These may not seem like big differences, but consider this: at these respective growth rates, it will take 116 years for China's population to double, whereas India's population will double in about fifty years and Nigeria's in just twenty-nine years! India is projected to pass China as the country with the world's largest population sometime in the decade 2030–2040—and with only about one-third of the land.

However, the compulsory, intrusive nature of China's family planning program and the extensive use of abortion as one of the major means of birth control have led to much international criticism. Because their family income now depends on having more people to work, many farmers have evaded the one-child policy by not reporting births and other means. Furthermore, the still widespread belief that male children will contribute more economically to the family and that a male heir is necessary to carry on the family line causes some rural families to take drastic steps to make sure that they have a son. Female infanticide and the abandonment of female babies have increased dramatically. Ultrasound technology has led to large number of sex-selective abortions of female fetuses. As a result, China has an unusual gender balance among its young population. One estimate suggests that there are 70 million more males in China than females. Such a surplus of males (India has a similar situation) may cause a number of serious social problems, including the abduction and selling of young girls as "wives"; some scholars have even argued that it could lead the country to become more militarily aggressive.

Partly in response to rural resistance and international pressure, the Chinese government has relaxed its population policies. Forced abortion and infanticide is now infrequent, although sex-selective abortion is not. Rural couples are often allowed to have two children. The government is also offering special pensions to those who have only one son or two daughters so they will be less dependent on their children for support in their old age. In the cities, where there has been more voluntary compliance with the policy because of higher incomes and limited living space, the one-child policy is still basically in effect. ❖

movements and associations of its citizens and can no longer easily limit access to information and ideas from abroad. Some forms of protest also appear to be increasing and may come to pose a serious challenge to the authority of the party-state.

Summary

Representation of citizen interests and political participation are important parts of China's "socialist democracy." But they are carried out under the watchful eye of the Chinese Communist Party. The National People's Congress, the legislature of the PRC, has become more active and independent as the country's focus has shifted from revolutionary politics to economic development. Elections, particularly at the local level, have become more open and democratic. The Communist Party has also changed significantly, not just welcoming workers, peasants, and political activists into its ranks, but even recruiting members from among China's growing capitalist class of private business owners. Although they are much more open than during the Maoist era, the media, the arts, and education are still ultimately under party supervision. Communist ideology is declining as a unifying force for the country, and the ability of the communist party-state to control and influence its citizens is weakening. The Internet, religion, consumerism, and popular culture are growing in influence. These all present a challenge to the CCP, which now emphasizes Chinese nationalism and pride as sources of citizen identity. Some of the greatest political tensions in China are in parts of the country with high concentrations of non-Chinese ethnic minorities, such as in Tibet and the Muslim areas of the northwest. Protests by farmers and industrial workers with economic grievances have been on the increase, but these have not become large-scale or widespread.

SECTION 5

Chinese Politics in Transition

Political Challenges and Changing Agendas

FOCUS QUESTIONS
- What has been the political impact of China's rapid economic development?
- What are the major political challenges facing the CCP?
- What factors will influence the future of the democratic idea in China?

Scenes from the Chinese Countryside[10]

China has become a lot more modern and urban in recent years. But it is still largely a rural country with a majority of its people living in the countryside. However, depending on where you look in its vast rural areas, you will see a very different China. Take, for example, the following:

Huaxi, Jiangsu Province. This rural village looks much like an American suburb: spacious roads lined with two-story townhouses, potted plants on doorsteps, green lawns, and luscious shade trees. Homes are air-conditioned with leather living room furniture, studies with computers, and exercise rooms. Most families have at least one car. Huaxi has grown rich by developing a number of industrial and commercial enterprises. These have replaced agriculture as the main source of income.

Nanliang, Shaanxi Province. This village is in one of the areas known as China's Third World. Persistent poverty is still the common lot. Per capita income is less than fifty dollars a year. Most families live in one-room, mud-brick houses with no running water that they often share with pigs or other farm animals. One muddy waterhole is used for bathing—by both people and livestock. There are no paved roads. The children, dressed in grimy clothes and ragged cloth shoes, are not starving. But they do not seem to be flourishing either. Education, professional health care, and other social services are minimal or nonexistent. The poor quality land barely supports those who work it.

Beihe, Shandong Province. This may be a typical Chinese village, nowhere near as wealthy as Huaxi nor as poor as Nanliang. Per capita income is about $600 per year. Most people work in small, privately owned factories. Many residents have mobile phones and own consumer electronics. But they are worried. The local enterprises are struggling to survive fierce market competition. The village-owned malt factory has gone bankrupt. Many hope to revive village fortunes by leasing out land to expanding businesses.

Daolin, Hunan Province. A few years ago, thousands of angry farmers marched on the township government headquarters to protest excessive taxes and fees and the gross corruption of local officials. One farmer was killed and dozens injured when the police used clubs and tear gas to disperse the crowd. Shortly afterward, nine people suspected of being ringleaders of the protests were arrested. But the national government did step in and ordered a reduction in financial burdens. It punished some of the most corrupt local officials.

Beiwang, Hebei Province. This was one of the first villages to establish a representative assembly and hold democratic elections for local officials. Among the first decisions made by the elected officials and the assembly was to give just a few families contracts to tend the village's 3000 pear trees rather giving each family an equal number to look after. They believed that this would lead to better pear farming and would cause the non–pear-tending families to develop other kinds of economic activity. The local Communist Party branch objected that this would lead to too much inequality. The party leaders eventually agreed, under pressure, to go along with the new policy. In a short time, pear production zoomed. The new system proved to be beneficial not only to the few families who looked after the trees but also to the village as a whole because of economic diversification and the local government's share of the increased profits.

These scenes reflect the enormous diversity of the Chinese countryside: prosperity and poverty, mass protests and peaceful politics. It is worth remembering that about 60 percent of China's population—that's more than 600 million people—still live in the rural parts of the country. What happens in the rural towns and villages will have a tremendous impact on China's political and economic future.

Beiwang reminds us that not all politics rises to national or international significance. The question of who looks after the village pear trees may matter more to local residents than what happens in the inner sanctums of the Communist Party or U.S.-China presidential summit meetings. The victory of the Beiwang representative assembly and elected officials on the pear tree issue shows that even in a one-party state, the people sometimes prevail against those with power, and democracy works on the local level—as long as the basic principle of party leadership is not challenged.

The Huaxi scene shows the astonishing improvement in living standards in much of rural China. But huge pockets of severe poverty, like Nanliang, still persist, especially in inland regions far removed from the more prosperous coastal regions. Most of rural China falls between the extremes. And it is in these in-between areas, such as Beihe and Daolin, where the combination of new hopes brought about by economic progress and the tensions caused by blatant corruption, growing inequalities, stagnating incomes, and other frustrations may prove to be politically explosive.

Economic Management, Social Tension, and Political Legitimacy

China's rural areas illustrate a larger challenge facing the leaders of the PRC: how to sustain and effectively manage the economic growth on which the CCP's legitimacy as the ruling party is now largely based. The party is gambling that continued solid economic performance will literally buy it legitimacy and that most citizens will care little about democracy or national politics if their material lives continue to get better. So far this gamble seems to have paid off.

But failure to keep inequality under control, especially between city and countryside, or failure to continue providing opportunities for advancement for the less well off could lead to social instability and become a liability for a political party that still espouses socialist goals. One of the government's most formidable tasks will be to create enough jobs not only for the millions of workers who are expected to be laid off by the closure or restructuring of state-owned enterprises, but also for the twenty million or so new entrants to the labor force each year. This situation will very likely be compounded by those displaced from companies that are no longer competitive in China's increasingly globalized economy.

The collapse of China's welfare system under the pressures of market reforms and globalization poses a serious challenge to China's technocratic leadership. The public health system is in a shambles, with AIDS and other infectious diseases spreading rapidly. China also has a rapidly graying population, that is, the percentage of elderly people in the population is growing. The country lacks any kind of adequate pension or social security system to meet the needs of its senior citizens. As mentioned before, these kinds of problems are the target of Hu Jintao's emphasis on building a "harmonious society." It remains to be seen whether the Chinese government will be able to translate this ideal into action.

The considerable autonomy from the central government gained by China provinces has had important economic benefits. It has also fostered regionalism. This is a potential threat to the CCP's political control and government efforts to have a coordinated national economic policy. China's Communist Party leaders must also decide how to further nurture the private sector, which is the most dynamic part of the economy. Business owners and investors still face significant restrictions. Corruption affects the lives of most people more directly than does political repression. It is probably the single most corrosive force eating away at the legitimacy of the Chinese Communist Party.

China and the Democratic Idea

China has evolved in recent decades toward a system of what has been called "Market-Leninism,"[11] a combination of increasing economic openness (a market economy) and continuing political rigidity under the leadership of a Leninist ruling party that adheres to a remodeled version of communist ideology.

However, as the people of China become more secure economically, better educated, and more aware of the outside world, they will also likely become more politically active. The steadily expanding class of private business owners may want political clout to match their wealth. Scholars, scientists, and technology specialists may become more outspoken about the limits on intellectual freedom. The many Chinese who travel or study abroad may find the political gap between their party-state and the world's democracies to be increasingly intolerable.

China's long history of authoritarian rule going back to its imperial system and the hierarchical values of Confucian culture, which is still deeply influential, seem to be mighty counterweights to democracy. The political legitimacy of the CCP may be relatively weak, and some aspects of its social control have broken down. But the party-state's coercive power remains formidable. The PRC's relatively low per capita standard of living, large rural population, vast areas of extreme poverty, and state-dominated media and means of communications also hinder democratization. Finally, many people are apathetic about politics or fearful of the violence and chaos that radical political change of any kind, even democracy, might unleash.

But Taiwan, which also has a deeply rooted Confucian heritage, has enjoyed impressive success in democratization in the past two decades. This includes free and fair multiparty elections from the local level up to the presidency. Taiwan's political development strongly suggests that the values, institutions, and process of democracy are not incompatible with Confucian culture.

Furthermore, China has a higher literacy rate, more extensive industrialization and urbanization, a faster rate of economic growth, and a larger middle class than most countries at its level of economic development. These conditions are widely seen by political scientists as favorable to democracy.

A number of significant political changes in China may also be planting the seeds of democracy: the decentralization of political and economic power to local governments; the setting of a mandatory retirement age and term limits for all officials; the coming to power of younger, better educated, and more worldly leaders; the greater role of the National People's Congress in the policy-making process; the introduction of competitive elections in rural villages; the strengthening and partial depoliticization of the legal system; tolerance of a much wider range of artistic, cultural, and religious expression; the increasing activity and influence of nongovernmental organizations; and the important freedom (unheard of in the Mao era) for individuals to be apolitical.

Furthermore, the astounding spread of the democratic idea around the globe since the 1980s has created a trend that will be increasingly difficult for China's leaders to resist. The PRC has become a major player in the world of states. Its government must be more responsive to international opinion in order to continue the country's deepening integration with the international economy and growing stature as a responsible and mature global power.

Student demonstrators erected a statue called the "Goddess of Democracy" in Beijing's Tiananmen Square in late May 1989 to symbolize their demands for greater political freedom in China. In the background is an official portrait of former Chinese Communist Party leader Mao Zedong. Chinese troops toppled and destroyed the statue after they occupied the square on June 4, 1989, a process that also resulted in the death of many protestors. *(Source: AP Images)*

> **FOCUS QUESTIONS**
>
> Why has the Chinese communist-party state survived while the Soviet Union and most other regimes of that type collapsed more than a decade ago? In what ways is China still a developing country and a Third World state? What lessons might be drawn about China from the development experience of other East Asian countries, such as South Korea?

totalitarianism a political system in which the state attempts to exercise total control over all aspects of public and private life, including the economy, culture, education, and social organizations.

Chinese Politics in Comparative Perspective

China as a Communist Party-State

Dramatic economic restructuring and rapidly rising living standards have saved the CCP from the kinds of economic crises that greatly weakened and led to the collapse of other Communist systems, including the Soviet Union. China's current leaders believe that the last Soviet party chief, Mikhail Gorbachev, went much too far with political reform and not far enough with economic change. They believe their reverse formula is a key reason that they have not suffered the same fate.

The Chinese Communists won power through an indigenous revolution with widespread popular backing. They did not need foreign military support for their victory. This sets China apart from most of the East-Central European communist parties, which depended on the Soviet Union. Despite its very serious mistakes in governing China over the last six decades, the CCP has a deep reservoir of historical legitimacy among the Chinese people.

But China still has much in common with other past and current communist party-states, including some of the basic features of a totalitarian political system. **Totalitarianism** (a term also applied to fascist regimes such as Nazi Germany) describes a system in which the ruling party prohibits all forms of meaningful political opposition and dissent, insists on obedience to a single state-determined ideology, and enforces its rule through coercion and terror. Such regimes also seek to bring all spheres of public activity (including the economy and culture) and even many parts of its citizens' private lives (including reproduction) under the total control of the party-state in the effort to modernize the country and, indeed, to transform human nature.

China is much less totalitarian than it was during the Maoist era. The CCP appears to be trying to save communist rule in China by moderating or abandoning many of its totalitarian features. To promote economic development, the CCP has relaxed its grip on many areas of life. Citizens can now pursue their interests without interference by the party-state as long as they avoid sensitive political issues. Bold economic and social reform may, in time, nurture a slow transition to democracy. But so far these reforms have helped to sustain a political system that is basically still a partly totalitarian communist party dictatorship.

China as a Third World State

In 1949, China was a desperately poor country, with an economy devastated by a century of civil strife and world war. It occupied a very weak position in the international system. The PRC has made remarkable progress in improving the well-being of its citizens, building a strong state, and enhancing the country's global role.

Why has China been more successful than so many other nations in meeting some of major challenges of economic development? Third World governments have often served narrow class or foreign interests more than the national interest. Many political leaders and governments in Africa, Asia, and Latin

America have been a drain on development rather than a stimulus. Third World states have often become defenders of a status quo built on extensive inequality and poverty rather than agents of needed change. In contrast, the PRC's recent rulers have successfully created a **developmental state**, in which government power and public policy effectively promote national economic growth.

> **developmental state**
> a nation-state in which the government carries out policies that effectively promote national economic growth.

Much of the Third World seems to be heading toward political democracy without economic development—or at best very slow development. China, however, seems to be following the reverse course. The harsh political rule of the party-state contrasts sharply with its remarkable accomplishments in improving the material lives of the Chinese people. This contrast makes it difficult to settle on a clear evaluation of the overall record of communist rule in China, particularly in the post-Mao era. It is also hard to predict the future of the Chinese Communist Party. The regime's economic achievements could continue to provide it with the support, or at least compliance, it needs to stay in power despite its serious political shortcomings.

In keeping firm control on political life while allowing the country to open up in other important ways, CCP leaders believe they are wisely following the model of development pioneered by the newly industrializing countries (NICs) of East Asia such as South Korea and Taiwan. The lesson that the CCP draws from the NIC experience is that only a strong authoritarian government can provide the political stability and social peace required for rapid economic growth. According to this view, democracy—with its open debates about national priorities, political parties contesting for power, and interest groups squabbling over how to divide the economic pie—is a recipe for chaos, particularly in a huge and still relatively poor country.

However there is another lesson that can be drawn from the East Asian NICs. Economic development, social modernization, and globalization create powerful pressures for political change both from below and from abroad. In both Taiwan and South Korea, authoritarian governments that had presided over economic miracles in the 1960s and 1970s gave way in the 1980s and 1990s to democracy, largely in response to domestic demands from their own populations.

China's dynamic economic expansion and social transformation over the last quarter century suggest that the PRC is in a period of growth and modernization that will lead it to NIC status. However, in terms of the extent of industrialization, per capita income, the strength of the private sector of the economy, and the size of the middle and professional classes, China's development is still far below the level at which democracy succeeded in Taiwan and South Korea. Nevertheless, economic reform in China has already created groups and processes and given rise to interests and ideas that are likely to evolve as sources of pressure for more and faster political change. The experience of the NICs and other developing countries suggests that such pressures will intensify as the economy and society continue to modernize. At some point in the not-too-distant future, the Chinese Communist Party is very likely to face the challenge of the democratic idea once again. How China's new generation of leaders responds to this challenge is perhaps the most important and uncertain question about Chinese politics in the early twenty-first century.

Summary

What happens in China's countryside, where 600 million people still live, will have an enormous impact on the nation's future. Dealing with very serious rural problems is one of the major challenges facing China's current leaders. Economic development has created other major challenges: growing inequalities, rising unemployment, pervasive corruption, and loss of control over lower levels of government, to name just a few. The Communist Party is also very likely to face increasing demands for a political voice from different sectors of society as its citizens become more prosperous, well-educated, and worldly. In comparative perspective, China has proven more economically successful and politically adaptable than other communist party-states, including the Soviet Union, which collapsed in 1991. China has also been much more successful than most other developing countries in promoting economic growth but so far has not been part of the wave of democratization that has spread to so many other parts of the world.

Key Terms

communist-party state
Marxism-Leninism
autonomous regions
newly industrializing country (NIC)
authoritarian
guerrilla warfare
collectivization
socialism
Great Leap Forward
communism
Great Proletarian Cultural Revolution

technocrats
command economy
household responsibility system
iron rice bowl
sustainable development
martial law
cadres
guanxi
socialist democracy
totalitarianism
developmental state

Suggested Readings

Bergsten, Fred, et al. *China The Balance Sheet: What the World Needs to Know Now About the Emerging Superpower*. New York: Public Affairs, 2006.

Blecher, Marc J. *China Against the Tides: Restructuring Through Revolution, Radicalism, and Reform*, 2nd ed. London: Continuum, 2003.

Chang, Jung. *Wild Swans: Three Daughters of China*. New York: Simon & Schuster, 1991.

Cheek, Timothy. *Living with Reform: China Since 1989*. New York: Palgrave McMillan, 2007.

Denoon, David, ed. *China: Contemporary Political, Economic, and International Affairs*. New York: New York University Press, 2007.

Economy, Elizabeth C. *The River Runs Black: The Environmental Challenge to China's Future*. Ithaca: Cornell University Press, 2004.

Gao Yuan. *Born Red: A Chronicle of the Cultural Revolution*. Stanford, Calif.: Stanford University Press, 1987.

Goldman, Merle. *From Comrade to Citizen: The Struggle for Political Rights in China*. Cambridge, Mass.: Harvard University Press, 2006.

Grasso, June et al. *Modernization and Revolution in China*, 3rd ed. Armonk, N.Y.: M. E. Sharpe, 2004.

Hessler, Peter. *Oracle Bones: A Journey Between China's Past and Present*. New York: Harper Collins, 2006.

Kynge, James. *China Shakes the World: A Titan's Rise and Troubled Future—and the Challenge for America*. Boston: Houghton Mifflin, 2006.

Lampton, David M. *Same Bed, Different Dreams: Managing U.S.-China Relations, 1989–2000*. Berkeley: University of California Press, 2001.

McFarquhar, Roderick, and Michael Schoenhals. *Mao's Last Revolution*. Cambridge, Mass.: Harvard University Press, 2006.

Pei Minxin, *China's Trapped Transition: The Limits of Developmental Autocracy*. Cambridge, Mass: Harvard University Press, 2006.

Pomfret, John. *Chinese Lessons: Five Classmates and the Story of the New China*. New York: Henry Holt, 2006.

Spence, Jonathan. *Mao Zedong*. New York: Viking, 1999.

Notes

[1] See, Jonathan Spence, *The Gate of Heavenly Peace: The Chinese and their Revolution, 1895–1989* (New York: Viking Press, 1981).

[2] Mao Zedong, "Report on an Investigation of the Peasant Movement in Hunan," March 1927, in *Selected Readings from the Works of Mao Tsetung* (Beijing: Foreign Languages Press, 1971), 24.

[3] David Bachman, *Bureaucracy, Economy, and Leadership in China: The Institutional Origins of the Great Leap Forward* (Cambridge: Cambridge University Press, 1991), 2.

[4] See, for example, Nicholas D. Kristof and Sheryl WuDunn, *China Wakes: The Struggle for the Soul of a Rising Power* (New York: Time Books, 1994); and James Kynge, *China Shakes the World: A Titan's Rise and Troubled Future—and the Challenge for America* (Boston: Houghton Mifflin, 2006).

[5] Deng Xiaoping first expressed his "cat theory" in 1962 in a speech, "Restore Agricultural Production," in the aftermath of the failure and famine of the Great Leap Forward. In the original speech, he actually quoted an old peasant proverb that refers to a "yellow cat or a black cat," but it is most often rendered "white cat or black cat." See *Selected Works of Deng Xiaoping (1938–1965)* (Beijing: Foreign Languages Press, 1992), 293.

[6] Emily Honig and Gail Herschatter, *Personal Voices: Chinese Women in the 1980s* (Stanford, Calif.: Stanford University Press, 1988), 337.

[7] Li Cheng and Lynn White, "The Thirteenth Central Committee of the Chinese Communist Party: From Mobilizers to Managers, *Asian Survey*, vol. 28, no. 4 (Apr., 1988), pp. 371–399; and Kaiser Kuo, Made in China: The Revenge of the Nerds," Time.com, Jun. 27, 2001, http://www.time.com/time/world/article/0,8599,165453,00.html.

[8] Gordon White, *Riding the Tiger: The Politics of Economic Reform in Post-Mao China* (Palo Alto, Calif.: Stanford University Press, 1993), 20.

[9] For a report on this speech, see Joseph Kahn, "China's Leader Vows to Uphold One-Party Rule," *New York Times*, June 27, 2007.

[10] The following scenes are extrapolated from Jonathan Watts, "In China's richest village," *The Guardian*, May 10, 2005; Wang Zhe, "Behind the Dream of a Village," *Beijing Review*, June 14, 2001, 13–16; Lu Xueyi, "The Peasants Are Suffering, the Villages Are Very Poor," *Dushu* (Readings), January 2001, in U.S. Embassy (Beijing, China), PRC Press Clippings, http://www.usembassy-china.org.cn/sandt/peasantsuffering.html; Hannah Beech, "In Rural China, It's a Family Affair" Time/Asia, May 27, 2002; "The Silent Majority: A Rare Look inside a Chinese Village," *The Economist*, April 7, 2005; Erik Eckholm, "Heated Protests by Its Farmers Trouble Beijing," *New York Times*, February 1, 1999, A; Susan V. Lawrence, "Democracy, Chinese-Style: Village Representative Assemblies," *Australian Journal of Chinese Affairs*, no. 32 (July 1994): 61–68.

[11] Nicholas D. Kristof, "China Sees 'Market-Leninism' as Way to Future," *New York Times*, September 6, 1993.